Practical Planning:
Appeals and Inquiries

Practical Planning:
Appeals and Inquiries

Sandra Banks
Solicitor, Denton Hall

LONGMAN

© Longman Group Ltd 1994

ISBN 0752 00060 8

Published by
Longman Law, Tax and Finance
Longman Group UK Ltd
21–27 Lamb's Conduit Street
London WC1N 3NJ

Associated offices:
Australia, Hong Kong, Malaysia, Singapore, USA

A CIP catalogue record for this book is available
from the British Library

Printed and bound in Great Britain by Biddles of Guildford Ltd, Surrey

Contents

Preface

This book deals with planning appeals where the local authority to whom a planning application has been submitted has either issued an unsatisfactory consent or refusal or has failed to determine the application within the required timescale. Listed building consent, conservation area consent, enforcement appeals and appeals in respect of certificates of lawfulness of existing or proposed use are dealt with briefly in Chapter 13 with particular reference to their place in the planning appeal framework.

The planning appeal procedure represents a clear opportunity. The Planning Inspectorate's report for 1994 shows that 42.1 per cent of appeals dealt with by public inquiry were allowed and planning permission granted. The purpose of this book is to enable practitioners to take a measured view of the merits of their case and to increase their chances of success. It is a practical handbook, intended to provide a step-by-step approach to making informed decisions on whether to make an appeal, how to appeal and how to deal with the appeal procedure. It may be used as a first port of call in retrieving more detailed information. Basic information on where to get forms, addresses and fax numbers has been provided. Worked examples are given to put flesh on the bare bones of the procedures.

Advice drawn from practical experience is also included. Inevitably, not every experienced practitioner will agree with all the advice but it is hoped that this book will provide a structured approach which the busy practitioner can apply to his own work.

Finally, a word of caution. Planning is a specialised area, changing as ministers and policies come and go. Do not be afraid to seek specialist advice — preferably before things start going wrong.

Sandra Banks
London
October 1994

Table of Cases

Table of Statutes

Table of Statutory Instruments

Acknowledgments

I am most grateful for the help of my colleagues at Denton Hall who have taken the time to read and respond to the manuscript, in particular Stephen Ashworth, Paul Bolger, Margaret Casely-Hayford, David Cox, Helen Norris and Carole Pavitt. Writing this book would have been impossible without the help of my secretary Anna O'Donovan, whose intelligent co-operation I gladly acknowledge.

Useful Information

Planning appeals and
Listed building and conservation area consent appeals

Appeal forms and explanatory booklets are available from:

England
The Planning Inspectorate
Tollgate House
Houlton Street
Bristol BS2 9DJ

Tel: 0272 878000
Fax: 0272 878782

From 16 April 1995:
Tel: 0117 987 8000
Fax: 0117 987 8782

Wales
The Planning Inspectorate
Cathays Park
Cardiff CF1 3NQ

Tel: 0222 825493
Fax: 0222 825150

From 16 April 1995 the area
    code is 01222.

Enforcement appeals

Forms and explanatory booklets are available from:

England
Department of the Environment
(PINS 6)
PO Box 326
Bristol BS99 7XF

Tel: 0272 878000
Fax: 0272 878782

From 16 April 1995:
Tel: 0117 987 8000
Fax: 0117 987 8782

Wales
The Secretary
Welsh Office
Cathays Park
Cardiff CF1 3NQ

Tel: 0222 8273036
Fax: 0222 8273036

From 16 April 1995 the area
    code is 01222.

Miscellaneous

COMPASS (Computerised Planning Appeals Service)

Suite 3
Lower Quay Street
Gloucester
GL1 2LW

Tel: 0452 310566
Fax: 0452 310551
From 16 April 1995 the area code is 01452.

COMPASS operate a database of appeal inquiry decisions dating back to 1982. The service may be accessed by telephone and provides printouts of cases within given parameters and original decision letters.

Statutory and Other Sources

Planning law and procedure is based on statute, either Acts of Parliament or Statutory Instruments. The main statutes, circulars and guidance notes and the abbreviations used in the text are as follows:

Statutes and statutory instruments

Town and Country Planning Act 1990	the Act
Town and Country Planning (Listed Buildings and Conservation Areas) Act 1990	the Listed Buildings Act
Town and Country Planning General Development Order 1988	GDO
Town and Country Planning (Fees for Applications and Deemed Applications) Regulations 1989	Fees Regulations
Town and Country Planning Use Classes Order 1987	Use Classes Order
Town and Country Planning Appeals (Determination by Inspectors) (Inquiries Procedure) Rules 1992	the Inspector Rules
Town and Country Planning (Inquiries Procedure) Rules 1992	the Secretary of State Rules

Circulars

(Welsh Office references are given in brackets)

Planning and Noise	DoE Circular 10/73 (16/73)
The Use of Conditions in Planning Permissions	DoE Circular 1/85 (1/85)
Town and Country Planning (Appeals) (Written Representations Procedure) Regulations 1987	DoE Circular 11/87 (21/87)
Changes of Use of Buildings and Other Land: The Town and Country Planning (Use Classes) Order 1987	DoE Circular 13/87 (24/87)

Nature Conservation	DoE Circular 27/87 (25/87)
Town and Country Planning (Assessment of Environmental Effects) Regulations 1988	DoE Circular 15/88 (23/88)
Planning and Compensation Act 1991 Planning Obligations	DoE Circular 16/91 (53/91)
Award of Costs incurred in Planning and Other (including Compulsory Purchase Order) Proceedings	DoE Circular 8/93 (29/93)

Planning Policy Guidance Notes
PPG1 General Policy and Principles
PPG2 Green Belts (under review)
PPG3 Housing
PPG4 Industrial and Commercial Development and Small Firms
PPG6 Town Centres and Retail Developments
PPG7 The Countryside and the Rural Economy
PPG10 Strategic Guidance for the West Midlands (under review)
PPG11 Strategic Guidance for Merseyside
PPG12 Development Plans and Regional Planning Guidance
PPG13 Transport
PPG15 Planning and the Historic Environment
PPG16 Archaeology and Planning
PPG23 Planning and Pollution Control
PPG24 Planning and Noise

Regional Policy Guidance Notes
RPG1 Strategic Guidance for Tyne and Wear
RPG2 Strategic Guidance for West Yorkshire
RPG3 Strategic Guidance for London
RPG4 Strategic Guidance for Greater Manchester
RPG5 Strategic Guidance for South Yorkshire
RPG6 Regional Planning Guidance for East Anglia
RPG7 Regional Planning Guidance for the Northern Region
RPG8 Regional Planning Guidance for the East Midlands Region
RPG9 Regional Planning Guidance for the South East
RPG10 Regional Planning Guidance for the South West

Introduction to the Planning System

The planning system is very different from civil law in general and tribunal work in particular. However, like most tribunals, it is almost entirely statute-based, and there is little room for common law concepts.

An administrative and political system

Planning is an administrative and political system with the objective of regulating the development process fairly and in the public interest. It is political in the sense that it is a regulatory organ of the state and in that decisions are made by elected politicians both at local and national level. The system is driven by political policies and the objectives of the ruling party, although the ruling parties at national and local level are not always the same. Over the years certain issues have become entrenched. For failure to comply with the regulatory mechanism there may be criminal sanctions or civil remedies.

The appeal system is necessary in order to provide a review of decisions taken by locally elected politicians. The appeal is made to a member of the government of the day, the Secretary of State for the Environment. He will review the local decision in the light of local policies and the objectives and policies he has published.

Such a system could be prone to short-term political pragmatism and some believe that it is. However, the basic planning framework set out by statute is a straitjacket within which political forces are contained. Local planning authorities operate on the basis of published policies and in the light of government advice; the Secretary of State for the Environment is required to consider not only local policies but also his own policies in making decisions on appeal. Basic principles of administrative law continue to operate to strike out perverse decisions that no reasonable decision-maker could have reached and decisions that fail to meet the legitimate expectations of those involved in the system.

This political influence means that planning is not static. It is in a continuous state of flux, evolving with political change at local and national level and as published documents are updated to take account of the changes. The system does not lend itself to a superficial approach. Those who are involved in planning decisions must accept the complexities of the evolving policies and be prepared to weigh material considerations one against another. And inevitably, a decision properly reached one year is not the same decision that would be reached on the same facts a few years later.

The statutory mechanism

The system was set up after the Second World War by the Town and Country Planning Act 1947. As one might expect from a government which nationalised the railways and produced the national health service, the approach was to bring all development under public control. The system was not retroactive, and development which had taken place before 1 July 1947 did not require planning permission.

Development is widely defined. The present definition of development is contained in s 55 of the Town and Country Planning Act 1990 ('the Act') and reads as follows:

> 55(1) Subject to the following provisions of this section, in this Act, except where the context otherwise requires, 'development', means the carrying out of building, engineering, mining or other operations in, on, over or under land, or the making of any material change in the use of any buildings or other land.
>
> (1A) For the purposes of this Act 'building operations' include—
> (a) demolition of buildings;
> (b) rebuilding;
> (c) structural alterations of or additions to buildings; and
> (d) other operations normally undertaken by a person carrying on business as a builder.
>
> (2) The following operations or uses of land shall not be taken for the purposes of this Act to involve development of the land—
> (a) the carrying out of for the maintenance, improvement or other alteration of any building of works which—
>   (i) affect only the interior of the building, or
>   (ii) do not materially affect the external appearance of the building, and are not works for making good war damage or works begun after December 5, 1968 for the alteration of a building by providing additional space in it underground;
> (b) the carrying out on land within the boundaries of a road by a local highway authority of any works required for the maintenance or improvement of the road;
> (c) the carrying out by a local authority or statutory undertakers of any works for the purpose of inspecting, repairing or renewing any sewers, mains, pipes, cables or other apparatus, including the breaking open of any street or other land for that purpose;
> (d) the use of any buildings or other land within the curtilage of a dwellinghouse for any purpose incidental to the enjoyment of the dwellinghouse as such;
> (e) the use of any land for the purposes of agriculture or forestry (including afforestation) and the use for any of those purposes of any building occupied together with land so used;
> (f) in the case of buildings or other land which are used for a purpose of any class specified in an order made by the Secretary of State under this section, the

use of the buildings or other land or, subject to the provisions of the order, of any part of the buildings or the other land, for any other purpose of the same class;

[(g) the demolition of any description of building specified in a direction given by the Secretary of State to local planning authorities generally or to a particular local planning authority.]

(3) For the avoidance of doubt it is hereby declared that for the purposes of this section—

(a) the use as two or more separate dwellinghouses of any building previously used as a single dwellinghouse involves a material change in the use of the building and of each part of it which is so used;

(b) the deposit of refuse or waste materials on land involves a material change in its use, notwithstanding that the land is comprised in a site already used for that purpose, if—
 (i) the superficial area of the deposit is extended, or
 (ii) the height of the deposit is extended and exceeds the level of the land adjoining the site.

(4) For the purposes of this Act mining operations include—

(a) the removal of material of any description—
 (i) from a mineral-working deposit;
 (ii) from a deposit of pulverised fuel ash or other furnace ash or clinker; or
 (iii) from a deposit of iron, steel or other metallic slags; and

(b) the extraction of minerals from a disused railway embankment.

(4A) Where the placing or assembly of any tank in any part of any inland waters for the purpose of fish farming there would not, apart from this subsection, involve development of the land below, this Act shall have effect as if the tank resulted from carrying out engineering operations over that land; and in this subsection—
 'fish farming' means the breeding, rearing or keeping of fish or shellfish (which includes any kind of crustacean and mollusc);
 'inland waters' means waters which do not form part of the sea or of any creek, bay or estuary or of any river as far as the tide flows; and
 'tank' includes any cage and any other structure for use in fish farming.]

(5) Without prejudice to any regulations made under the provisions of this Act relating to the control of advertisements, the use for the display of advertisements of any external part of a building which is not normally used for that purpose shall be treated for the purposes of this section as involving a material change in the use of that part of the building.

Certain types of development were then specifically taken out of the regulatory framework in order not to overwhelm the system. Certain changes of use are deemed *not* to be development by virtue of the Town and Country Planning Use Classes Order 1987. Certain development is automatically permitted (subject to limitations) by the Town and Country Planning General Development Order 1988 (GDO).

The complexity of the system made it necessary to establish in some cases whether work already done was development which required planning permission and whether future work was development requiring planning permission.

Separate legislation in respect of listed buildings is based on different criteria in order to control alterations and demolition of such buildings. If work involves 'development', planning permission is required; if the work is to a listed building it will also, in most cases, require listed building consent. More recently conservation areas have been strengthened by the requirement that demolition of buildings within the conservation area requires consent, thus enabling the local authority to protect the character and appearance of the conservation area, even though the buildings are not listed.

The role of the practitioner

Once the basic nature of the system is understood, the role of the practitioner falls into place. Because the system differs fundamentally from other areas of legal work, much of the work of the planning practitioner may also be different. He may be involved in drafting documents and in statutory interpretation. But these documents will be greatly conditioned by public policy. The practitioner is also more likely to be seen as part of the development team rather than a troubleshooter called in to deal with the legal aspects of a particular case. Because planning appeals are not subject to restrictive rules on who can appear, planning lawyers have always had to provide value for money, which has been salutary. Good planning lawyers, in the author's experience, are proactive strategists with a firm understanding of the client's business purposes (if acting for the developer) or the local authority's planning objectives (if acting for the local authority).

Chapter 1

The Decision to Appeal

1.1   Introduction

This chapter considers the situations when an appeal should be lodged and those
when another course of action may be more appropriate. It is not good practice
to put in an appeal without being confident that it is worth doing. Procedural
rules are such that there will be very little time to get a case together or take
decisions once the appeal is lodged. Although no fee is required, the planning
appeal will involve time and trouble. In some cases there is a possibility of costs
being awarded against the appellant.

Having looked at the circumstances where an appeal can be lodged, the time
limits and the question of who can appeal, this chapter goes on to deal with the
process of weighing up the elements needed to enable an informed decision to
be made. PPG1, at the end of this chapter, contains government advice on
planning decisions.

1.2   The right to appeal

The Town and Country Planning Act 1990, s 78 gives a right to appeal to the
Secretary of State for the Environment in the following circumstances:
  (1) The refusal of planning permission. There is no right of appeal against
       notification by a local authority under s 70A of the Act when the authority
       has declined to determine the application because it is similar to an
       application determined on appeal within the preceding two years.
       However, the applicant's right of appeal in respect of non-determination
       at the expiry of the eight-week period remains, so that if the local authority
       inadvertently fails to issue notification of its decision under s 70A within
       the eight-week period the applicant may appeal. He should do so
       immediately because if the local authority's determination is received
       before the appeal is lodged, the right of appeal will have been lost (the
       time for appeal in respect of non-determination is discussed in para 1.4).
  (2) The grant of planning permission subject to conditions.
  (3) Refusal of an application made under s 73 of the Act to develop land
       without complying with any condition previously imposed or the
       conditional grant of such a permission.

(4) Refusal of an application made under s 73A for retrospective permission when development has already taken place. The procedure for such appeals is identical to that applying under previous sections. Special considerations apply to dealing with such appeals because of the enforcement dimension. These are therefore dealt with in the context of enforcement appeals in Chapter 13.

(5) The refusal or conditional grant of any consent, agreement or approval required by a condition of a planning permission (normally an application for approval of reserved matters pursuant to an outline application).

(6) Failure to obtain approval from the local authority that is required under a development order. Some permitted development rights in the GDO are subject to approval of matters such as siting.

(7) The failure of the local authority to issue a decision within the 'prescribed period' (ie eight weeks, or 16 weeks in the case of an application submitted with an environmental statement) or such longer period as has been agreed between the parties.

Note that s 79(6) of the Act enables the Secretary of State to decline to determine an appeal if planning permission could either not have been granted or not have been granted otherwise than subject to the conditions imposed.

1.3   Appeals against decisions

In all cases except (7) above (the failure of the local authority to issue a decision), the applicant will receive a document from the local authority. This will either be a refusal notice or a grant of permission subject to conditions. Both will contain reasons. The decision and the reasons will form the starting point for consideration of an appeal. The date shown on the decision will be the date from which the six-month period for lodging appeals begins to run (see para 1.7). Once the local authority have issued a notice of their decision they can take no further action in relation to that application.

1.4   Non-determination appeals

If no decision has been made by the local authority, the situation is a little more complicated. If an appeal is being considered because of the failure by the local authority to determine an application, there will be no reasons for refusal set out in writing. The appellant cannot therefore be expected to draft full grounds of appeal.

In some cases there may be an advantage, if time permits, in allowing the local authority time to issue a refusal notice before appealing, because the reasons for refusal will assist in evaluating the appeal.

If the local authority are considering declining to determine an application under s 70A of the Act because it is similar to an application refused on appeal within the previous two years, then it is essential that an appeal is lodged, if it is to be lodged at all, immediately upon the expiry of the eight-week period.

Once the local authority have formally indicated that they decline to determine the application under s 70A, there is no right of appeal.

1.5 The prescribed period and extensions of time

If no refusal notice is issued, an appeal can be lodged after the expiry of the relevant 'prescribed period' unless the applicant has agreed with the local authority that the authority will be allowed further time to reach a decision. If a refusal notice has already been issued, the 'prescribed period' is irrelevant.

The 'prescribed period' is set out in art 23 of the GDO. It is eight weeks (or 16 weeks for cases involving an environmental assessment). Time begins to run from the time that a valid application is received by the local authority, including the correct fee and ownership certificates. If the fee is paid by a cheque which is subsequently dishonoured, time ceases to run against the local authority until payment has been received.

It is good practice, if this time limit is likely to be important and where circumstances allow, to ensure that the application and its supporting documents are delivered by hand and checked at the public counter of the local authority offices. A note should be made by the person delivering the documents. Local authorities may take days to register an application: the vital date is the date when it reaches them, not the date on which they register it. The date quoted by the local authority when acknowledging the application is likely to be the date of registration, inadvertently causing calculation of the prescribed period (incorrectly) from that date.

In *Camden London Borough Council v ADC Estates* (1991) P&CR 347 Glidewell LJ held that: '. . . the date on which an application is made is the date of the earliest moment when the application is received by its intended recipient. So I would hold that an application for planning permission is not made until it has been communicated to or received by the local planning authority to whom it is to be made'. He refused to speculate on what the position might be if a document had been received in the planning office but not looked at for two days. This is not an uncommon occurrence. Indeed one local authority has been known not to open incoming post for some days. In the author's view, once a complete application form has been physically delivered to the planning desk of the local authority the prescribed period begins to run (subject to a cheque for the planning fee not being dishonoured) from that date. To allow the time period to run from the date when the local authority take some active step such as registering the application would in effect give the authority control over the time period in a way that the legislator cannot have intended.

Local authorities frequently send a form to applicants asking for an extension of time. An applicant should not agree to this without considering whether he wishes to co-operate in this way or whether he wishes to hold the local authority to the prescribed period, leaving the option open of lodging an appeal once it has expired. If the applicant agrees an extension of time, an appeal cannot be lodged until that time period has expired unless a decision has been issued in the meantime. If he does not agree an extension of time, this does not affect the local authority's ability to process the application and issue a decision outside the prescribed period. The position is unaffected until an appeal is lodged.

The only occasion when no extension of time should be allowed to an authority and the appeal should be lodged forthwith is where the local authority is contemplating a refusal to determine an application under s 70A of the Act because a similar application has been refused on appeal within the preceding two years (see para 1.4).

If time is simply needed by the authority to deal with outstanding issues but a satisfactory approval is likely to be forthcoming, an applicant may prefer to agree an extension of time. If it appears that the application is likely to be refused, however, an applicant may not wish to postpone the date on which an appeal can be lodged. If indications are unclear, or if the applicant wishes to preserve the possibility of negotiating a consent while at the same time exploiting the opportunity of making an early appeal, this can be done by using a duplicate application, which is dealt with in para 1.8.

There may, however, be reasons for allowing the authority extra time, even where they have indicated that the application is likely to be refused planning permission. The extra time may be used to allow the applicant to resolve outstanding issues with consultees, eg highway authorities, thereby limiting the issues to be taken forward at the appeal stage.

1.6   Who can appeal?

Section 78 of the Act grants a right of appeal only to the person or persons mentioned on the application form as applicant. This limitation has two important consequences: it restricts the ability of a person to appeal despite the fact that for one reason or another he or she may be interested in taking the matter to appeal. Secondly, owners of the land concerned, neighbours or other interested parties are excluded.

The effect of this rather narrow right of appeal means that those wishing to avail themselves of an appeal opportunity because they want to promote the development must take care to ensure that they are in a position to ensure that the appeal avenue is kept open for them.

Any person buying land or interested in the development of land where an application is still before the local authority or where there is the likelihood of appeal should make arrangements with the applicant that the applicant will, if required, take steps to initiate and deal with any appeal. This will usually be at the cost of the interested party and it is usual in such arrangements to name that person's solicitor or planning consultant as agent for these purposes. Provision should be made for a full indemnity in respect of *all* conceivable costs, including any award of costs against the appellant for which the 'named person' may be liable. Some practitioners take the view that this rather artificial device weakens the position on appeal because the underlying reality may become apparent. Objectively, this argument is difficult to sustain. Planning permission is not normally concerned with the identity of the party seeking it and it is certainly not necessary for such a person to own any interest in the land. However, there may be circumstances which make for a stronger case on appeal where the appellant has a known identity. This is often best left to be dealt with at the evidential stage by explaining that the new person is the intended occupier or proposed operator and producing evidence such as a contract to purchase conditional on obtaining planning permission.

If there is real difficulty as to whether the newcomer can deal with an appeal, a better course may be for the purchaser to resubmit the application to the local authority in his own name and appeal that resubmitted application at the end of the prescribed period.

1.6.1   Third party right of appeal

The second significant effect of the statutory limitation on lodging an appeal is that it excludes people such as the owners of the land concerned, neighbours and other interested parties, despite the fact that they may have made representations at the planning application stage. It is this limitation which means that there is no right of appeal by a person who objects to the granting of planning permission or conditions attached to such a grant. However, once an appeal has been lodged such people do have some rights to make their views known in the course of the appeal procedure and such representations will be taken into account. The only way third parties can directly attack the local authority's decision is by an application for judicial review to the High Court under Ord 53 of the Rules of the Supreme Court.

1.6.2   Third party right of appeal against the Secretary of State

However, an application to the High Court under s 288 of the Act as a result of a decision of the Secretary of State or his inspector on appeal can be made by parties other than the appellant. A disappointed third party may be better placed to intervene after the decision on appeal (if planning permission is granted) than after the decision by the local authority. This is dealt with in Chapter 12.

The local authority naturally have no right to appeal to the Secretary of State against a decision they have made or conditions they have imposed. At first glance it is difficult to conceive of reasons why a local authority would wish to appeal. However, there are circumstances where a local authority might wish, perhaps as a result of new information becoming available, to reconsider a decision. Once the decision notice has been issued or an appeal lodged for non-determination the local authority cannot appeal under s 78 of the Act or reconsider the application.

1.7   Six-month time limit on lodging appeal

In accordance with art 26 of the GDO, an appeal must normally be lodged within six months of the local authority's decision (or the expiry of the 'prescribed period' if the appeal is in relation to non-determination). Article 26 gives the Secretary of State power to allow a longer period for lodging an appeal. He has indicated that although he has the power to accept a late appeal he will generally do so only in exceptional circumstances where the appellant can demonstrate that every reasonable attempt was made to give notice within the six-month period (Circular 22/88, para 48).

If the time period is close to expiry, the best advice must be to lodge an appeal form, by fax if necessary, indicating that details of grounds of appeal, etc will follow. If the appeal is well out of time, it may be better to resubmit the application to the local authority and wait until the eight-week period has expired before appealing that application.

The Town and Country Planning (Fees for Applications and Deemed Applications) Regulations 1989 (the Fees Regulations) provide that there is normally no fee for submitting an identical application within 12 months of the refusal of a previous application.

1.8 Duplicate applications

There may be circumstances where it is worth submitting applications in duplicate from the outset. This enables one application to be appealed when the prescribed period has expired while the other application remains before the local authority so that discussions may continue. Two sets of fees, however, may be payable. In addition, the local authority could regard this as a hostile act and refuse both applications simultaneously.

If it looks as if a decision will be delayed, the better course may be to submit one application and only submit a duplicate application a few days before the expiry of the prescribed period. The first application can then be appealed, leaving the duplicate before the authority. Alternatively, a second application may be submitted after an appeal has been lodged. If the application that is the subject of the appeal has been refused, there may be no fee payable. (For particular circumstances regarding exemption from fees see the Fees Regulations.)

However, some local authorities will either not process a duplicate application with any sense of urgency while an appeal is pending or will simply refuse it quickly on the basis that there has been no change in the circumstances. (See further para 2.3.)

1.9 Should you appeal?

1.9.1 Collecting the information

The first stage of deciding whether to appeal is to collect the papers that will be needed. These will normally be:
  (1) The refusal notice or conditional consent.
  (2) Application, plans and the original ownership certificate.
  (3) The committee report and background papers for the application (unless the decision was delegated to officers).

(4) Notes of any meeting with the local authority, correspondence and the planning history of the site, eg previous applications, decisions and notices.

(5) All responses to consultation and letters received by the local authority.

(6) The development plan (county structure plan, district local plan or the unitary development plan) marking relevant policies.

Is there a local plan review? What are the changes and what stage has it reached? Are the changes relevant to your appeal? What stage have they reached? Is there still time to lodge objections? Lodging an objection may form part of the appeal strategy.

(7) Relevant government advice: PPGs and circulars.

(8) Any other relevant material, eg is there any question of enforcement action? Is there an associated listed building or conservation area issue? Are there similar schemes on competing sites which should be decided together? If so, consider the implications for the appeal process.

This point was considered in *Edwards (PG) v SOSE* [1994] EGCS 60. The Department of Transport had specified one service area only on each side of the A47 in Norfolk. Seven applications to provide the service areas were made and all were appealed. Mr Edwards had lodged an appeal and he requested that all the appeals should be heard at a single inquiry. The Secretary of State was unwilling to delay the other appeals where the written representation procedure rather than public inquiry had been chosen. The Court of Appeal, however, held (in upholding the decision at first instance) that the appeals should have been dealt with together as they were alternative sites in a situation where only one planning permission could be granted.

1.9.2 Obtaining copies of documents

Most local authorities will co-operate with a person seeking information in connection with an appeal. Development plans are public documents and should be available for purchase from the local authority concerned. Alternatively, it may be sufficient simply to inspect a copy to check whether there are any relevant policies and to photocopy the relevant sheets. Most public planning counters have photocopying facilities, although a charge is usually made.

The refusal notice, previous applications and decisions are part of the planning register (which is open for public inspection) at the local authority's offices and copies can be obtained from the local authority. There are sometimes copyright difficulties in obtaining plans. Attention is drawn to the provisions of s 47 of the Copyright, Designs and Patents Act 1988 and the Copyright (Material Open to Public Inspection) (Making of Copies of Plans and Drawings) Order 1990. The 1988 Act provides that where material is open to the public for inspection under a statutory requirement, copyright is not infringed by copying it to the public (with the authority of the appropriate officer of the local authority). The 1990 Order provides that the exception from copyright only applies to plans and drawings marked in a specific manner.

If the plans cannot be copied under these exceptions they will either have to be copied manually or requested formally once the appeal has been lodged. Alternatively an approach can be made to the original applicant or architect for consent.

Where an application has been decided by the planning committee of the local authority (and this will be the case for most applications of substance), the application, the representations and all other background papers are open for public inspection by virtue of ss 100B to 100F of the Local Government Act 1972 as amended by the Local Government (Access to Information) Act 1985. Members of the public are permitted normally to take copies subject to paying a reasonable charge. In case of real difficulty, it may be better to wait until an appeal has been lodged when any such document can legitimately be requested from the local authority as part of the appeal process.

Some applications will be dealt with by planning officers under delegated authority. In these cases the Access to Information provisions will not apply. However, it is hoped that local authorities will co-operate by allowing relevant material to be copied. If they will not, the point should be formally raised with the Inspectorate once the appeal has been lodged.

PPGs, circulars and other government advice are normally published by HMSO. The most important and commonly used of these documents are listed among the statutory and other sources at the front of this book. Many planning reference books such as the *Encyclopaedia of Planning Law and Practice* are regularly updated and contain these documents.

1.10   Background to the decision-making process

Once the documentation relevant to the appeal has been assembled, it is helpful to consider how the inspector will deal with this information in reaching his decision. By virtue of s 79(1) of the Act, the Secretary of State (and the inspector appointed to make the decision) will deal with the application as if it had been made to him in the first instance. This means the inspector will make an independent decision in the light of all the relevant issues in exactly the same way as the local authority did. Requirements imposed on the local authority will apply equally to inspectors on appeal.

Two sections of the Act have particular relevance to this decision-making process:

> 70(2)   In dealing with such an application the authority shall have regard to the provisions of the development plan, so far as material to the application, and to any other material considerations.

Additional strength to the development plan is given by:

> 54A   Where, in making any determination under the planning Acts, regard is to be had to the development plan, that determination shall be made in accordance with the plan unless material considerations indicate otherwise.

The relationship between the provisions of the development plan and other material factors is spelt out in PPG1, 'General Policy and Principles' which is reproduced at the end of Chapter 1. Since the inspector will pay particular attention to the statutory requirements and government advice as set out in PPG1, it is essential that the appellant takes them into account when considering the merits and structure of his appeal.

Paragraph 25 of PPG1 makes clear that s 54A introduces a presumption in favour of development proposals which are in accordance with the development plan. It follows from this that an application for development which is clearly in conflict with the development plan will need to include convincing reasons to demonstrate why the plan should not prevail. However, such a presumption sits uncomfortably with government advice as set out in para 5 of PPG1:

> 5. The planning system should be efficient, effective and simple in conception and operation. It fails in its function whenever it prevents, inhibits or delays development which should reasonably have been permitted. It should operate on the basis that applications for development should be allowed, having regard to the development plan and all material considerations, unless the proposed development would cause demonstrable harm to interests of acknowledged importance.

Applying these policy factors to any particular case is the task of the inspector. Ensuring that the salient facts are properly exposed and the inspector is fully advised in any particular case is the task of the parties. The underlying purpose of the guidance is to move towards a plan-led system and to discourage arbitrary decisions on a case-by-case basis either by the local authority or on appeal.

A number of cases have been taken to the High Court recently, with decisions illustrating the balance to be struck. If conflict with the development plan is given as a reason for refusal, this area should be given particular attention (*St Albans District Council v Secretary of State for the Environment* [1993] 1 PLR 88 and *R v Canterbury City Council ex p Spring Image Ltd* [1993] NPL 125).

1.10.1   A practical approach

This book suggests a practical rather than an academic approach, on the following lines:

- Does the development plan contain relevant policies? If it does not, it will not influence the decision and can be disregarded.
- If there are relevant development plan policies they should form the starting point for consideration of the merits of an appeal.
- Consider the status of the relevant development plan. Is it recently adopted and up to date? Has it yet to be formally adopted but has it nonetheless completed consultation or public inquiry stages? Have objections been made to the policy during the course of local plan preparation?
- Once the existence of relevant development plan policies and their status have been established, consider whether the application is clearly in conflict with the policies cited or whether they have been referred to purely as a make-weight by the local authority.

In any particular case a proposal may accord with some policies, perhaps employment generation policies, but conflict with others, eg those seeking to curtail or restrict development in the open countryside. The nature and weight of such policies should be carefully considered. Some policies are firm and will be extremely difficult to overturn but other policies may be more easily outweighed by other factors.

● Having established the nature and weight of any policies against which the proposal is found to be in conflict, it will then be necessary to consider whether there are other 'material considerations' to outweigh that conflicting policy.

In most cases there will be. The following paragraphs look at the question of 'material considerations' in more detail.

● Having collected all relevant considerations, a metaphorical balance can be struck by placing each factor in the plus or minus side of an imaginary scale.

1.11   Material considerations

The term 'material considerations' in the planning context is a term of art. It is an important concept in evaluating the strength of the case. However valid and however 'right' an issue appears, if it is not a material consideration it should not be taken into account in the decision-making process and should be discarded as soon as possible.

There are very significant dangers in testing the limits of what is material. If you persuade an inspector that an issue is a material consideration and it later transpires it is not, that will undermine the decision that has been reached. On the other hand, it is important to ensure that all legitimate points are taken and properly documented in the appeal process. The weight which can be attached to a material consideration is quite a different thing and very difficult to challenge. This is an area where established decisions may not be especially helpful. Unless a particular point has been decided the better course is to consider the issue from basic principles.

Over 20 years ago the leading case of *Stringer v Minister of Housing and Local Government* [1971] JPL 114 established the correct approach to determining what is a material consideration. Paragraph 23 of PPG1 refers to this approach when it states:

> 23.   In principle . . . any consideration which relates to the use and development of land is capable of being a planning consideration. Whether a particular consideration falling within that broad class is material in any given case will depend on the circumstances' *(Stringer v MHLG* 1971). Material considerations must be genuine planning considerations, ie they must be related to the purpose of planning legislation, which is to regulate the development and use of land in the public interest. The considerations must also fairly and reasonably relate to the application concerned *(R v Westminster CC ex parte Monahan* 1989). Much will depend on the nature of the application under consideration, the relevant policies in the development plan and the surrounding circumstances.

Material consideration was helpfully defined in the *Monahan* case as a factor which

(1) is relevant to the facts, policies or submissions under consideration;
(2) has or can have a significant bearing on the matters at issue in the determination to be made; and
(3) is a planning consideration.

There is thus no easy answer. There is no handy list of what is material and what is not material in any particular case. However, it is possible to deduce certain broad principles of what, in most cases, will be material and what are unlikely ever to be material considerations. The weight that may be attached to a material consideration in any particular case is quite a different question. As a strategy, therefore, it is possible to accept an issue as material, but argue that it has little importance in reaching a particular decision.

The following matters are always material considerations:

● Relevant development plan policies.
● Government advice as set out in PPGs and circulars.
● An environmental impact statement submitted as a requirement of the Town and Country Planning (Assessment of Environmental Effects) Regulations 1988, as amended.
● The effect on listed buildings: ss 66 and 67 of the Planning (Listed Buildings and Conservation Areas) Act 1990 requires the local authority, or the Secretary of State (and an inspector) on appeal, to have 'special regard' to the desirability of preserving the building or its setting or any features of special architectural or historic interest which it possesses in considering a planning application affecting the building or its setting.
● The effect on conservation areas: ss 72 and 73 of the Planning (Listed Buildings and Conservation Areas) Act 1990 require the local authority to pay special attention to the desirability of preserving or enhancing the character or appearance of a conservation area when considering planning applications within it.
● The planning history of the site: is there an existing consent which could be implemented? Have similar proposals already been refused either by the local authority or on appeal?

    This aspect was canvassed in the case of *North Wiltshire District Council v Secretary of State for the Environment* [1992] 3 PLR 113. Planning permission for a house and garage had been refused on appeal in 1982. In 1989 a similar application was refused and appealed. The second inspector granted planning permission but made no reference to the previous decision. The court held that in the circumstances of that case the previous appeal decision was a material consideration and the inspector's reasons for departing from the previous decision should have been included in the decision letter. The omission meant that it was not possible to say with any certainty that the inspector had considered all material considerations as he is required to do.

- Representations received from owners and agricultural tenants of the land concerned as required by the GDO, art 22A.
- Any responses received as a result of consultation either at the planning application stage or as a result of the appeal consultation.

The following matters may be material considerations in certain circumstances:

- Third party interests. The private rights of owners and occupiers may not always be relevant. A person has no right (in planning law) to continue to enjoy a view which would be restricted by new development. On the other hand, issues such as overlooking by a new development and general amenity considerations may well be material.
- The identity of an applicant and his particular needs will not normally be relevant. However, there will be cases where the identity of the occupier may be material, eg in considering the requirements of a disabled person or in securing development for a local business, to tie a development to local agricultural need or for social housing.
- Financial or other personal considerations, which may become relevant in particular circumstances.

  It may thus be a material consideration that an existing building cannot be economically repaired and will be left empty as an eyesore and subject to vandalism, or that the existing use will not continue (even if planning permission is refused).

  Social policy issues, such as social housing, are at the moment under particular scrutiny and should be carefully considered in the light of the most up-to-date views.

  It may be relevant that the development will release profits to be used for restoration of other buildings (*Brighton Borough Council v SOSE* [1979] JPL 173 and also *R v Westminster City Council ex p Monahan* [1989] JPL 107).

- Planning gain: community gain in the shape of recreational facilities or highway improvements may be a material consideration but is subject to limits. Since most such gain comes forward by way of planning obligations this is dealt with in Chapter 8.

Certain matters cannot be material considerations. These are:

- Issues not related to land use. An ulterior purpose, however worthwhile, should not influence a planning decision, eg a local authority cannot use their planning powers to preserve the rights of a particular tenant (*Westminster City Council v British Waterways Board* [1985] AC 676). However, if there is an underlying planning purpose then the fact that the policy will inevitably protect certain occupiers does not render it unlawful (*Westminster City Council v Great Portland Estates* [1985] AC 661).
- Bias and conflict of interest. The local authority may not use their powers as planning authority to further their interests as land owner (*Steeples v Derbyshire County Council* [1981] JPL 582).

Because planning applications are decided at local level by elected councillors it may well be the case that the local authority may have, wearing another hat as housing authority or otherwise, preferred projects. Providing that the planning application is considered properly on its merits without fettering the council's discretion such other issues are unlikely to affect the validity of a planning decision (*R v Carlisle City Council ex p Cumbrian Co-operative Society* [1985] 276 EG 1161).

The crux of the difficulty for the appellant is that if he uses an issue as part of his case which is doubtful as a material consideration, he may find it open to challenge.

It is important for advisers to form a clear view of the central non-contentious area and to be aware of the dangers of moving to the peripheral areas. If a decision is taken to rely on such a peripheral area this should be a conscious decision, taken because the issue concerned is seen to be vital for the case. The risks and delays of a challenge should be weighed up at an early stage. If the question of materiality is not picked up right from the outset, one could be caught up unexpectedly in a challenge on a point which was not essential or without having prepared the ground to meet the challenge. If it is intended to challenge the limits of 'material considerations', it must be sensible to involve counsel before the appeal is lodged.

It should also be borne in mind that inspectors are not usually lawyers. They have no doubt a quite human desire to avoid their decisions being challenged in the High Court. They are likely, therefore, to refuse to break new ground in the acceptance of the materiality of an issue presented to them or to indicate in the decision letter that the issue in question has been accorded very little weight and has not therefore affected the decision. The courts have consistently held that they will not interfere with the judgment of the decision-maker as to questions of weight and it is extremely difficult to challenge such a decision. See further Chapter 12 on High Court challenge.

The advice in a practical handbook such as this must be to concentrate on the central planning arguments and to avoid the temptation to be legally inventive. In the author's experience, fine legal arguments are out of place in most appeals. They distract attention from the planning merits and are often counter-productive as far as the inspector is concerned. If the matter is proceeding by way of written representations or informal hearing, it is possible that the inspector will adjourn the proceedings and require a public inquiry to be held so that contentious legal issues can be properly addressed.

One final academic question may arise once the pieces of the jigsaw have been assembled and before the reasons for refusal of a particular case are looked at. The question is whether in the particular case benefit can be derived from the presumption in favour of development unless it would harm interests of acknowledged importance (PPG1, para 5).

It seems now quite clear that the fact that there is a relevant policy opposed to the proposals is not in itself sufficient reason to justify a refusal. One is entitled to look at the purpose of the policy and to examine the question of whether harm will result.

The gloss which seems to be implied is that we have a plan-led system but not yet a prescriptive plan system. Contrary policy can be attacked on two fronts:
- that the policy is 'weak', eg fails to deal adequately with present circumstances for one reason or another; and
- that the proposals themselves will not harm planning objectives.

But care is needed: consistency and precedent are also issues of acknowledged importance. The fact that your proposal may weaken the system generally may also be a factor.

1.12   The balancing act

Having assembled all the relevant documents and considered the application of the Act and material considerations, the next stage for the practitioner will be to weigh up the reasons for refusal, or the objections as they have emerged from discussions with the local authority, against this background. Most of the work will have already been done. It will be relatively easy thereafter to reach a conclusion as to whether an appeal should be lodged and if so, the grounds for appeal and strategy for the appeal procedure.

1.12.1   Reasons for refusal and grounds of appeal

If there is a decision notice, this should form the starting point for considering the grounds of appeal. Consider the reasons carefully one by one, as they can be illuminating. On some occasions, they will be trite, but on others they are an indication that the local authority have taken a wrong turning or had real difficulty in substantiating a reason for refusal. This is particularly likely in cases where the application was refused by members of the committee against officer advice. If the reasons have a delphic inscrutability (eg 'to protect local amenity'), remind the local authority of the need to give reasons, making reference to Circular 1/85, para 8 and ask for a clear explanation in ordinary English.

Most reasons fall into two categories: first, that the proposals are contrary to policy, either local development plan policies or central government advice as set out in PPGs or circulars, and secondly, the site-specific arguments referring to the adverse impact of the proposals.

1.12.2   Policy issues

If reasons for refusal relate primarily to policies, consider the strength of those policies and the local plan position. Is the policy a nationally recognised and enforced one, such as the green belt? A successful appeal would be unlikely. On the other hand, is it a local plan policy which is out of date or so newly formulated that it is a part of a local plan that has not yet formally reached the end of its statutory journey to adoption? If the proposals are contrary to an up-to-date adopted policy, consider the weight that s 54A of the Act attaches to such policies and the real likelihood of an inspector being constrained to decide an appeal in accordance with such policies.

It is important to be objective. Planning is all about balancing competing pressures for the use of land. Many cases are not clear cut. This may be a good moment to consider taking advice from an experienced planning practitioner who can give his assessment of how an inspector is likely to approach the policy issues in the particular circumstances.

What kind of evidence will an inspector need? The inspector will not simply consider the local authority's reasons. He or she will deal with the appeal as if it were a new application. Some appeals are extremely expensive to run, requiring a great deal of specialist evidence.

1.12.3   Site-specific issues

If the reasons for refusal are site-specific, they should also be weighed up carefully. More information may now be available. A professional adviser may indicate that evidence can be brought quite easily to refute a point. Is the reason for refusal primarily one of subjective appraisal, eg the appearance of a building? In this kind of case the inspector may take a different view of what is essentially a matter of taste. In any event local authorities are advised not to impose their taste on an applicant (PPG1, Annex A). In non-determination cases there will be no reasons for refusal. Discussions with the local authority should already have indicated where difficulties lie.

If an applicant has no clear idea of the local authority's view of his application, it might be better to persevere with the application until the authority's position is clear. Even if an applicant refuses to grant the local authority an extension of time, the local authority can continue to consider the application until either they make a decision or an appeal is lodged.

1.13   Making the decision to appeal

Having spread the net widely and considered all material considerations in the light of the reasons for refusal, the prospective appellant can take the final step of identifying the relevant issues and the strengths and weaknesses of the case. At this stage it is important to see the wood for the trees. If all issues have been thoroughly rehearsed, little is likely to emerge at a later stage to interfere with the appeal strategy.

It may be now helpful to produce a position statement reflecting all relevant issues and how they are to be dealt with. This will not only be useful in formulating the grounds of appeal but it can also be amended and amplified as the case becomes clearer and as the procedure progresses. It is quite possible to be even more sophisticated and attempt to weight the relevant factors and thus arrive at some objective assessment as to the chances of success. This can be useful to counteract the natural tendency to believe one's own arguments and to discount those of others. This approach also ensures that all the issues have been addressed. Inevitably when an application is refused in circumstances where the applicant thinks it should not have been, he may focus on one particular element where he believes the local authority have been unreasonable. Aspects which did not concern the local authority may concern the inspector; likewise matters about which the local authority were concerned may be easily answered on appeal. A comprehensive list of issues will go some way towards anticipating such changes.

There is a danger that because some issues have been dealt with extensively at the application stage, they have been emphasised beyond their real importance. An appeal is an opportunity to re-present the merits of the case and the issues should be looked at afresh.

Scoping, or taking objective stock of the realities of the case, is important in deciding whether to appeal and ensuring that the correct decisions are taken right from the beginning as to which issues are important, which are not and which should be discarded entirely. In this way, the right team can be assembled to deal with the issues and they will be working purposefully from the outset.

1.13.1   Amending the scheme

It is surprising what can emerge from a genuine, unblinkered reassessment of the case. One factor which may emerge is that the application could be improved, thus enhancing the chances of success. If it becomes evident in the course of the appeal that some change is desirable, it is necessary to consider the extent to which such changes can be made.

The Act makes no specific provision for the amendment of appeal proposals, but it is beyond doubt that such changes can be made (*Brittania (Cheltenham) v Secretary of State for the Environment* [1979] JPL 534). Indeed the emphasis now placed on consultation, particularly after the application is refused and during the early stages of the appeal, may well encourage the consideration of changes (see in particular Circular 18/86, para 7). It would, however, clearly be wrong to permit fundamental changes on appeal. The result might be that planning permission would be granted for a development which had not gone through the normal consultation processes and would thus prejudice third parties.

The test to be applied to changes was laid down in the case of *Bernard Wheatcroft Ltd v Secretary of State for the Environment and Another* (1980) P&CR 43. There the application was for 420 houses on 35 acres. The appellant at the appeal stage attempted to hedge his bets by indicating that he would put forward at the inquiry alternative proposals for 250 dwellings on 25 acres to be considered by the inspector if the scale of development was critical. The Secretary of State declined to consider the revision. It was held in an application under what is now s 288 of the Act that the proper test was whether the effect of a grant of planning permission would be to allow development that was substantially different from that for which permission had been applied.

It could be argued that in the *Wheatcroft* case no third party could be injured by granting planning permission for a development which was of the same nature as the original application but little more than half the size. Somewhat predictably the enlargement of a site was rejected in the case of *Breckland District Council v Secretary of State for the Environment* and *Hill* [1993] JPL 1140. The site area of a proposed caravan site was extended from 0.47 hectares to 0.6 hectares but the number of pitches remained the same. Although the local authority had been consulted, they had drawn attention to the fact that the parish council and local residents had not been notified. The inspector's decision to accept the amendment and grant permission on the basis of the amended site was held to be unreasonable and invalid.

However, it must be admitted that schemes, particularly in relation to design details, are often amended even in the course of the appeal. Amendment is a useful way of taking in points which have emerged from the detailed examination of a scheme during the appeal process. It is often only at the appeal stage that the appellant's architect may have the opportunity of meeting and discussing in detail shortcomings of development proposals with the local authority architect. As a general rule, providing such changes are within the *Wheatcroft* principle, the local authority should be asked whether they object to the changes being introduced on appeal. If the local authority accept the revisions, the inspector should be asked whether he will consider them. Even if the local authority do not accept the revisions, they can still be put forward at the inquiry but this of course makes the changes contentious and makes it more likely that the inspector will be reluctant to consider them.

If there is any real doubt as to whether the changes are so substantial as to alter the nature of the proposals, or if the changes are opposed by the local authority, the better course may well be to consider alternatives to lodging an appeal. If the appeal is already running, consideration should be given to abandoning the variations and, if this substantially affects the chances of success, withdrawing the appeal (although here the question of costs must be borne in mind).

1.14   Withdrawing the appeal

Lodging an appeal is not something to be undertaken lightly, but nor is it necessarily a commitment to see the procedure through to the end. Somewhat perversely, it may be as well to consider the opportunities and implications of withdrawal before the appeal is lodged. The question of withdrawal should also be reviewed by advisers during the course of the appeal as the case develops. The author believes that, strictly speaking, an appeal can be withdrawn at any time until the decision letter is stamped and sent by the Inspectorate. However, there may be resistance to allowing this to be done at a very late stage. Whether this is, at any stage, the right course is now considered, together with the consequences flowing from such a withdrawal.

1.14.1   Reasons for withdrawal

1.14.3   One of the commonest reasons for withdrawing an appeal is that the appellant has thought better of it. If the preparatory work has been done thoroughly, this is seldom the case, as it results in a waste of time and money for the appellant. However, it may be inevitable if an appeal has been lodged as a precautionary measure because the six-month time limit was about to expire. Once a decision is taken that an appeal is not the right course, the submission of the 'holding' appeal will have achieved its objective and should be withdrawn immediately.

If the preparatory work has been carefully done and a meaningful dialogue opened with the local authority, agreement may be reached to achieve an acceptable application. In this case, an appellant may wish to submit a revised application to the local authority rather than try to amend the current appeal and possibly fall foul of the *Wheatcroft* principle (see para 1.13.1). He will also avoid the costs and uncertainty inherent in the appeal process. Appellants may consider requesting the Inspectorate to hold the appeal in abeyance while a new application is processed by the local authority because until planning permission is actually issued there can be no certainty. The Inspectorate will usually grant a limited extension of time, particularly at the beginning of the appeal process. However, if the appeal has progressed, and particularly if the date for a public inquiry has been fixed, then there may be considerable reluctance to delay the appeal. The Inspectorate is now working to reduce time taken to deal with appeals.

In practice, the Inspectorate are usually willing to assist an appellant to sort out a problem if this is supported by the local authority. If the appeal cannot be delayed, the appellant may be forced to withdraw the appeal to avoid committing further resources. The costs position will need to be considered.

The materiality of planning considerations may change during the course of the appeal procedure, as may the weight to be attached to them. Revised local plans or government advice may have a considerable impact on the inspector's consideration of the appeal. In these circumstances, an appellant may think it prudent to withdraw the appeal rather than risk a refusal on the planning record.

It is also possible that the appellant's interest in the appeal may wane. If he is a prospective developer, he may have decided not to proceed with the project. An appellant who has lent his name to a prospective developer for the purposes of prosecuting an appeal, might have no choice but to withdraw an appeal since the agreement will normally require him to do so if requested. If a prospective developer has lost interest in the site, another party might be interested in developing the site, and the time gained by taking over an appeal may be valuable. It may also be of use to the landowner, whether or not he was involved in the appeal process, to consider ensuring that the appeal continues because if it is successful it will enhance the value of the land.

1.14.2   Consequences of withdrawal

There are two main consequences of withdrawing an appeal. The first relates to costs and the second affects the future planning of the site. An appellant must at all stages bear in mind the risk of costs being awarded to other parties and payable by him if an appeal is withdrawn. The risk increases as time progresses, particularly once a date for a public inquiry has been fixed. Awards of costs are dealt with in Chapter 11.

It is worth discussing withdrawal with the local authority and any third party who may be in a position to ask for a costs award. Local authorities do have resource pressures and will often readily agree not to ask for costs if an appeal is withdrawn. They are aware that there can never be any certainty of receiving costs. If they refuse their agreement, the appellant could decide to press on with the appeal in any event. Other third parties may be less amenable to this argument but the appellant will consider carefully the reality of costs being awarded, particularly if there is a legitimate objective reason for withdrawing the appeal.

1.14.3 Time for withdrawing appeal

An appeal should be withdrawn immediately it becomes clear that that is the right course of action, and all other parties should be notified. When the question of the reasonableness of conduct comes to be looked at in the context of a costs award (if one is in issue), the fact that the appellant has reacted promptly to new circumstances will be of value. It is part of the professional adviser's role as the appeal progresses to assess whether original assumptions cease to hold valid. Matters should not be allowed to drift and the decision on withdrawal, however unpalatable, should be discussed and a prompt decision made. Many successful costs awards arise because the situation is allowed to drag on, involving the other parties in unnecessary additional work. The impact on the future planning of the site should also be considered. In the ordinary way, it is possible to re-submit an application to the local authority and begin the process again. Where this is not the case, the balance may tip in favour of continuing with the appeal despite the changed circumstances. This would be the case, for instance, where there is an application for approval of reserved matters and the three-year limit for submission of details has passed. If the appeal is withdrawn, the outline permission will normally become incapable of implementation. If there has been a change in the circumstances, a similar outline application to the local authority may not readily be approved. The ability to proceed with an appeal based simply on the limited issues arising from an existing consent may therefore be extremely valuable.

If timing is crucial, the time lost in starting again from scratch could be unacceptable. An appellant might choose to take a chance on the revised circumstances, even though he might not have submitted the appeal in the first place had the circumstances been the same. There is always uncertainty as to the outcome of planning appeals. A change may in fact be given less weight by the inspector if it arises very late in the appeal process. In particular, changes in the local plan which emerge in the course of the appeal are likely to be at an early stage and not yet have been subject to full public consultation.

1.14.4   Is there an alternative to withdrawal?

It is always possible to change the procedure adopted. If the chances of success do not now warrant the expense of a public inquiry, consideration should be given to requesting a change to the written representations procedure. Local authorities are aware of the costs, preparation and hearing time required for public inquiries and will normally welcome a change to the written representations procedure. If the local authority agree, this will not normally be resisted by the Inspectorate unless a case is clearly unsuitable for the written representations procedure. Local authorities will very often agree not to ask for costs on such a change.

From the appellant's point of view, if the preparation has been thorough, very little additional work will be required to assemble a written dossier to place before the inspector. This will enable the appeal to progress and a decision to be issued at little additional cost.

Advisers should not be mesmerised by fear of an award of costs. In a public inquiry case, most of the costs relate to the hearing itself and the period immediately before the hearing when proofs are exchanged. Even if costs are awarded in such a situation, provided an appeal is withdrawn before the inquiry, costs are likely to be substantially less than those that would have been expended in any event by the appellant in running the inquiry itself.

1.15   Is there an alternative to appeal?

1.15.1   Submitting an amended scheme

In the course of the consideration of an application, new information may emerge which will enable an application to be improved. The local authority may have indicated, for instance, that they find the siting or elements of the design unacceptable. It may be sensible to submit a revised application to the local authority rather than embark on an appeal on proposals which are not as good as they might be. It can be tactically advantageous to tackle all the points that can be dealt with in a revised application. If this is refused, an appeal can be lodged on the few outstanding issues identified between the parties rather than leaving the inspector to deal with a whole host of issues. Although the inspector is free to take his own view of the proposals, he is unlikely to refuse an application on appeal for reasons which the local authority have not raised.

There is something to be said for compromising on, say, the size of an extension in order to obtain a planning permission from the local authority without the expense and uncertainty of an appeal. It will be possible at a later date to make a further application.

1.15.2   Intervening in the local plan process

If the appeal is contrary to policy, consider intervening in the local plan process. Applications which accord with the local plan are more likely subsequently to receive a planning permission without difficulty. In some cases, such as development on the edge of the green belt, it may be virtually impossible to persuade an inspector to grant an application which does not conform. The only realistic option will be to ensure the site is taken out of the green belt by way of the local plan process. It may also be possible in the local plan process to identify a particular site for a particular use. This again will ensure that a subsequent planning application is not contentious.

1.15.3   Unacceptable conditions

Is it only a condition imposed on a consent that is unacceptable? If an appeal is lodged against the consent, there is a risk that the inspector (who has the right to consider all issues anew) could decide that the application as a whole should be refused. This will effectively overturn the previous consent. It may therefore be preferable to use the procedure under s 73 of the Act whereby an application can be made to the local authority for permission to carry out the development without complying with the specific condition. Although the local authority may refuse consent to remove or alter the condition, an appeal against this refusal will not put the original consent at risk.

Sections 91 and 92 of the Act require certain time limits for the commencement of development to be imposed. The usual time limit on a detailed planning permission is that it must be implemented within five years. Where outline planning permission has been granted, the application for approval of reserved matters must be submitted within three years of the date of grant of the planning permission (s 92(3) of the Act). Applications can be made under s 73 of the Act to extend these time limits. An application can also be made to renew a planning permission. Special provisions governing renewal applications are contained in the Town and Country Planning (Applications) Regulations 1988.

If time limits are close to expiry it may be important to consider a safe option. Once the three years for submission of applications for approval of reserved matters under an outline permission have expired, it is no longer possible to submit details and in effect that part of the development becomes incapable of implementation. In the same way once the five-year period has expired without the planning permission being implemented, it will be incapable of implementation. In both cases there is a real risk that if the local authority are unhappy with the situation, and they may be if the original consent was granted on appeal, there will be difficulties in either extending the time periods or renewing the application.

In order to keep the permissions alive, it may be essential to ensure either that the application for approval of reserved matters is submitted within the three-year period, in a form where the local authority cannot reasonably refuse it. Or, if a detailed planning permission is in issue, it should actually be implemented in accordance with s 56 of the Act. The effect of this action is twofold, preserving the development opportunity granted by the original planning permission and enabling any subsequent application and appeal proceedings to be dealt with against a planning history which includes the ability to carry out such development.

This procedure may also be useful where either circumstances have changed or where it is believed that the local authority had little evidence to impose the condition. It sometimes happens that conditions are imposed simply as a result of public pressure.

The question of conditions and their validity is dealt with in more detail in Chapter 7.

1.15.4   Offering conditions and planning obligations

Can objections be overcome by offering conditions or a planning obligation? A condition limiting the hours of operation or a binding planning obligation may meet the case. In other cases, perhaps in relation to a new business unit, a temporary consent may give time for the unit to establish its operational base. If an appeal is lodged, draft conditions will have to be put forward and discussed with the local authority in any event as part of the appeal process. It will not be wasted time to consider these issues at this stage.

Planning conditions are dealt with in Chapter 7 and planning obligations in Chapter 8.

1.15.5   Was the planning application properly dealt with?

Planning procedure has to comply with principles of administrative law. This means that not only do the principles of natural justice and fairness operate but the procedural rules must also be adhered to.

Judicial review under RSC Ord 53 is technically available to challenge an improper decision of a local authority made in the course of considering a planning application. This may be the only avenue open to a person affected by a planning decision if no appeal is lodged (see Chapter 14). However, there may be occasions when the applicant himself takes exception to the way a planning application or associated matters have been handled. This was the case in *R v Swansea City Council ex p Elitestone* [1992] JPL 1143. An application for judicial review was made by the owner of land who wished to demolish the chalet-type wooden structures on the land and replace them with conventional housing. The planning authority declared the area a conservation area at a meeting of two members where the requisite three clear days' notice of the meeting as required by the access to information provisions of the Local Government Act 1972 had not been given. In that particular case the application for judicial review was academic because the local authority subsequently declared the area a conservation area at a properly convened meeting.

The question arises as to whether an applicant who believes that a refusal results from the improper processing of his application should take this as a separate point. This will only very rarely be the case where an applicant is in a position to lodge an appeal. If the local authority have for some reason neglected to carry out a proper notification and consultation exercise in accordance with s 65 of the Act, s 79 permits these steps to be carried out by the Secretary of State once an appeal has been lodged to remedy the matter. If the complaint relates to what was taken into account or said at the time the decision was made by the local authority, this will automatically be rectified by the appeal process because the inspector will not be simply considering the local authority's decision but will be making his own decision in the light of all relevant factors. This is also the case where an applicant believes that members wrongly disregarded the professional advice tendered to them. In most cases an applicant will be better advised to proceed with an appeal.

An application for judicial review will normally result in the decision in question being remitted to the local authority to carry out the decision-making process again. The court will not *grant* the planning permission sought (see Chapter 14 on judicial review). There is nothing to prevent an appellant raising such issues as part of his case in order to undermine the stance adopted by the local authority. In this way, he may persuade the inspector to accord less weight to the propositions put forward by the authority than might otherwise be the case.

1.16   Is now the best time?

Consider whether this is the right time to lodge an appeal. Will the situation be better or worse in a year's time? Are you prepared to wait and try again in a few years when circumstances may have changed? This may be particularly important where need for the development is an element of the case. In times of recession it may be difficult to make an outstanding need case. The view may be taken that circumstances are unlikely to improve or are likely to become much more difficult. This may well be true of green belt protection, development involving the open countryside and development involving conservation areas.

1.17   Back to the drawing board?

Reconsider the project as a whole. It is disappointing to put work into a planning application and to have it refused. It may take courage to look afresh at the development proposals and start again from scratch. However, this may be a better use of resources than pursuing an expensive and uncertain appeal.

Projects take on a life of their own and it is not easy to advise a client not to throw good money after bad. There are cases where a client is better advised to move to a new location where his proposals are not contentious in planning terms rather than dissipate time, energy and money in trying to force through proposals. If making widgets is his business he should be concentrating on making widgets.

If there are serious doubts as to whether an appeal is the right course of action, go over the ground again. Once a refusal on appeal is on the planning record it will be difficult to overcome in future. Although there is no precedent, strictly speaking, inspectors are required to have regard to previous appeal decisions (*North Wiltshire District Council v Secretary of State for the Environment* [1992] 3 PLR 113). There is a natural tendency towards consistency unless there has been a significant change in circumstances.

PPG1: GENERAL POLICY AND PRINCIPLES

Introduction

1.   This Planning Policy Guidance Note is a revision of PPG1, first published in January 1988, which it supersedes. The guidance in the earlier version has been reviewed and amended to reflect changes introduced by the Planning and Compensation Act 1991 and developments in policy stemming, in particular, from the White Paper 'This Common Inheritance', published in September 1990. It sets out the general principles under which the planning system is to operate and incorporates advice on some specific issues not covered elsewhere in PPGs.

2.   The town and country planning system is designed to regulate the development and use of land in the public interest. The system has served the country well. It is an important instrument for protecting and enhancing the environment in town and country, preserving the built and natural heritage, conserving the rural landscape and maintaining Green Belts.

3.   The Government has made clear its intention to work towards ensuring that development and growth are sustainable. It will continue to develop policies consistent with the concept of sustainable development. The planning system, and the preparation of development plans in particular, can contribute to the objectives of ensuring that development and growth are sustainable. The sum total of decisions in the planning field, as elsewhere should not deny future generations the best of today's environment.

4.   The planning system has a positive role to play in guiding appropriate development to the right place, as well as preventing development which is not acceptable. It must make adequate provision for development (for example, the new houses and workplaces the nation needs, and associated services such as roads and schools), and at the same time take account of the need to protect the natural and built environment. It must also take account of international obligations. In this way, properly used, the planning system can secure economy, efficiency and amenity in the use of land.

5.   The planning system should be efficient, effective and simple in conception and operation. It fails in its function whenever it prevents, inhibits or delays development which should reasonably have been permitted. It should operate on the basis that applications for development should be allowed, having regard to the development plan and all material considerations, unless the proposed development would cause demonstrable harm to interests of acknowledged importance. The approach that decision makers should take to the consideration of planning applications is set out in paragraphs 25–31 below.

6.   It is not the function of the planning system to interfere with or inhibit competition between users and investors in land, or to regulate the overall provision and character of space for particular uses for other than land-use

planning reasons. Where development is acceptable, it is a matter for landowners, developers and/or tenants as to whether or not to proceed with it.

Speed of operation

Unnecessary delays in the planning system can result in extra costs, wasted capital, delayed production, reduced employment opportunities, and lost income and productivity. The Government and local planning authorities therefore have a responsibility to ensure that delays in preparing development plans, and in determining planning applications and appeals are minimised. Local planning authorities should aim to decide 80% of applications within eight weeks.

The target handling times for appeal cases decided by Inspectors are being reviewed in preparation for the Planning Inspectorate's transition to a 'Next Steps' Executive Agency on 1 April 1992. The targets, which will be published, will be compatible with the standards of efficiency and effectiveness that the Government wishes to see reflected elsewhere in the planning system. Where the Secretaries of State take the decision on appeals, they will aim to decide 80% of cases within eight weeks of receiving the Inspector's report.

Legislation

7.   The primary legislation is now contained in three consolidating Acts of Parliament:
      the Town and Country Planning Act 1990 (referred to in this guidance as 'the 1990 Act');
      the Planning (Listed Buildings and Conservation Areas) Act 1990; and
      the Planning (Hazardous Substances) Act 1990 (when brought into force).
Each of these Acts has been amended by the Planning and Compensation Act 1991 (referred to in this guidance as 'the 1991 Act').

8.   The main instruments of subordinate legislation are: the Town and Country Planning General Development Order 1988 (the GDO) and the Town and Country Planning (Use Classes) Order 1987 (the UCO), both of which have been amended; and the Town and Country Planning (Development Plan) Regulations 1991.

Planning permission

9.   Planning permission is required for any development of land. 'Development' is defined in section 55 of the 1990 Act as 'the carrying out of building, engineering, mining or other operations in, on, over or under land, or the making of any material change in the use of any buildings or other land'. The definition of building operations will be amended (when section 13 of the 1991 Act is brought into force) to include the demolition of buildings. A

direction by the Secretaries of State and amendments to the GDO will have the effect that most types of demolition will either not involve development or will be permitted development.

10.   Section 55 also provides that certain works and uses do not constitute development under the Act. These include:

works of maintenance, improvement or alteration which affect only the interior of a building or which do not materially affect its external appearance;

the use of buildings or land within the curtilage of a dwellinghouse for any purpose incidental to the enjoyment of the dwellinghouse as such;

the use of land for the purpose of agriculture or forestry; and

change of use of land or buildings from one use to another within the same class of the UCO.

11.   Moreover, the GDO, as amended, gives a general permission for certain defined classes of development or use of land, mainly of a minor character. The most commonly used class permits a wide range of small extensions or alterations to dwellinghouses. Schemes for Enterprise Zones and Simplified Planning Zones (see PPG5) also confer planning permission for developments of types defined in the scheme concerned.

12.   The general permission which the GDO grants for a particular development or class of development may be withdrawn in a particular area by a direction made by the local authority or by the Secretaries of State under Article 4 of the GDO. Where this is done, specific permission for the development in question must be sought, although refusal of permission in these circumstances or the granting of permission subject to conditions (other than those imposed by the GDO) entitles those with an interest in the land to claim compensation from the local planning authority under sections 107 and 108 of the 1990 Act, for any financial loss and/or depreciation in the value of the land.

13.   Currently over 500,000 planning applications are received by English local authorities annually, and nearly 40,000 by those in Wales. About 80% are granted. The Secretaries of State may require applications to be referred to them for decision, but this call-in power has in recent years only been exercised in around 130 cases each year in England, and in about 10 in Wales. The policy of the Secretaries of State is to be very selective about calling in planning applications, and such action is generally taken only if planning issues of more than local importance are involved. Examples are applications which could have wide effects beyond their immediate area, or give rise to substantial controversy nationally or regionally, or conflict with national policy on important matters, or where national security or the interests of foreign governments are involved.

14.   Under section 78 of the 1990 Act, an applicant may appeal to the respective Secretary of State against a local planning authority's decision to refuse planning permission or to grant it subject to conditions, or against the authority's

failure to notify its decision within 8 weeks or within a longer period that may have been agreed between the applicant and the authority. The Department of the Environment and the Welsh Office currently receive some 25,000 planning appeals a year, of which about one-third are allowed. The overwhelming majority (98%) of the planning permissions granted in England and Wales each year result from decisions by local planning authorities; only 2% from decisions by the Secretaries of State or Planning Inspectors following call-in or on appeal.

15.   Planning authorities have an extensive and flexible range of discretionary enforcement powers with which to deal with breaches of planning control. The 1991 Act introduces a new planning contravention notice, a breach of condition notice and a provision for obtaining an injunction to restrain a breach of planning control, in addition to improving and strengthening the present powers to issue an enforcement notice and serve a stop notice. These new provisions will make the planning powers more effective. Guidance on their use is given in PPG18 and DOE Circular 21/91 (WO 76/91).

16.   In deciding whether to grant planning permission, decision-makers must refer to the provisions of the development plan (see paragraphs 25–31 below) and to all other material considerations. In every case where a proposal for development is not acceptable, the local planning authorities must state clearly and precisely the full reasons for refusing planning permission. Similarly, where the Secretaries of State refuse a planning application on appeal, or following a call-in, they must give their reasons for that decision. Local planning authorities should also be prepared on request to explain to a statutory consultee, where they decide to approve an application against the advice of that consultee, the reasons for their approval.

Development plans

17.   Full guidance on the preparation of development plans is given in PPG12, and for Wales in PPG12 (Wales). Development plans are prepared following a statutory process of public consultation and debate. Such plans, which should be consistent with national and regional planning policy, provide the primary means of reconciling conflicts between the need for development, including the provision of infrastructure, and the need to protect the built and natural environment. Although their provisions are not prescriptive, they are intended to provide a firm basis for rational and consistent decisions on planning applications and appeals. Statutorily approved and adopted plans provide all concerned with development in a locality — residents and amenity bodies, developers and other business interests, and those responsible for providing infrastructure — with a measure of certainty about what types of development will and will not be permitted.

18.   A number of different plans may together comprise the development plan — depending on the subject and the area where development is proposed. These plans comprise:

   (i)   *structure plans*, setting out strategic policies in non-metropolitan areas;

   (ii) *local plans, waste local plans* and *minerals local plans*, all of which set out detailed development policies for non-metropolitan areas;

   (iii) *unitary development plans* in which planning authorities in Greater London and metropolitan areas combine the functions of (i) and (ii); and for a transitional period:

   (iv) *old-style development plans* approved under legislation up to and including the Town and Country Planning Act 1962 and not yet replaced by local plan provisions; and

   (v) any local plan saved under Schedule 4 to the 1991 Act.

Structure plans are already in place for all areas in England and Wales. Unitary development plans are in preparation for all metropolitan areas and Greater London, The 1991 Act makes mandatory the preparation of district-wide and National Park-wide local plans, and of county-wide and National park-wide minerals and waste local plans. The Secretaries of State expect coverage of area-wide local plans to be substantially complete by the end of 1996.

19.   The Secretaries of State are statutory consultees in the preparation of development plans, and have powers of intervention — they can object to a draft plan on deposit, or direct that a draft plan should be modfied, or ultimately they can call in all or part of a draft plan for their own determination.

Statements of the government's planning policies

20.   The Courts have held that the Government's statements of planning policy are material considerations which must be taken into account, where relevant, in decisions on planning applications. Such policy statements may be found in White Papers; Planning Policy Guidance Notes (PPGs); Minerals Planning Guidance Notes (MPGs); Regional Planning Guidance (RPGs) [England only]; Development Control Policy Notes (DCPNs); Departmental Circulars; and Ministerial Statements. PPGs, MPGs and RPGs are now the principal source of policy guidance on planning matters; DCPNs are being progressively withdrawn, and planning Circulars will tend to focus on legislative and procedural matters.

21.   The Department's policy statements cannot make irrelevant any matter which is a material consideration in a particular case. But where such statements indicate the weight that should be given to relevant considerations, decision-makers must have proper regard to them. If decision-makers elect not to follow relevant statements of the Government's planning policy they must give clear and convincing reasons (*EC Gransden and Co Ltd v SSE and Gillingham BC* 1985).

22.   Emerging policies, in the form of draft Departmental Circulars and policy guidance, are capable of being regarded as material considerations, depending on the context. It may not be appropriate to disregard such drafts completely, since their very existence may indicate that a relevant policy is under review, and the circumstances which have led to that review may need to be taken into account.

Other material considerations

23.   'In principle . . . any consideration which relates to the use and development of land is capable of being a planning consideration. Whether a particular consideration falling within that broad class is material in any given case will depend on the circumstances' (*Stringer v MHLG* 1971). Material considerations must be genuine planning considerations, ie they must be related to the purpose of planning legislation, which is to regulate the development and use of land in the public interest. The considerations must also fairly and reasonably relate to the application concerned (*R v Westminster CC ex parte Monahan* 1989). Much will depend on the nature of the application under consideration, the relevant policies in the development plan and the surrounding circumstances.

24.   The Courts are the arbiters of what constitutes a material consideration. Over the years the scope of what can be regarded as material has been clarified by judicial authority. All the fundamental factors involved in land-use planning are included, such as the number, size, layout, siting, design and external appearance of buildings and the proposed means of access, together with land-scaping, impact on the neighbourhood and the availability of infrastructure.

Determining planning applications and appeals

25.   The approach that decision-makers should take to the consideration of planning applications is set out in sections 70(2) and 54A of the 1990 Act (the latter inserted by section 26 of the 1991 Act). Section 70(2) requires the decision-maker to have regard to the development plan, so far as it is material to the application, and to any other material considerations. Where the development plan is material to the development proposal, and must therefore be taken into account, section 54A requires the application or appeal to be determined in accordance with the plan, unless material considerations indicate otherwise. In effect, this introduces a presumption in favour of development proposals which are in accordance with the development plan. An applicant who proposes a development which is clearly in conflict with the development plan would need to produce convincing reasons to demonstrate why the plan should not prevail. (The plan to which sections 70(2) and 54A apply is the approved or adopted development plan for the area, and not any draft plan which may exist — but see paragraph 32 below).

26.   Those deciding planning applications or appeals should therefore look to see whether the development plan contains policies or proposals which are relevant to the particular development proposal. Such material policies and proposals may either give support to a development proposal in a particular location or indicate that it is not appropriate. If the development plan does contain material policies or proposals and there are no other material considerations, the application or appeal should be determined in accordance with the development plan.

27.   Where there are other material considerations, the development plan should be taken as a starting point, and the other material considerations should be weighed in reaching a decision. One such consideration will be whether the development plan policies are up-to-date and apply to current circumstances, or whether they have been overtaken by events (the age of the plan is not in itself material). For example, policies and proposals in the plan may have been superseded by more recent planning guidance issued by the Government, or developments since the plan became operative may have rendered certain policies or proposals in the plan incapable of implementation or out of date.

28.   In those cases where the development plan is not relevant, for example because the plan does not contain a policy relating to a particular development proposal, or there are material policies in the plan which pull in opposite directions so that the plan does not provide a clear guide for a particular proposal, the planning application or appeal should be determined on its merits in the light of all the material considerations.

29.   Since the commencement of section 54A, the Secretaries of State have been examining development plans carefully to identify whether there appear to be conflicts with national or regional policy guidance. They will continue to do so and will normally draw the attention of local authorities to those conflicts which do not appear to be justified by local circumstances. If necessary they will make a formal intervention (see paragraph 19 above); if no such intervention is made, local authorities may take it that the Secretaries of State are content with the plan at the time of adoption and will attach commensurate weight to it in decisions they make on appeals or called-in applications.

30.   Local planning authorities or the Secretaries of State may find it appropriate, on occasion, to permit a development proposal which departs from the development plan because the particular contribution of that proposal to some local or national need or objective is so significant that it outweighs what the plan has to say about it. Such a consideration might be, for example, compelling argument by the applicant or appellant that a particular proposal should be allowed to proceed because of the contribution it will make to fulfilling an international commitment, or to some other particular objective which the plan did not foresee or address. Certain departures (see the Town and Country Planning Development Plans Directions 1992 for England and Wales) must be notified to the Secretary of State concerned so that he can decide whether to call in the application for his own decision.

31.   There will be occasions when a planning authority can show that the determination of a planning application for a proposed development is in accordance with an operative plan which is up-to-date and consistent with national and regional policies, and has substantiated this in its reasons for refusal of permission and in its written statement on an appeal. In such circumstances, the applicant will risk an award of the authority's costs against him if he pursues the appeal to a hearing or an inquiry but is unable to produce substantial evidence

to support the contention that there are material considerations which would justify an exception to the policies in the plan. An applicant who presses to appeal a matter which is dealt with in a well-advanced draft development plan, where the planning authority has refused the application on grounds of 'prematurity' (see paragraphs 32–34 below), also risks having costs awarded against him if his action in pressing the appeal in advance of the plan's adoption is found to be unreasonable.

Prematurity

32.   The weight to be attached to emerging development plans which are going through the statutory procedures towards adoption, depends upon the stage of preparation — the weight will increase as successive stages are reached — and upon the degree of any conflict with the existing plans. If no objections have been lodged to relevant policies in a deposited plan, then considerable weight may be attached to those policies because of the strong possibility that they will be adopted and replace those in the existing plan.

33.   Questions of prematurity may arise where a development plan is in preparation or under review, and proposals have been issued for consultation, but the plan has not yet been adopted or approved. In these circumstances it may be justifiable to refuse planning permission on grounds of prematurity in respect of development proposals which are individually so substantial, or likely to be so significant cumulatively, as to predetermine decisions about scale, location or phasing of new development which ought properly to be taken in the development plan context. However, whenever possible, planning applications should continue to be considered in the light of current policies. Where planning permission is refused on grounds of prematurity, at a time when the development plan is being prepared or reviewed, the planning authority will need to indicate clearly how the grant of permission for the development concerned would prejudice the outcome of the development plan process; rejection on grounds of prematurity would not normally be justified in cases where the effect on the plan would be marginal.

34.   Where there is a phasing policy in the development plan [see paragraphs 5.38–5.42 of PPG12, and 5.36–5.40 of PPG12 (Wales)] there may be circumstances in which it is necessary to refuse planning permission on grounds of prematurity if the policy is to have effect.

Other legislation

35.   Decisions on individual applications should be based on planning grounds only, and must be reasonable. Planning legislation should not normally be used to secure objectives achievable under other legislation. This principle of non-duplication should be maintained even though the powers and duties resulting from the other legislation may also be the concern of local authorities. But even where consent is needed under other legislation, the planning system may have

an important part to play, for example in deciding whether the development is appropriate for the particular location. The grant of planning permission does not remove the need to obtain any other consents that may be necessary, nor does it imply that such consents will necessarily be forthcoming.

36.   For example, the Building Regulations impose requirements on how most non-domestic buildings should be designed and constructed to secure specific objectives relating to health and safety, access for disabled people and energy conservation. It would not be appropriate to use planning legislation to impose *separate* requirements in these areas, although development plan policies can seek to ensure that consideration is given to the provision of adequate access for disabled people in the preparation of site layouts and in the relationship between buildings and their carparking areas and other public access points. Such factors can also be taken into account in determining planning applications. However, detailed attention to the precise standard of provision — for example, the specifications for steps, ramps and doors — should not be dealt with under planning legislation. Similarly, a planning application for, say, an amusement centre should be considered on its land-use planning merits and not on the basis of issues which are immaterial to those considerations, such as moral grounds or because it is considered that the demand for such facilities is already met in the area. Licences for amusement centres offering prizes must be obtained under the Gaming Acts. The grant of such licences is at the discretion of local authorities who may take into account, among other things, the fact that the demand for such facilities is already adequately met in a particular area.

37.   Provided a consideration is material in planning terms, however, it must be taken into account in dealing with a planning application notwithstanding that other machinery may exist for its regulation. For example, planning permission may be refused on the ground that the land concerned forms part of a proposed road widening scheme, even though an alternative procedure is specified in the Highways Act (*Westminster Bank Ltd v MHLG* 1971).

Personal circumstances

38.   Unless otherwise specified, a planning permission runs with the land and it is seldom desirable to provide for any other arrangement. Exceptionally, however, the personal circumstances of an occupier, personal hardship, or the difficulties of businesses which are of value to the character of the local community, may be material to the consideration of a planning application. In such circumstances, a permission may be made subject to a condition that it is personal to the applicant (see paragraph 73 of Annex to DOE and WO Circular 1/85). Such arguments will seldom outweigh the more general planning considerations. If the proposed development entails works of a permanent nature they will remain long after the personal circumstances of the applicant have ceased to be material.

Third party interests

39.   The planning system does not exist to protect the private interests of one person against the activities of another, although private interests may coincide with the public interest in some cases. In fact 'the public interest . . . may require that the interests of individual occupiers should be considered. The protection of individual interests is one aspect, and an important one, of the public interest as a whole' (*Stringer v MHLG* 1971).

40.   It is often difficult to distinguish between public and private interests, but this may be necessary on occasion. The basic question is not whether owners and occupiers of neighbouring properties would experience financial or other loss from a particular development, but whether the proposal would unacceptably affect amenities and the existing use of land and buildings which ought to be protected in the public interest. Good neighbourliness and fairness are among the yardsticks against which development proposals can be measured, for example it might be material to consider the question of 'overlooking' or loss of privacy experienced by a particular resident. Furthermore, planning permission may be refused where a proposed development would have an adverse effect on a nearby existing development provided there is a planning purpose or other special consideration involved, eg the siting of a ready-mixed concrete plant adjacent to a high precision plant requiring especially clean air (*RMC Management Services Ltd v SSE* 1972).

41.   The Government recognises the importance of public awareness of, and participation in, the development control process. It is committed to requiring publicity for all planning applications to augment the legislation which already provides for registers of all planning applications to be available for public inspection. Local inquiries and hearings into planning appeals and called-in applications are held in public and members of the public have an opportunity to express views on the proposed development. Similarly, when appeals are decided on the basis of written representations, the planning authorities notify those likely to be affected by the development proposal and it is open to them to express their views in writing.

42.   In general, the elected members of the local planning authority represent the interests of the community in planning matters. But when determining planning applications they must take into account any relevant views on planning matters expressed by neighbouring occupiers, local residents and any other third parties. For example, opponents of a development proposal may highlight factors, such as traffic problems or the scale of a proposed development in relation to its surroundings, which are land-use planning issues and thus comprise material considerations; these must be taken into account, along with all other material considerations, in deciding the case. Nevertheless, local opposition to a proposal is not in itself a ground for refusing planning permission, unless that opposition is founded upon valid planning reasons which can be substantiated. While the substance of local opposition must be considered, the duty is to decide each case on its planning merits.

Environmental assessment

43.   Environmental Assessment (EA) is a process by which information about the likely environmental effects of certain major projects is collected, assessed and taken into account by the local planning authority in deciding whether planning permission should be granted. The Town and Country Planning (Assessment of Environmental Effects) Regulations 1988, which implement a European Community Directive, set out two lists of projects. For those in Schedule 1 (such as crude oil refineries, major aerodromes and the disposal of radioactive or other toxic waste), EA is required to be carried out in every case. For the wider list in Schedule 2 (including the chemical, food, textile and rubber industries, minerals extraction and the disposal of non-toxic waste), EA is required if the particular development proposed is judged likely to have significant effects on the environment by virtue of factors such as its nature, size or location.

44.   Where EA is required, the applicant must prepare and submit an environmental statement with the planning application. An applicant may submit an environmental statement voluntarily, but otherwise it will fall to the local planning authority to decide whether EA is necessary. An applicant who is dissatisfied with the authority's request for EA may seek a direction from the relevant Secretary of State as to whether EA is required.

45.   Further information on these requirements is given in DOE Circular 15/88 (WO 23/88) and in the Department's booklet 'Environmental Assessment — A Guide to the Procedures' (HMSO, November 1989).

Planning conditions

46.   The ability of local planning authorities and the Secretaries of State to impose conditions on a planning permission can enable many development proposals to proceed where it would otherwise be necessary to refuse planning permission. The sensitive use of conditions can improve the quality of development control and enhance public confidence in the planning system. To achieve these ends, conditions should be used in a way which is clearly seen to be fair, reasonable and practicable. Conditions should only be imposed where they are:
- necessary
- relevant to planning
- relevant to the development to be permitted
- enforceable
- precise
- reasonable in all other respects.

47.   In considering whether a particular condition is necessary, one key test is whether planning permission would have to be refused if the condition were not imposed. If not, then such a condition needs special and precise justification.

The same criteria and test should be applied in deciding whether to dispense with an extant condition. More detailed advice about planning conditions is given in DOE Circular 1/85 (WO 1/85), and for mineral developments in MPGs 2 and 7.

Planning obligations

48.   Guidance on the operation of section 106 of the 1990 Act, as substituted by section 12 of the 1991 Act, and on the use of planning obligations, is given in DOE Circular 16/91 (WO 53/91).

Listed building control

49.   The Planning (Listed Buildings and Conservation Areas) Act 1990 sets out an additional system of control for listed buildings and conservation areas. Under these provisions listed building consent is needed for any works to demolish a listed building, or to alter it or extend it in any manner which would affect its character as a building of special architectural or historic interest. Separate controls also apply to the demolition of most unlisted buildings in conservation areas. These controls are additional to any planning permission or other consents which may be necessary. Advice on the operation of listed building and conservation area controls in England and Wales is given respectively in DOE Circular 8/87 and WO Circular 61/81.

Design considerations

50.   Guidance on design considerations is given in Annex A.

Crime prevention

51.   Crime prevention is one of the social considerations to which, in accordance with the Town and Country (Development Plan) Regulations 1991, regard must be given in development plans. Local plans may establish standards for the design and layout of new development which can make crime more difficult to commit and/or increase the risk of detection for potential offenders. Local authorities may also wish to consult Police Architectural Liaison Officers (ALOs) on planning applications for those developments where there is potential to eliminate or reduce criminal activity through the adoption of appropriate measures at the design stage. Because there are very few ALOs they should be consulted mainly on applications which involve a large number of people or properties, for example new housing estates, industrial estates, shopping centres, leisure complexes and car parks. More detailed advice on crime prevention will be contained in a future Circular.

Hazardous substances

52.   The controls in the Planning (Hazardous Substances) Act 1990,   when brought into force, will enable local authorities to decide if the presence of a significant quantity of a hazardous substance is appropriate, taking into account existing and prospective development in the vicinity. The controls will be concerned with the storage and use of substances which could present major fire, explosion or toxic hazards to people in the surrounding area. Hazardous substances consent will be required where a hazardous substance is to be present at or above a specified amount, known as the 'controlled quantity'.

53.   Although local planning authorities have been able to exercise some control over the siting of hazardous substances by imposing conditions on planning permission, hazardous substances may be introduced on to land without development being involved. The new provisions will thus enable control to be exercised in circumstances other than where development requiring planning permission is proposed.

Noise

54.   Noise can affect health and have a direct impact on local amenity. Its impact can therefore be a material planning consideration. It may, for example, be a factor in proposals to use or develop land near an existing source of noise, or where a proposed new development is likely to generate noise. Local planning authorities should therefore make a careful assessment of likely noise levels before determining planning applications. Advice on planning and noise is contained in DOE Circular 10/73 (WO 16/73). Updated advice on this issue, to replace and expand that given in Circular 10/73, will be given in a forthcoming PPG. Advice on the control of noise from mineral workings will be provided in a forthcoming MPG Note.

Access

55.   The development of land and buildings provides the opportunity to secure a more accessible environment for everyone, including wheelchair users and other people with disabilities, elderly people, and people with toddlers or infants in pushchairs. Developers and local authorities are encouraged to consider the issue of access at an early stage in the design process. Local planning authorities should ensure that they are fully informed about ways in which access needs can be met, and can offer appropriate advice to developers. The appropriate design of spaces between and around buildings and of parking provision is particularly important in ensuring good access to buildings. When a new building is proposed, or an existing building is being extended or altered, developers should consider the needs of disabled people who might use the building as a place of work, or as visitors or customers.

56.   Where it is not clear from a planning application that provision for disabled people is being considered, it will always be preferable to resolve the problem

through negotiation. Where the public are to have access to the building, the local planning authority should consider the extent to which the securing of provision for disabled people can be justified on planning grounds. The sphere of planning control is limited in this context. Conditions attached to planning permissions which have no relevance to planning matters, will be *ultra vires*. More detailed advice on access issues will be contained in a future Circular.

Cancellation of advice

57.   The following advice is hereby cancelled:
PPG1 (January 1988)
Paragraphs 1–4 and 18–21 of DOE Circular 22/80 (WO 40/80)

Annex A: design considerations

A1.   The appearance of proposed development and its relationship to its surroundings are material considerations, and those who determine planning applications and appeals should have regard to them in reaching their decisions.

A2.   Good design should be the aim of all involved in the development process, but it is primarily the responsibility of designers and their clients. Applicants and planning authorities should recognise the benefits of engaging skilled advisers and encouraging high design standards. In considering a development proposal, authorities should recognise the design skills and advice of architects and consider carefully the advice of their own professionally qualified advisers, although the final decision remains that of the authority itself.

A3.   Planning authorities should reject obviously poor designs which are out of scale or character with their surroundings. But aesthetic judgments are to some extent subjective and authorities should not impose their taste on applicants for planning permission simply because they believe it to be superior. Authorities should not seek to control the detailed design of buildings unless the sensitive character of the setting for the development justifies it.

A4.   Applicants for planning permission should demonstrate wherever appropriate that they have considered the wider setting of buildings. New developments should respect but not necessarily mimic the character of their surroundings. Particular weight should be given to the impact of development on existing buildings and the landscape in environmentally sensitive areas such as National Parks, Areas of Outstanding Natural Beauty and Conservation Areas, where the scale of new development and the use of appropriate building materials will often be particularly important.

A5.   The appearance and treatment of the spaces between and around buildings is also of great importance. Where these form part of an application site, the landscape design — whether hard or soft — will often be of comparable importance to the design of the buildings and should likewise be the subject of consideration, attention and expert advice. The aim should be for any development to result in a 'benefit' in environmental and landscape terms.

A6.   Development plans and guidance for particular areas or sites should provide applicants with clear indications of planning authorities' design expectations. Such advice should avoid excessive prescription and detail and should concentrate on broad matters of scale, density, height, massing, layout, landscape and access. It should focus on encouraging good design rather than stifling experiment, originality or initiative. Indeed the design qualities of an exceptional scheme and its special contribution to the landscape or townscape may justify departing from local authorities' design guidance.

A7.   Planning authorities should encourage applicants to consult them before formulating development proposals. Authorities' consideration of proposals will be assisted if applicants provide appropriate illustrative material, according to the circumstances, to show their proposals in context. It may sometimes be helpful for the applicant to submit a short written statement setting out the design principles of the proposal.

This 'Planning Policy Guidance Note' is Crown Copyright and is reproduced by kind permission of the Department of the Environment Welsh Office and the Controller of Her Majesty's Stationery Office.

Chapter 2

Appeal Strategy

2.1 Introduction

Once the decision has been taken to lodge an appeal, further decisions have to be made before the appeal papers are prepared. This chapter deals with those issues. Chapter 3 deals with the paperwork involved in submitting the appeal and the appeal procedures.

Copies of appeal forms, guidance notes and a free booklet on appeals is obtainable from the Planning Inspectorate, Tollgate House, Houlton Street, Bristol BS2 9DJ. The local authority may also be willing to supply these to individuals, and it may be useful to obtain these at this stage. The first part of this chapter deals with general matters relevant to all appeals. The second part outlines the three procedures available and examines factors which will influence the choice of procedure.

The three types of appeal procedure are:
- written representations;
- informal hearing;
- public inquiry.

In many cases there will be no clear right or wrong choice, and the factors have to be weighed up. Figure 2.1 illustrates the questions that the practitioner and client should be asking to ascertain the most appropriate choice. A more detailed analysis occurs later in this chapter. The choice of procedure is not entirely within the appellant's control. It is possible to change procedures once an appeal is underway.

The annual report of the Inspectorate for 1994 reveals that for cases decided by inspectors 80 per cent of appeals were dealt with by written representation procedure, 12 per cent by informal hearings and 8 per cent by public inquiries. Virtually all applications are decided by inspectors: only 2 per cent are decided by the Secretary of State himself. Eighty per cent of inspector cases are decided within 17 weeks in the case of written representations. The figures for informal hearings and public inquiries are 28 weeks and 40 weeks respectively. In 1993/94, 33.8 per cent of written representation appeals were allowed and planning permissions issued accordingly. Comparable figures for informal hearings and public inquiries are 40.4 per cent and 42.9 per cent respectively.

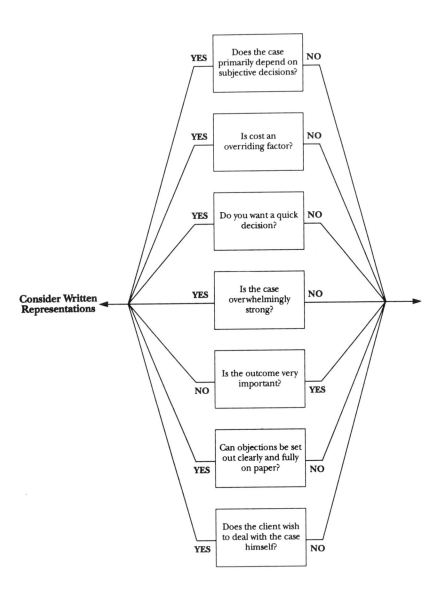

Figure 2.1 Selection of appeal procedure

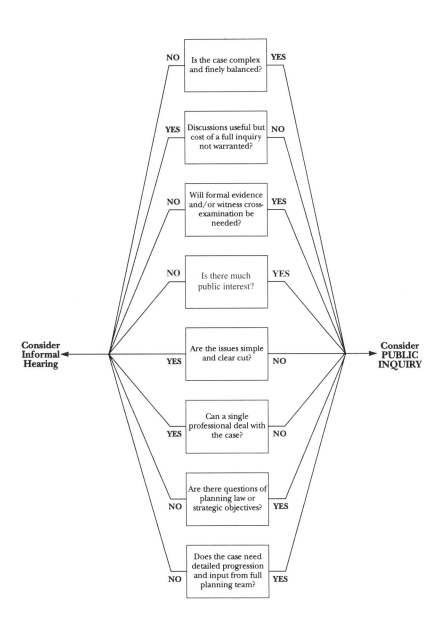

Figure 2.1, *cont.*

However, it is unwise to conclude that the best chance of success is by public inquiry. There is a feeling among practitioners that many hopeless cases are dealt with by the written representation procedure, which affects the statistics. On the other hand it is probably also true that many cases go to public inquiry because the issues they present are very difficult and there may be an argument that the overall success rate for reasonable cases at public inquiry is somewhat better than the figures might imply.

The figures are probably most helpful in indicating that if over 40 per cent of public inquiry appeals are allowed, then the chances for an appeal in a case which does not fall into the hopeless category and which is carefully prepared and argued must be substantially higher.

2.2   Issues common to all appeals

2.2.1   Six-month time limit

The six-month time limit on lodging appeals is not an absolute statutory bar but late appeals are accepted only in exceptional circumstances. If the time limit is about to expire it is usually preferable to lodge an appeal within the time limit even if this is in a skeleton form (see para 1.7). When completing the form, the box asking for a public inquiry should preferably be ticked in cases where time is tight. It will be possible to change to another procedure once consideration has been given to the best procedure. If there is little information, the grounds of appeal can simply give the obvious reasons with an indication that full grounds and details will follow as soon as possible.

2.2.2   Secretary of State decisions

Inspectors deal with 98 per cent of appeals. Some proposals which involve a significant departure from the development plan or are of more than local importance or particularly sensitive because of their scale or location may be dealt with by the Secretary of State (the Secretary of State for Wales if the land is in Wales). In such cases the Secretary of State will notify the parties of this. The procedure for such appeals is dealt with in Chapter 10.

2.2.3   Changing the type of procedure

If a decision is made to lodge an appeal on the basis of written representations, it is open to the local authority to suggest that the appeal is more suitable for one of the other methods. The Secretary of State may decide that the case should be heard by a public inquiry and if this is so the case will proceed on that basis. If the appellant requests a public inquiry he is entitled to be heard in that way although an informal hearing is frequently offered by the Inspectorate if this procedure is suitable for the case. The appellant need not agree to such an offer.

It is possible to change the procedure during the early stages of the appeal if it becomes apparent that another procedure is preferable. It can happen that when the local authority's statement of case is received, the issues have been simplified and perhaps on that basis a ground of appeal has to be withdrawn. In these circumstances an informal hearing may be appropriate to the new circumstances. There is usually little difficulty in removing a case from the public inquiry procedure to informal hearing or written representations provided that this is done early in the proceedings. Care should be taken if an inquiry date has already been fixed because the appellant could be liable for wasted costs. In such a case discussion should always take place with the local authority. The authority may be prepared to agree to the revised procedure and agree not to ask for costs in the circumstances.

If an appeal is proceeding on the basis of written representations or an informal hearing and it becomes evident that a public inquiry would be a better method, it will usually be possible, particularly at an early stage, to request a public inquiry.

Particular difficulties can arise during the course of an informal hearing if the inspector takes the view that the matter should be dealt with by public inquiry. This will result in an adjournment of the informal hearing and a public inquiry date being fixed. Inevitably there will be additional costs and a delay. This is most likely to happen when the appellant brings considerable evidence to an informal hearing or raises legal issues. The inspector in such circumstances may feel that the more structured approach of a public inquiry is the best way of ensuring a fair hearing. No attempt should therefore be made to push through by the informal inquiry route a case which demands a number of witnesses and detailed examination of conflicting evidence or legal arguments.

2.3 Duplicate applications

Once an application has been refused or an appeal has been lodged, the local authority can take no further action in respect of it. Where there is still a possibility of negotiations with the local authority resulting in the grant of permission, it may be worth considering putting in a second application identical to the one under appeal. In these circumstances, a duplicate application may be helpful, although some local planning authorities will not negotiate on a duplicate application once an appeal has been lodged.

The usefulness of duplicate applications has also been undermined to a certain degree by the recent speeding up of the appeal process which leaves little time for negotiation on the duplicate application and by the fact that an appellant may be exposed to costs if an appeal is withdrawn at the last minute even if it is withdrawn on the basis that the local authority has granted planning permission for development identical to the appeal proposal. However, a duplicate application may give a local authority an opportunity to reconsider the position because it offers a way of avoiding the costs and uncertainties of appeal. The same holds true for the appellant: it is always preferable to have a planning permission from the local authority rather than embark on the risk and delay of an appeal if they can be avoided.

In some circumstances it may be tactically advisable to offer with the duplicate application further information which has come to light and which will be used in the appeal in an endeavour to persuade the local authority to change its mind. In other circumstances, however, the battle lines may be clearly drawn and an appellant will wish to keep his powder dry and use the appeal process as the primary route for gaining planning permission.

2.4 Team building

As part of the strategy for preparing the appeal, consideration should be given to the team required to process the appeal. If specialists are to be used, the earlier their expertise is drawn into the process the better. They may have an input into the decision as to which appeal strategy should be used.

2.5 Evidence

Consideration of the evidence required is an essential part of choosing the correct appeal strategy. Before choosing the strategy advisers should have a clear idea of the issues, the arguments and the evidence which is needed to support the case; and what further work is required.

2.6 Confidentiality

Section 321 of the Town and Country Planning Act 1990 requires a public inquiry to be held, as the name indicates, in public. Furthermore the documentary evidence is also open to public inspection. The section provides that evidence may be heard in camera and documents refused to the public where the Secretary of State directs that a public disclosure would result in the disclosure of information in relation to national security or the measures to be taken to ensure the security of any premises or property *and* that such disclosure would be contrary to the national interest.

These are very narrow grounds. They would, for example, enable a government department such as the Prison Service to give evidence in private relating to the effects of development in the vicinity of a prison. For most purposes, it is apparent that any evidence tendered to an inquiry must be public. Local newspapers and the national press may attend and are likely to receive copies of the documents if they request them.

2.6.1 Neighbours

Individuals often overestimate the interest of others in their own affairs, and publicising certain matters may not be as damaging as they fear. However, if they wish, for instance, to give evidence against their neighbour as to what he has been doing, they cannot do so under the cloak of confidentiality. This aspect of neighbour confidentiality is generally most acute in relation to enforcement appeals where neighbours are often the best witnesses of when events occurred and what exactly has been happening over the last few years. The neighbour against whom enforcement action is being taken may not appreciate the public spirited nature of such evidence but the ability of an inspector or the Secretary of State to receive evidence confidentially in a public inquiry is clearly extremely limited.

2.6.2 Commercial confidentiality

Commercial confidentiality often constitutes a difficulty. Those running shops in a town centre may object to the effect of a large new store on their trade. Their interest goes beyond their own financial interest (which is not a material planning consideration) to the health and vitality of the town centre (which *is* a material planning consideration). Most such traders will be loath to reveal figures of their turnover and profitability, fearing the commercial repercussions. In a sense they are forced to fight this type of competition on commercial grounds without releasing the base information. The same may be true of farmers and other businesses who wish to bring commercial viability evidence in support of their own planning applications. Finally, certain applications, particularly development of listed buildings, may require commercial evidence of current rent levels and future viability.

In practice, it will be difficult to keep confidential representations or evidence tendered in the course of written representation appeals or informal hearings. How is the inspector to deal with this in his decision letter? It is suggested that all appeals should be dealt with on the basis that evidence cannot be subject to secrecy and will reach the public domain. The decision on whether to use information always will be for the client, but practitioners should take a view on how important sensitive evidence may be to the success of the appeal and advise the client accordingly.

2.7 Objections by members of the public

Careful consideration should be given to dealing with objections by members of the public and amenity groups. If such objectors can be reassured, they may be willing to withdraw their objections. In certain cases, there might be a role for a public relations programme. Appellants, however, should take care that they are not seen to impede in any way the voicing of objections. Further information on handling the public is given in Chapter 9. Cases with outstanding third party objections of substance are likely to be dealt with by public inquiry because this may be the most suitable forum for dealing with those public representations, whether or not the appellant agrees.

2.8 Appeal by way of written representations

This type of appeal is handled without a hearing: the papers are laid before the inspector. He or she will consider them and carry out a site visit, either accompanied or unaccompanied. A decision letter will then be sent to the appellant and the local authority. Detailed information on this procedure is given in Chapter 4. No costs are at present awarded in written representation cases, but the power to award costs is in force and the position could change at any time.

2.8.1   Cases appropriate for written representations

If cost is the overriding factor, the written representation procedure is the cheapest of the three, but it is easy to take the cheapest option now and regret it later. Both the other procedures can be managed efficiently and may be well worth it. A refusal on appeal on the planning record is difficult to overcome subsequently.

Where time is of the essence, it is usually the quickest procedure. It is recommended for cases with clearly defined and limited arguments, which can be set out fully on paper. It is useful, too, for a weak case where the result is not particularly important but the appellant wants to test the water. There is at present no risk of a costs award.

The procedure is suitable for cases where objections by neighbours or interest groups are better dealt with on paper so that public hearing of the objections can be avoided and time saved. It is also suitable where the case is overwhelmingly strong and little can be said against the proposals, or where the case depends primarily on subjective decisions such as bulk, design and the impact on the surrounding area. For example, an appeal based on refusal because of the detrimental effect on the character and appearance of a conservation area may be decided largely on the inspector's reading of the plans and his site inspection. Face-to-face discussion may not add much.

2.8.2   Cases not appropriate for written representations

In cases where there is considerable disagreement on the facts, policies or relevant law, written representations should not be used. There is no opportunity to meet the inspector, argue the case and correct any omissions, which may be damaging. The results from appeals by way of written representations tend to be a little more inconsistent than appeals by way of the other procedures; for this reason, the procedure is not recommended for cases where the outcome is very important to the appellant.

2.9   Appeal by way of informal hearing

Informal hearings take the form of a round table discussion between a planning officer from the local authority and the appellant and/or his representative. Papers are submitted in much the same way as for written representations but the inspector will lead the discussion. Legal representation is discouraged and the procedure is normally unsuitable if the client wishes to be legally represented. After the hearing and site visit, the decision letter will be written by the inspector and sent to the appellant and the local authority.

A customer satisfaction survey carried out for the Inspectorate indicated a considerable level of satisfaction by those involved in informal hearings. This is a useful half-way house between written representations and public inquiry.

2.9.1 Cases appropriate for informal hearing

The informal hearing procedure enables a beneficial discussion of the issues without the client incurring the costs of a public inquiry where the issues will benefit from exploration and discussion between the parties but the differences are not such that formal evidence must be presented and tested.

The procedure is useful in cases where members of the public have little contribution to make, and in cases where the issues are simple and clear cut but of sufficient importance to the client to justify being explored in a hearing. In cases where, the issues may be ones of subjective appraisal, it is helpful to place them vividly before the inspector. Finally, the procedure may be adopted in cases which can be dealt with substantially by one professional, whether a planner or architect, without relying on other evidence.

2.9.2 Cases not appropriate for informal hearing

Complex cases where there are substantial areas of disagreement on which evidence needs to be presented by witnesses and tested in cross-examination are not appropriate. Nor are cases where formal evidence is needed, on oath if necessary, or witness summons issued. There are also situations where the client wishes to deal with the case entirely himself, and it is usually easier for an inexperienced client to deal with the written representation procedure.

2.10 Appeal by way of public inquiry

Public inquiries are the most expensive of the three procedures. It will usually take longer before a decision is issued because of the time required to set up the inquiry, the hearing itself and the writing of the inspector's report. It is, however, by far the best procedure because it results in the most thorough examination of the appeal proposals and the objections to them.

The pre-inquiry procedure ensures that issues are defined and information exchanged between the parties through exchange of statements of case and proofs of evidence in good time to allow their proper consideration. These issues are then tested through cross-examination at an oral hearing. There will be an accompanied site visit before the decision is made.

2.10.1 Cases appropriate for public inquiry

Where the outcome is crucial for the client's plans and the cost can be justified in commercial or personal terms, public inquiry is the best course. It is suitable when the issues are complex and finely balanced, and a number of different fields need to be covered by several witnesses. The public inquiry is the appropriate forum when the arguments are technical and require oral presentation and discussion, and if there are evidential weaknesses which cannot be dealt with properly in writing. The inquiry can handle questions of planning law or strategic objectives. It enables the appeal proposals to benefit from the detailed progression of the inquiry procedure and strategic input of a full planning team.

2.10.2   Cases not appropriate for public inquiry

A public inquiry should be avoided where the value of a planning permission or the chances of success do not warrant the expenditure. It should also be avoided if the case may not stand up to the detailed scrutiny of a public inquiry and, should not be chosen in cases where the client wishes to rely on one witness for advocacy and evidence. This usually results in severe practical difficulties, and the client may be advised to opt for an informal hearing if he is not prepared to employ a separate advocate and witness.

Chapter 1 considered whether an appeal should be lodged and this chapter has analysed the procedures available. Once the decision has been made to appeal and the method chosen, the appeal has to be lodged. Chapter 3 deals with lodging the form of appeal and the following chapters look in detail at the appeal procedures.

Chapter 3

Lodging the Appeal

3.1 Introduction

This chapter explains how to lodge the appeal and what information should accompany it. General points relevant to lodging all three types of appeal are dealt with first, and each type of appeal is then covered in detail in subsequent chapters. The three types of appeal are:
- written representation;
- informal hearing;
- public inquiry.

An example of each is provided at the end of the relevant chapters.

3.2 General

An appeal is made by sending the official form to the Planning Inspectorate if the land is in England. In Wales the form should be sent to the planning division of the Welsh Office. Scottish appeals are not covered in this book although many of the procedures are similar. Enforcement appeals and listed building appeals are subject to different requirements, which are dealt with in Chapter 13.

No fee is at present payable for lodging an appeal. Each side is normally expected to bear their own costs. Costs are awarded only exceptionally for unreasonable behaviour. Costs awards are dealt with in Chapter 11. The Department of the Environment does not at present award costs in respect of written representation appeals (Circular 8/93).

The six-month rule must not be forgotten and if time is short, the form may be faxed to the Inspectorate with the grounds of appeal in outline. A complete form should be sent as soon as possible and the Inspectorate kept informed. You are required to send a copy of the appeal form to the local authority concerned. The Inspectorate may notify you that in addition copies are to be sent to certain other parties. A sound general rule is to circulate copies of all correspondence among the parties, both to the Inspectorate and the local authority. This means that all parties are kept up to date with developments and there is no room for misunderstanding.

3.3   The appeal form

Most of the appeal form will be completed in the same way whatever the procedure chosen. The following sections of the appeal form will be completed differently according to the procedure chosen:

(1) Section D (procedure) requires the appellant to choose the procedure he wishes.
(2) Section E (supporting documents) will require close scrutiny.
(3) Section G (grounds of appeal).

3.3.1   Section A: information about the appellant

In most cases the information will be identical to that appearing on the planning application which is being appealed. The identity of the appellant must be the same as the applicant for planning permission. If a person other than the original applicant wishes to appeal, arrangements will have to be made with the original applicant (see para 1.6). The usual arrangement is that the original applicant permits his name to be used for the appeal procedure but the new party's professional advisers appear as his agents. All correspondence will then be addressed to the agent for the new party. If there is an agent, the agent's box should be completed. This can be the solicitor, planning consultant, surveyor or whoever is advising. The reference of the particular person dealing with the matter should be inserted. All correspondence will be sent to the agent concerned. If the agent is a professional, the address and daytime telephone number of the appellant may be omitted. Any queries by third parties will then be addressed to the agent.

3.3.2   Section B: details of the appeal

Details will be identical to the details appearing on the planning application except that the application will by this time have a local authority reference number which should appear at the bottom of this sheet in the box provided.

3.3.3   Section C: the appeal

Delete as appropriate: there should be no difficulty.

3.3.4   Section D: procedure

By now the method of appeal will have been chosen and the appropriate box indicating whether the written representations procedure is agreed or a public inquiry or hearing is to be requested should be ticked. If a public inquiry is requested, the Inspectorate may respond by offering an informal hearing for suitable cases.

3.3.5   Section E: supporting documents

Much of the information on the form is factual and should be available from the original planning application. However, this section can cause difficulties in two areas: site ownership certificate (box 2) and boxes 3 and 5 (documents and other relevant correspondence). The 'article 12(A) certificate' referred to in box 2 is the original certificate of ownership submitted with the application. This will often form part of the original application form and must be sent in with the appeal.

An applicant for planning permission does not have to own the land but it is only right that those parties who do have a legal interest in the land concerned should be notified of planning applications and appeals on their land.

If there has been a change in ownership then the certificate to be submitted in connection with the appeal will differ from that originally submitted. Provided the certificates correctly reflect the land ownership at the time they are given, this does not matter. Information on ownership certificates for the appeal itself is given in para 3.3.7.

The third box requires each of the plans, drawings and documents sent to the local authority as part of the application to be submitted. The fifth box refers to all relevant correspondence with the local authority being forwarded at this time. There is sometimes uncertainty as to how much of the correspondence and how many of the documents which were exchanged between the local authority and the applicant in the course of processing the application should be submitted at this stage. The appeal form indicates that everything should be submitted. The author takes the view that selection may be advisable.

Art 26 of the Town and Country Planning General Development Order 1988 requires the following to be submitted:

(1) the application the subject of the appeal;
(2) all plans, drawings sent to the local authority in connection with the application;
(3) all correspondence with the local authority relating to the application;
(4) any art 12A certificate;
(5) any other plans, documents or drawings relating to the application which were not sent to the local authority;
(6) the decision notice; and
(7) if in respect of an application for approval of certain matters conditional on a planning permission, that application, plans and permission.

Some of the documents and correspondence will have been overtaken by events. The appellant may feel that it is more helpful to the inspector that the information which he needs to decide the inquiry should be presented and explained by his witness rather than requiring him to wade through a large amount of correspondence, much of which is no longer relevant. This is particularly the case where ground has shifted significantly in the course of dealing with the planning application or there are new professional advisers who were not involved with the application.

An Environmental Statement, where submitted as part of the application, must clearly accompany the appeal papers, but informal appraisals may best be left to be dealt with by witnesses at the inquiry.

The safe course, if in doubt, is to send all documents to the Inspectorate. Appellants should consider also discussing these issues with the local authority to decide, for example, which drawings need to be considered and which drawings have been superseded and are no longer relevant.

Whichever method of appeal is being used, the appellant will wish to present a coherent and reasoned case. It may be more appropriate to introduce correspondence as part of this case rather than just copying the file and sending it on. Either the appellant or the local authority may have developed their case since the time original documents were submitted and it may be positively unhelpful to allow these to cloud the issues which both parties now know to be central.

3.3.6   Site plan

The sixth box requires a site plan. In most cases the original site drawing submitted with the application can be copied and used for these purposes. It is the convention that the site is outlined in red; adjoining land owned by the appellant is outlined in blue.

The final three boxes of this section (boxes 7 to 9) refer to documents to be enclosed in appropriate cases. If the appeal is in respect of reserved matters, the relevant outline application, the plans submitted and the outline permission should be sent. Box 8 invites the appellant to send copies of documents sent to the local authority but not part of the submitted application. Unless such drawings are clearly still relevant (as, for example, illustrative plans), they should not be sent. Similar reservations apply as for box 5 above. Any difficulties should be discussed with the local authority.

The final box will rarely be used. Normally any additional plans or drawings will be sent as part of the reasoned case when this is prepared.

3.3.7   Section F: serving notice of ownership and certificate for appeal

A new Art 12A certificate must be submitted with the appeal. This will be identical to the original certificate unless there has been a change in ownership (see para 3.3.5). Ownership details should be checked to see that they are still correct.

Notice must be served on each person who was, 21 days before the date the appeal is lodged, any one of the following:
   (1)   the freehold estate owner;
   (2)   a person with a leasehold of which not less than seven years remain unexpired;
   (3)   the tenant of an agricultural holding, any part of which is comprised in the land to which the appeal relates.

Requirements for serving the notice are set out in s 329 of the Town and Country Planning Act 1990. What is required is the service of a notice on relevant owners and then the signing of a certificate on the appeal form that this has been complied with.

If no one coming within the above categories, apart from the appellant, has an interest in the land, no notices need to be served and the certificate can be filled in accordingly. If the client has bought the land or an interest in the land and the vendor is allowing the purchaser to lodge the appeal in his name then the agent will have to serve the notice on the new purchaser in accordance with these provisions.

A certificate is not required for an appeal against refusal or deemed refusal of applications for approval of reserved matters. The reason for this is that the outline consent was the planning permission as such and this application does therefore not require notification in the same way.

Section F of the appeal form includes the form of certificate prescribed by Art 12A of the GDO. The appeal form should have with it a copy of the notice which needs to be served on owners or occupiers. If not, this is set out in the GDO. The forms are prescribed by the GDO and it is wise to follow the instructions exactly, simply deleting those portions which do not apply. The temptation to strike out the whole of that part of the certificate should always be avoided. All facts need to be carefully checked.

Where the identity of all the owners cannot be established by reasonable inquiry, there is a procedure, set out in Art 12 of the GDO, whereby advertisements in local papers may be inserted.

The Inspectorate will not register an appeal unless it is accompanied by a certificate indicating that the requirements have been complied with. Failure to serve notice on an owner could have the effect of invalidating any subsequent planning permission, although this will depend on the precise circumstances. In the leading case of *Main v Swansea City Council* [1984] 49 P&CR 26 the court upheld a planning permission although an owner of part of the site had not been notified: he was not in that particular case prejudiced. The best course is to make sure the certificate and notification are correct. If there are a number of owners and the situation is unclear, it may be advisable to carry out a land registry search and make enquiries on the site. Care is needed with certificates: it is an offence knowingly or recklessly to issue a certificate which contains a statement which is false or misleading in a material particular (s 65(6) of the Act).

Appeals in relation to mineral applications or underground working also require additional advertisements and site displays (see Art 12(2) of the GDO).

3.3.8   Notification

The local authority are required to carry out appropriate publicity, eg advertise applications and notify neighbours when they receive applications but this need not be repeated at the time an appeal is lodged providing the local authority carried out appropriate publicity when the application was received. Local authorities are required to certify to the Inspectorate that they have carried out appropriate notification at the application stage. In due course, the local authority will notify those who made representations in relation to the original application that an appeal has been lodged and offer them the opportunity of making further representations in respect of the appeal.

3.3.9   Section G: grounds of appeal

Different considerations apply to the different types of appeal. With word processors now in common use, it may be easier to use a separate piece of paper rather than type on the form itself. 'See attached sheets' can simply be written in the space provided.

3.3.10   Grounds of appeal: written representation appeals

Complete grounds of appeal and full supporting documents should be sent with the appeal form. In written representation cases the appeal form is not simply the starting point but the appellant's substantive case. The advice given in respect of public inquiry grounds of appeal may be a useful starting point for drafting written representation grounds of appeal. However, having identified the grounds of appeal, each needs to be underpinned by the evidence which establishes those grounds. The relevant evidence should also be attached. In view of the fact that in written representations, the appeal form is in fact the substance of the appellant's case, it is dealt with in detail in Chapter 4.

3.3.11   Grounds of appeal: informal hearings

This is a non-statutory procedure. The appeal form will be completed by ticking box D.2. Grounds of appeal will follow the same broad principle as for public inquiries. Thereafter, the procedure will be different (see Chapter 5).

3.3.12   Grounds of appeal: public inquiries

If the advice in Chapters 1 and 2 has been followed, a clear idea of why the local authority's decision is not acceptable should have emerged. What is required here is not the evidence upon which the case rests; this will be brought out later in the statement of case and the written proofs of evidence. Nor should the grounds of appeal go into great detail. The objective at this stage is to give a clear concise position statement of why the appellant disagrees with the local authority's decision, leaving room for manoeuvre to structure the case in its final form when more information is available on one's own case and the local authority's case.

A sensible approach is to consider the reasons for refusal given by the local authority and to answer them point by point. The temptation simply to contradict the local authority should be resisted. This does not normally provide sufficient information to establish why the appellant disagrees.

Having set out why the local authority's reasons are not acceptable, one should consider additional points which the local authority may have neglected to cover in their reasons, particularly positive aspects of the proposals. These additional points should be made as briefly as possible.

It is important to cover the ground fully. If the local authority are not alerted to all elements of the appellant's case in the grounds of appeal, they will not be able to respond in their statement of case. The appellant will thus lose the benefit of discovering their views at an early stage.

If the appeal is against non-determination, s 78(2) of the Act provides that the application is to be treated as refused. In many cases the appellant will be aware from his discussions with the local authority where the objection lies and may be able to frame brief grounds of appeal. However, as it is for the local authority to show why the application is unacceptable, it may be sensible in non-determination cases to submit terse grounds of appeal, stating simply that the appeal is for non-determination, that the appeal proposal causes no harm to interests of acknowledged importance and should therefore be allowed. This leaves the appellant free to build his detailed case once the local authority's formal statement of case is received.

In many local authorities once an appeal is received the matter will be returned to the planning committee. No decision can be taken (once the appeal is lodged the local authority is no longer in a position to take a decision on the matter), but the committee can state the reasons which it would have given for refusal had an appeal not been lodged. This enables the officers of the local authority to frame their statement of case appropriately and is helpful to the appellant. Very occasionally, the committee may indicate that it does not oppose the grant of planning permission. If this happens, contact should be made to establish whether this appeal should be pursued or a new application submitted.

3.4   Final details

The local authority do not need to receive additional copies of the documents they already have, such as the application and plans. Often the only document sent to the local authority is the appeal form, including the grounds of appeal and the ownership certificate. The declaration should be signed and a check made that everything is complete. A copy should be retained.

Once the Inspectorate have received the appeal and checked that it is in order, they will send an acknowledgment to the appellant and further information. They will also notify the local authority and send them a questionnaire requesting other relevant information.

Chapter 4

Written Representation Appeals

4.1 Written statement

The appeal form is unlikely to provide sufficient space for the written representation grounds and supporting statement. It is suggested that the words 'see attached file' should be typed on the form. This enables the appeal documents to be assembled and bound separately in a folder or ringbinder. Advice on the structuring of a written statement is contained in Circular 18/86, Appendix 1.

The first sheet should contain a summary and contents page. In this way, the brief reasons can be set out in order and allocated a section number. Each discrete topic will therefore have an individual section. Depending on the nature of the supporting material, it may make sense for each section to be self-contained. In other cases, documents such as the local plan may be relevant to different sections and are usually included as a separate appendix to which reference is made within individual sections. An introduction drawing together the strands of the case will be useful.

The tendency to amass a thick dossier should be resisted. The inspector will be influenced by how pertinent the evidence is, not its extent. Strict rules of evidence do not apply. Letters from neighbours, newspaper articles and the like can be pressed into service. The greatest weight will be attached to the best evidence. If traffic is an issue, a proper traffic survey will make the point better than a statement that the appellant knows the area and there have never been traffic hold ups on that road. The question of conditions to be imposed can usually be left until the local authority's statement has been received.

Where the appeal is against non-determination, it will be difficult for the appellant to produce concise reasons and the evidence to support them. If there is real doubt as to what the local authority see as the issues, the appeal form may have to be relatively brief and indicate that a full case will be submitted in response to the information from the local authority.

Once the appeal and supporting papers have been lodged, the procedure will be commenced by the Inspectorate and culminate in the receipt of the decision letter. Early correspondence will indicate who is the 'case officer' at the Inspectorate. He or she is an important source of information. It is in a party's own interest to be prompt and courteous in dealing with the case officer.

4.2   Procedural steps

The procedure is governed by the Town and Country Planning (Appeals) (Written Representations Procedure) Regulations 1987. Circular 11/87 provides additional advice and information. Annex A of the circular provides a useful diagram of the written representation appeal procedure and this is reproduced in Figure 4.1. For ease of reference the rules are discussed in the order in which they appear.

4.2.1   Regulation 3: application

The regulations apply to all appeals received after the 5 May 1987 where the appellant has expressed a wish for the appeal to be determined by this procedure. Regulation 3 also makes provision for the change of procedure in two circumstances. Firstly, where the appellant or the local authority inform the Secretary of State that an appeal previously entered under the informal hearing or public inquiry procedure is to be dealt with by this procedure. The Secretary of State can therefore apply these regulations having regard to steps already taken. Secondly, the regulations cease to apply if the Secretary of State informs the appellant and the local authority that he intends to deal with the appeal by way of inquiry or informal hearing. Upon such changes taking place the parties will be notified of the further steps required and the time for carrying them out.

4.2.2   Regulation 4: notification of receipt of appeal

When the appeal is received the Inspectorate will immediately notify both the appellant and the local authority of the date of receipt, which is 'the starting date' for the subsequent time periods, the reference number allocated to the appeal and the address to which correspondence should be sent. Notification of the starting date is not necessarily an indication that the appeal is valid (see Circular 11/87, para 5).

4.2.3   Regulation 5: notice to interested persons

Once the local authority have received notice of the appeal from the Inspectorate, they must within five working days notify the following parties:

  (a)   any authority or any person notified or consulted in accordance with the Act or a development order about the application which has given rise to the appeal; and

  (b)   any other person who made representations to the local planning authority about that application.

  The notice to these parties gives them the information they need about the appeal; where copies of representations can be seen; the fact that earlier representations will be forwarded to the Inspectorate as part of the appeal process but that modifications, elaborations or withdrawal of those representations should be sent directly to the Inspectorate within 28 days of the

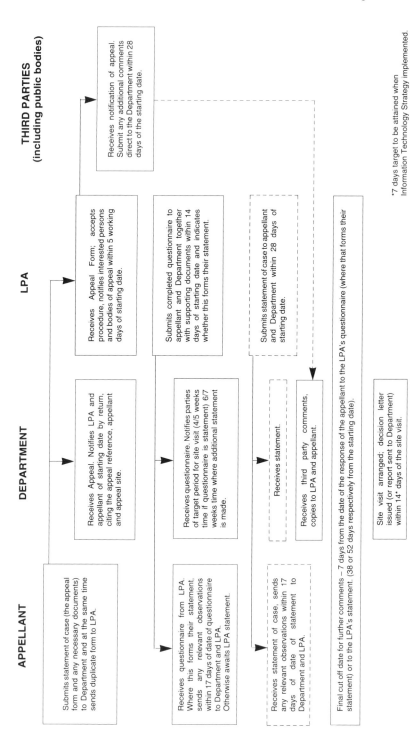

Figure 4.1. Procedure for written representations appeals, from Annex A of Circular No. 11/87: The Town and Country Planning (Appeals) (Written Representations Procedure) Regulations 1987, reproduced by kind permission of the Controller of Her Majesty's Stationery Office.

starting date. Annex B of the circular contains a model letter to be sent to such interested persons.

This notice will ensure that all those who expressed a view in respect of the original application have an opportunity to make further representations (or withdraw previous representations) at the appeal stage. For an appellant it is important that such representations receive special care as part of the appeal process and further advice is given on this in Chapter 9. People who buy neighbouring property after the application has been dealt with have no *right* to be notified of an appeal even if the local authority knows a neighbouring property has changed hands (*Robson v Secretary of State for the Environment, Tynedale District Council and Troldahl*). Not being a statutory party nor a person who made representations at the application stage, they will not fall within the scope of the rule.

4.2.4   Regulation 6: appeal questionnaire

The Inspectorate has supplied local authorities with an appeal questionnaire which they are required to send to the Inspectorate and to the appellant within 14 days of the starting date. The questionnaire contains information on such matters as whether the building is listed and whether there are any related inquiries or development plan provisions. Annexed to the questionnaire will be copies of correspondence with interested parties and directions from statutory consultees, the planning officer's report to committee (if any) and committee minutes and extracts from the local plan and any other relevant documents.

The local authority may indicate on the appeal questionnaire that this documentation contains the totality of their case. Alternatively, they can indicate that they are going to prepare a further statement to explain the reasons for their decision.

The questionnaire and its documents are important from the appellant's point of view. He will want to check carefully that the representations and responses to consultations match those he has already obtained from the local authority. The local authority may have letters received after the time when he asked for copies. If the local authority have indicated that this is their whole case he will then begin to consider whether there is anything he needs to add to the initial documentation submitted with the appeal or whether the exchange of information is complete. Where the local authority have indicated on the questionnaire they intend to make a further statement the appellant should wait for that statement before responding to the questionnaire (Circular 11/87, para 11). As para 12 of Circular 11/87 makes clear, the appellant should not respond to the local authority's representations unless there is something he needs to add. The sooner the exchange of representations is complete, the quicker the decision.

4.2.5   Regulation 7: representations

Regulation 7 states that the notice of appeal and the supporting documentation shall comprise the appellant's representations in relation to the appeal. This is an important distinction between the written representation and the public inquiry procedure. In the public inquiry procedure, the grounds of appeal do not include the evidence and there is a further refining of the issues.

Where the local authority wish to put in further representations over and above the appeal questionnaire, they have 28 days from the starting date to submit such additional information. It is usually possible for them to make additional representations if these are required.

Regulation 7(4) enables the appellant to make further representations by way of reply within 17 days of receipt either of the questionnaire, if this is the totality of the local authority's case, or within 17 days of the submission of their further representations in accordance with this regulation. It is at this stage that the appellant will have to consider the proposed conditions to be attached to any planning permission granted and will respond, indicating if these are accepted and putting forward a revised set with his reasons.

Copies of all representations, whether by the appellant or the local authority, must be copied to the other side. Representations made by third parties and sent to the Inspectorate will be copied to the local authority and the appellant who have not less than seven days in which to reply.

In practice written representation appeals often do not conform to these time limits. Further representations can be submitted up to the time the inspector makes his decision. However, if the appeal has been properly prepared there should be no need for an on-going exchange of representations. The impulse to answer every point as it is made should be resisted. The appellant should have dealt fully with his case initially. Lengthy exchange of correspondence usually blurs the issues and fails to concentrate on the important elements of the case which the appellant has identified and set out in his initial representations and response to the local authority's representations.

One of the difficulties of the written representation procedure is that, with no opportunity to meet the inspector and talk through the issues, an appellant sometimes feels that he must engage in lengthy correspondence. If this begins to happen or further issues emerge, it may be an indication that the appellant would be better served by requesting a change to an informal hearing or a public inquiry. The later such a request is made, the greater the practical difficulties, costs and delay.

4.2.6   Regulation 8: Power to set later time limits

Circular 11/87 makes it clear that time limits will be extended only in exceptional circumstances, eg the failure of another party to abide by a time limit; the appellant's need for extra time to respond to the local authority's statement in a non-determination case; or the linking of the appeal to another type of appeal where different time limits apply. These give flexibility to the regulations. It is always the right thing to comply with time limits or to request an extension of time. Provided the Inspectorate are warned at an early stage that further representations are on their way, the inspector will not reach a decision until he is satisfied that he has received all relevant information. But there is a power to strike out appeals on the grounds of delay under s 79(6A) of the Act. In practice, a warning will be received, but there is the risk that it might be mislaid. It is better to keep in close contact with the case officer at the Inspectorate.

4.2.7 Regulation 9: decision on appeal

This regulation indicates that a decision may be made taking into account only written representations submitted within the relevant time limits. A decision may also be made despite the fact that no written representations have been made within the time limit if it appears to the inspector that he has sufficient material to reach a decision on the merits.It is unlikely that this regulation will be activated while any of the parties have indicated that further representations are to be made. Appellants should, however, be aware that the Inspectorate have a brief to speed up the appeal process. It is therefore dangerous to delay unduly in collecting the information required and forwarding it to the Inspectorate. The power of the Secretary of State to dismiss appeals for undue delay under s 79(6A) of the Act should not be overlooked.

Copies of documents must be sent with the relevant written representations. It is not normally necessary to send to the local authority copies of documents they already have. However, if the file is not too bulky it may be more satisfactory to make up a complete dossier and simply copy it for the inspector, the local authority and the client, with one or two spare sets. In this way, everyone has an exact duplicate.

4.3 Site visits

A site visit will be held. Paragraphs 24 and 25 of Circular 18/86 explain that the aim is to carry out the site visit within a two week target period following the closing date for representations and to issue a decision letter within two weeks of the site visit.

Site visits are normally unaccompanied if the inspector can see the site from a public place. The appellant should consider whether this is the case and whether he would wish to be present at a site visit, even though the site can be seen from a public place. The opportunity to show the inspector the site and point out the issues of importance is valuable. If appropriate an accompanied site visit should be requested.

The inspector will then consider the issues and send each party an identical letter indicating his decision and the reasons for it. More detailed information on the decision letter is given at the end of Chapter 6 and in Chapter 12 on High Court challenge.

A worked example of a simple written representation procedure appeal is given for general information.

Worked Example

3 Leafy Lane
Surbiton
SU0 000
19.2.94

Director of Planning
Surbiton Borough Council
Town Hall
Surbiton
SU0 OO1

Dear Sir

I have pleasure in enclosing an application form, the fee, a sketch plan and a location plan.

I have discussed this with Mr Green, the Area Planning Officer, who told me that this application was likely to be refused because it did not meet the Council's design guidelines.

I would like to explain that a new extension is absolutely necessary because the house itself is very small and both kitchen and bathroom and toilet facilities are contained in the present substandard rear extension. This means that the toilet has to be accessed directly from the kitchen which does not meet modern requirements and the Environmental Health Officer has been on to me about this. The simplest solution seems to replace this single-storey extension with a double-storey extension so that the bathroom and toilet can be built on the first floor. This will result in a much more satisfactory housing layout and meet health requirements.

I have shown these plans to my two neighbours, Mr White and Miss Blue, both of whom support my application.

Would you please deal with this application as quickly as possible as I have arranged for the builder to start in three weeks.

Yours sincerely

S. Black

Please read the *GUIDANCE NOTES* before completing this form

APPLICATION FOR PLANNING PERMISSION

CHIEF PLANNING OFFICER

SURBITON BOROUGH COUNCIL

Send at least four copies (preferably five) of the application forms and the same number of each set of plans together with the correct fee to:

Application No.

1 Name and address of APPLICANT

Mr. & Mrs. S Black
3 Leafy Lane, Subiton

Post Code

Telephone No. 081–993 5432

2 Name and address of AGENT (if any)

Post Code

Telephone No.

3 Full address or Location of Site

3 Leafy Lane, Subiton

Post Code

Site Area   Acres/Hectares

4 Describe the proposed development

double storey rear extension to form new kitchen and bathroom

5 What is the applicant's interest in the land or buildings ? (Owner, Tenant, Prospective Purchaser etc.)

owner

6 Does the applicant own or control any adjoining land or buildings?

no

If YES, edge in blue on the location or site plans.

7 State present use of the site or buildings or state last previous use and the date last used

private house

8 Indicate whether the proposal involves:

New Building(s)	no
Alteration or Extension to building(s)	yes
Construction of new access to highway	no
Alteration of access to highway	no
Change of Use	no
Other Operations	

9 Indicate which ONE of the following the application is for:

	OUTLINE planning permission (for erection of a building(s) only)*
	APPROVAL of reserved matters (Give ref. no. of outline permission)**
yes	FULL planning permission (includes CHANGE OF USE and CONVERSIONS)
	RENEWAL of temporary/previous permission (Give previous ref. no.)
	REMOVAL OF CONDITION. Give condition no. [ ] permission no:

* For outline permission, ring any of the following for which approval is sought now:

SITING   DESIGN   EXTERNAL APPEARANCE   MEANS OF ACCESS   LANDSCAPING

** State any of the above reserved matters NOT applied for:

10 Give details of proposed means of:

Surface water disposal   as existing

Foul sewage disposal

Water supply

11 List plans submitted:

Site Plan DRW 1
elevations DRW 2

12 State manufacturer, type and colour of ALL external wall and roof materials   to match existing

13 Further information will be required for the following development:

Offices	☐	Industry ☐	Shopping ☐	Warehousing ☐		Tick the correct box to indicate that you have filled out the relevant extra form
Farm Buildings	☐	Farm Dwellings ☐	Waste Disposal ☐	Mineral Extraction ☐		

14 If the applicant

-owns all of the site or buildings, then complete Certificate A and the Agricultural Holdings Certificate
-owns none or part of the site, then complete Certificate B and the Agricultural Holdings Certificate
-does not know who owns any part of the site, refer to the GUIDANCE NOTES for further advice

15 CERTIFICATE A**

I certify that at the beginning of the period 21 days ending with the date of the accompanying application, nobody except the applicant, was the owner** of any part of the land to which the application relates

SIGNED   S. Black   *On behalf of   Date   19.2.94

────────────────────────── OR ──────────────────────────

CERTIFICATE B**   not applicable

I certify that I have/The applicant has* given the required notice to everyone else who, at the beginning of the 21 days ending with the date of the accompanying application, was the owner of any part of the land to which the application relates as listed below.

Owners name   Address at which notice was served.   Date notice served.

SIGNED   S. Black   *On behalf of   Date   19.2.94

* See GUIDANCE NOTES   ** Delete if not applicable

16 AGRICULTURAL HOLDINGS CERTIFICATE

Whichever is appropriate of the following alternatives must form part of Certificates A,B,C and D. If the applicant is the sole agricultural tenant he/she must delete the first alternative and insert "not applicable" as the information required by the second alternative.

*None of the land to which the application/appeal** relates, is, or is part of, an agricultural holding.
**I have/The applicant has/The appellant has* given the requisite notice to every person other than my/him/herself* who, on the day 21 days before the date of the application/appeal* was a tenant of an agricultural holding on all or part of the land to which the application/appeal* relates, as follows:-

Tenant's name   Address at which notice was served.   Date notice served.

SIGNED   S. Black   *On behalf of   Date   19.2.94

* See GUIDANCE NOTES   ** Delete if not applicable

17 I/We hereby apply for permission to carry out the development described in this application and on the accompanying plans.

SIGNED   S. Black   *On behalf of   Date   19.2.94

This Form is reproduced with the kind permission of North Wiltshire District Council, Monkton Park, Chippenham, Wiltshire, SN15 1ER.

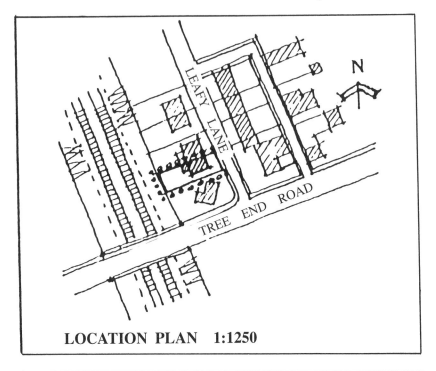

LOCATION PLAN   1:1250

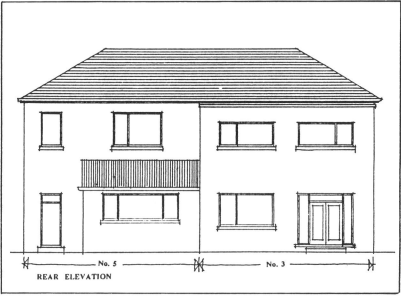

Figure 4.2. Illustrative example: architect's drawings showing proposed domestic extension (not to scale).
Key: OOOOO site boundary (shown in red on architect's drawings).

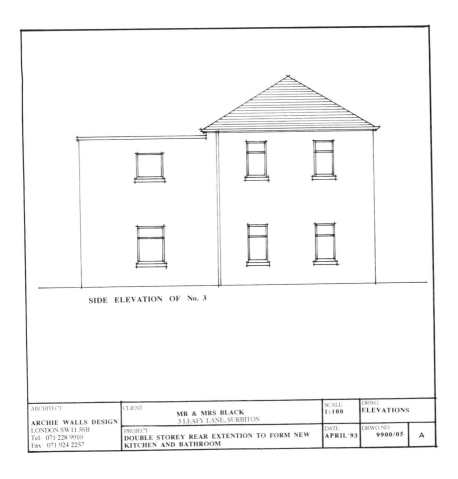

SIDE ELEVATION OF No. 3

ARCHITECT **ARCHIE WALLS DESIGN** LONDON SW11 5SB Tel: 071 228 9910 Fax: 071 924 2257	CLIENT **MR & MRS BLACK** 3 LEAFY LANE, SURBITON	SCALE **1:100**	DRWG **ELEVATIONS**	
	PROJECT **DOUBLE STOREY REAR EXTENTION TO FORM NEW KITCHEN AND BATHROOM**	DATE **APRIL '93**	DRWG NO **9900/05**	**A**

[Figure continues]

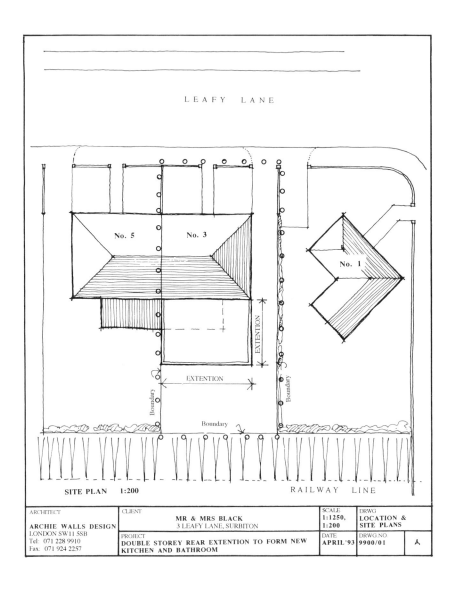

Figure 4.2, *cont.*

Surbiton Borough Council

Reference No: SC/120/94

Refusal Notice

TOWN & COUNTRY PLANNING ACT 1990

Full Planning Application SC/120/94

Drawing No./Date Stamped: 12.2.94

The Council as Local Planning Authority REFUSES planning permission for the following development for the reason(s) set out in the schedule below:—

Proposal: Double-storey rear extension to form new kitchen and bathroom.

Location: 3 Leafy Lane, Surbiton SU0 000.

REASONS FOR REFUSAL

The proposals do not conform to the Council's adopted design guidelines for domestic extensions and are seriously detrimental to the amenity of neighbouring properties.

Dated 3.4.94

The Planning Inspectorate

An Executive Agency in the Department of the Environment and the Welsh Office

FOR OFFICIAL USE ONLY

Date received

PLANNING APPEAL TO THE SECRETARY OF STATE
TOWN AND COUNTRY PLANNING ACT 1990
TOWN AND COUNTRY PLANNING GENERAL DEVELOPMENT ORDER

The appeal must reach the Inspectorate within 6 months of the date of the Notice of the Local Planning Authority's decision, or within 6 months of the date by which they should have decided the application.

A. INFORMATION ABOUT THE APPELLANT(S)

Full name: MR. & MRS. S. BLACK

Address   3, LEAFY LANE, SURBITON

Postcode _____
Failure to provide the post code may cause delays in processing your appeal.

Daytime Telephone number _____   Reference _____

Agent's name (if any)   SMITH & JONES

Agent's Address _____ 134, NEWTOWN ROAD, NEWTOWN

Postcode   N43 12AP
Failure to provide the post code may cause delays in processing your appeal.

Daytime Telephone number   081-550 1234   Reference   2/GUN

B. DETAILS OF THE APPEAL

Name of the Local Planning Authority (LPA)   SURBITON BOROUGH COUNCIL

Description of the development

   Double storey rear extension to form new kitchen and bathroom

Address of the site ___ 3 Leafy Lane, Surbiton

National Grid Reference (see key on OS map for instructions).
Grid Letters: Grid Numbers
eg TQ: 298407

Postcode _____
Failure to provide the post codee, if any, may cause delays in processing your appeal.

Date and reference no. of the application in respect of which you are appealing.   SC/120/93   19.2.94

Date of LPA notice of decision (if any).
3.4.94

(REV 1994)

C. THE APPEAL

THIS APPEAL IS AGAINST the decision of the LPA:- (✔)

1. to *refuse/~~grant subject to conditions,~~ planning permission for the development described in Section B. ✓

2. to *refuse/grant subject to conditions, approval of the matters reserved under an outline planning permission.

3. to refuse to approve any matter (other than those mentioned in 2 above) required by a condition on a planning permission.

Or the failure of the LPA:-

4. to give notice of their decision within the appropriate period on an application for permission or approval.

*Delete as appropriate

D. PROCEDURE

1a. Do you agree to the written procedure? (ie an exchange of written statements with the LPA and a visit to the site by an Inspector). If yes, please tick opposite and answer question 1b below. ✓

1b. Tick if the whole site can clearly be seen from a road or other public land. (An unaccompanied site visit will be arranged if the Inspector can adequately view the site from public land).

OR

2. Do you wish to appear before and be heard by an Inspector? If yes, please tick.

3. If the LPA agree and the Inspectorate considers your appeal suitable, do you wish to proceed by way of a hearing rather than a local inquiry? If yes, please tick.

E. SUPPORTING DOCUMENTS

A copy of each of the following should be enclosed with this form.

1. The application submitted to the LPA; ✓

2. Any Article 12(A) certificate (site ownership details) submitted to the LPA; ✓

3. Plans, drawings and documents forming part of the application submitted to the LPA; ✓

4. The LPA's decision notice (if any); ✓

5. Other relevant correspondence with the LPA - Please identify the correspondence by date or otherwise

6. A plan showing the site in red, in relation to two named roads (preferably on an extract from the relevant 1:10,000 OS map)

Copies of the following should also be enclosed, if appropriate:

7. If the appeal concerns reserved matters, the relevant outline application, plans submitted and the permission;

8. Any plans, drawings and documents sent to the LPA but which do not form part of the submitted application (eg drawings for illustrative purposes);

9. Additional plans or drawings relating to the application but not previously seen by the LPA: Please number them clearly and list the numbers here

2

F. APPEAL CERTIFICATION

IMPORTANT: THE ACCOMPANYING GUIDANCE NOTES SHOULD BE READ BEFORE THE APPROPRIATE CERTIFICATE IS COMPLETED.

SITE OWNERSHIP CERTIFICATES

PLEASE DELETE INAPPROPRIATE WORDING WHERE INDICATED (*) AND STRIKE OUT INAPPLICABLE CERTIFICATE

CERTIFICATE A

I certify that:
On the day 21 days before the date of this appeal nobody, except the appellant, was the owner (*see Note (i) of the Guidance Notes*) of any part of the land to which the appeal relates.

OR

CERTIFICATE B

I certify that:
I have/The appellant has* given the requisite notice to everyone else who, on the day 21 days before the date of this appeal, was the owner (*see Note (i) of the Guidance Notes*) of any part of the land to which the appeal relates, as listed below.

Owner's Name	Address at which notice was served	Date on which notice was served

Signed   Smith & Jones   (on behalf of) MR. & MRS. S. BLACK

Name (in capitals) SMITH & JONES   Date   3.7.94

AGRICULTURAL HOLDINGS CERTIFICATE (TO BE COMPLETED IN ALL CASES)

* None of the land to which the appeal relates is, or is part of, an agricultural holding.

OR

* I have/The appellant has given the requisite notice to every person other than my/him/her* self who; on the day 21 days before the date of the appeal was a tenant of an agricultural holding on all or part of the land to which the appeal relates, as follows:-

Tenant's Name	Address at which notice was served	Date on which notice was served

*Delete as appropriate. If the appellant is the sole agricultural tenant the first alternative should be deleted and "not applicable" should be inserted below the second alternative.

Signed Smith & Jones   (on behalf of) MR. & MRS. S. BLACK

Name (in capitals)   SMITH & JONES   Date   3.7.94

G. GROUNDS OF APPEAL If the written procedure is requested, the appellant's FULL STATEMENT OF CASE **MUST** be made - otherwise the appeal may be invalid. If the written procedure has not been requested, a brief outline of the appellant's case should be made here.

Please see documents attached.

continue on a separate sheet if necessary

PLEASE SIGN BELOW

I confirm that a copy of this appeal form and any supporting documents not previously seen by the LPA has been sent to them. I undertake that any future documents submitted in connection with this appeal will also be copied to the LPA at the same time.

Signed   Smith & Jones   (on behalf of)   MR. & MRS. S. BLACK

Name (in capitals)   SMITH & JONES   Date   3.7.94

CHECKLIST

- This form signed and fully completed.

- Any relevant documents listed at Section E enclosed.

- Full grounds of appeal/outline of case set out at Section G.

- Relevant ownership certificate A, B, C or D completed and signed.

- Agricultural Holdings Certificate completed and signed.

Send one copy of the appeal form with all the supporting documents to:

> The Planning Inspectorate
> Tollgate House
> Houlton Street
> Bristol BS2 9DJ

A copy of the appeal form **must** be sent to the LPA at the address from which the decision on the application (or any acknowledgements, etc) was received, enclosing only copies of those documents not previously seen by the LPA.

Cdf 106170/6/B09955 10m 9/93 DTP

This Form is Crown Copyright and is reproduced by kind permission of the Planning Inspectorate, Houlton Street, Bristol BS2 9DJ.

Mr and Mrs Black
3 Leafy Lane
Surbiton
SU0 000

APPEAL BY WRITTEN REPRESENTATIONS
AGAINST REFUSAL OF PLANNING PERMISSION
BY SURBITON BOROUGH COUNCIL DATED 3.4.1994

---

1. The original sketch plans have now been replaced with architect's drawings and copies are attached. The Council have no objection to the revised drawings superseding the previous sketch plans.

2. The extension is needed to provide modern facilities and cannot be made any smaller. The Council design guidelines for extensions do not cover this situation.

3. The extension will be invisible from the front of the house and there is a railway line to the rear. The only two people affected are the immediate neighbours, Mr White and Miss Blue, both of whom are aware of the appellant's difficulties and support these proposals.

    The side window is now to be in obscure glass to avoid any risk of overlooking.

Conclusion

4. The appellant has done everything possible to meet the Council's objections but the reality is that the Council are rigidly enforcing their guidelines despite the special circumstances of this case.

5. I look forward to welcoming the inspector on site so that he may see for himself. I have also arranged with my two neighbours for access to the rear of their properties.

6. I am sure that when the inspector sees the state of the rear extension he will agree that planning permission should be granted.

Annex

1. Revised drawings

2. Excerpts from Council's extension policies

3. Letters from Mr White and Miss Blue

4. Suggested conditions including obscured glazing requirements

COUNCIL'S WRITTEN REPRESENTATIONS

1. The Council has received revised drawings from Mr Black and has no objection to these drawings being substituted. While they do represent an improvement on the original sketch plans, the Council's objections are ones of principle and are not overcome by the cosmetic changes.

2. The Council's design guidelines for residential extensions were adopted by the Council for development control purposes and have been included as policy D3 in the Deposit Draft of the Local Plan and a copy is attached.

3. The house faces east onto Leafy Lane and as a result the two-storey bulk will substantially overshadow the properties to the north.

4. In addition, the position of the extension will result in very considerable overlooking and loss of privacy and visual amenity to neighbouring properties on both sides.

5. The Council's design guide indicates that a two-storey extension is inappropriate in these circumstances because of these adverse effects.

   A single storey extension to match the existing would be in accordance with the design guideline and the Council would have no objection to the extension being a little longer than the present building.

6. The fact that the existing kitchen and bathroom do not meet modern standards and that the present neighbours do not object does not justify the erection of a permanent double-storey extension which contravenes the Council's guidelines and has a detrimental effect on the built environment.

   The inspector is urged to support the Council's policies and refuse this appeal.

The Council encloses the following documents:

1. Draft Deposit Local Plan

2. Design Guide

3. Daylight indicators for midday, winter and summer

Chapter 5

Informal Hearing Appeals

5.1 Introduction

There is no statutory procedure for informal hearings as there are for written representation appeals and public inquiries. There is, however, a Code of Practice published by the Department of the Environment and if this procedure is chosen a copy will be sent to the appellant.

The procedure for informal hearings is illustrated in Figure 5.1. If it is appropriate, the Inspectorate will normally offer an informal hearing within five working days of receipt of an appeal. If it is accepted by the local authority and the appellant, an informal hearing date will then be arranged, normally within 12 weeks. At least 28 days' notice is given. The hearing will normally be held at the offices of the local authority.

Paragraph 2 of the Code of Practice makes it clear that the procedure is intended to save time and money and the inspector will lead a discussion on the issues raised by the appeal. Everyone, including interested third parties, should get a fair hearing but in a less formal setting than a public inquiry.

As para 3 of the Code of Practice makes clear some cases are not appropriate to this procedure:

> A hearing will not be appropriate if many members of the public are likely to be present; if the appeal raises complicated matters of policy; if there are likely to be substantial legal issues raised; or if there is a likelihood that formal cross-examination will be needed to test the opposing cases.

It is important to remember that the procedure is informal. If parties are late in supplying their full statements of case in accordance with the Code of Practice or if there is a complex exchange of information between the local authority and the appellant, the inspector may take the view that the case should be dealt with by public inquiry.

Paragraph 8 of the code makes it clear that arrangements for the hearing are designed to foster discussion. Wherever possible inspectors are advised to sit round a table. This very informality can be a danger if either the appellant or third parties are likely to try to dominate the proceedings or there is a great deal of heat on one side or another. The inspector can at any time close the informal hearing and decide to hold a public inquiry.

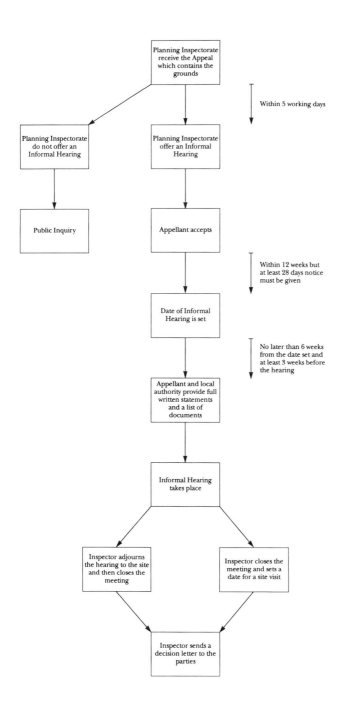

Figure 5.1. Procedure for informal hearings.

5.2   Who can appear?

There is no statutory limit on appearance. The inspector may permit anyone to appear and speak. In some cases the appellant may himself feel that he can explain the position to the inspector and take part in the discussion. In most cases, the informal hearing will benefit from the disciplined approach and experience of a planning professional, usually a chartered town planner. There is no reason why a chartered town planner should not deal with the technical evidence while the appellant in person deals with matters within his own knowledge, such as the need for the development.

5.3   Procedure

As with the written representation appeal, the local authority will notify interested parties of the arrangements. Third parties will be notified so that they can inspect copies of pre-hearing statements and also be advised that they may, at the discretion of the inspector, participate in the discussion.

Grounds of appeal will already have been provided on the appeal form. At least three weeks before the hearing and no later than six weeks from the date that a hearing is agreed, both the appellant and the local authority must provide a full written statement and list of documents (para 6 of the code). It is suggested that a proposed list of conditions to be imposed should be included. It may be useful for the parties to discuss them informally before the hearing: if they can be agreed, so much the better. If not, those conditions which are not agreed can be specifically drawn to the inspector's attention.

The inspector will use this exchange of documents to brief himself on the important issues so that he can lead the discussion properly. At the hearing he will indicate what he considers are the main issues and where he needs further information. The appellant is usually asked to start the discussion.

Because the written material has been exchanged, it will not normally be read out at the hearing. Those participating are encouraged to ask questions as the discussion progresses. The appellant will be given the opportunity to make any final comments before the discussion is closed. The inspector will control the hearing and may refuse to allow questions to be put which are not relevant and may require any person who is behaving in a disorderly manner to leave. The hearing can be conducted in a way which is not possible in the more formal context of a planning inquiry. The inspector may decide to continue the informal hearing at the site itself rather than closing the hearing and then going on a site visit.

Paragraph l4 of the code explains the circumstances when the inspector will adjourn the hearing to the site. He will do this only when he is satisfied that:

● weather conditions are suitable;
● the discussion could proceed satisfactorily;
● no one involved would be at a disadvantage;
● all parties present at the hearing will have the opportunity to attend;

- no one participating in the hearing has objected to the discussion being continued on the site.

If the informal hearing is not adjourned to the site, the inspector will, before closing the informal hearing, ask the parties whether they wish to accompany him on the site visit. If any of them does, he will arrange the date and time of the visit.

At the site visit the appellant, landowner and representative of the local authority may attend, as may any party appearing at the hearing, at the discretion of the inspector and with the consent of the landowner. Discussion on site may be more important in informal hearings than it is at public inquiries, particularly if the hearing is not closed before the site visit, as the more relaxed rules make it possible to continue the discussion of issues raised in a way which is not possible in formal public inquiry procedure.

5.4   Comparison with public inquiry

An appellant should bear in mind the significant differences between informal hearing and public inquiry. It is open to the inspector to discontinue the informal hearing procedure and remit the appeal to be heard by public inquiry if he thinks that this is the correct course of action, and the local authority or any third party can make representations to this effect. The appellant is entitled at any stage to discontinue the informal procedure and ask for a formal public inquiry but he may find that a change of mind will be 'unreasonable behaviour', leading to an award of costs (see Chapter 11).

A number of factors may cause the informal hearing procedure to be aborted, resulting in considerable delay in the appeal decision. Legal representation is not normal at informal hearing. If the appellant brings lawyers and a number of witnesses, the inspector may believe the hearing is moving away from a round table discussion. He may, during the course of the hearing itself, decide that a public inquiry must be held.

Sometimes an appellant becomes aware after the appeal has been lodged that he needs witnesses to make his case and deal with the local authority's objections. It is likely that the inspector will see when the documentation is exchanged that the amount of material is unsuitable for a round table discussion and should be dealt with by the more structured approach of calling evidence and cross-examination at a public inquiry.

It sometimes emerges at a late stage that there are important policy issues, legal issues or differences of evidence. In these cases, the inspector may consider that the more formal public inquiry procedure would enable these issues to be better explored.

5.5 Advance notification of decision and post-hearing matters

It is possible to ask for an advance notification of the decision if the appellant and the local authority agree. If the inspector feels it is appropriate to offer this service, he will write within 24 hours giving simply the decision, ie whether he will allow or dismiss the appeal. The formal decision with reasons will follow in due course.

Once he has concluded the informal hearing, the inspector will consider the evidence and write his decision letter. This will be sent to the parties. More detailed consideration of the decision letter is given at the end of Chapter 6 (para 6.23) and in Chapter 12 on High Court challenge.

Any application for costs should be made before the hearing is closed.

An example of an informal hearing appeal follows.

Worked Example

Please read the *GUIDANCE NOTES* before completing this form

APPLICATION FOR PLANNING PERMISSION

CHIEF PLANNING OFFICER

NORTH COUNTRY DISTRICT COUNCIL

Send at least four copies (preferably five) of the application forms and the same number of each set of plans together with the correct fee to:

Application No. ☐☐☐☐☐☐☐☐

1 Name and address of APPLICANT

Mr. F Giles
The Old Cottage, Mildmay, Cheshire

Post Code

Telephone No.

2 Name and address of AGENT (if any)

Post Code

Telephone No.

3 Full address or Location of Site

The Twenty Acre Field, Crooked Usage, Mildmay

Post Code

Site Area 20   Acres/Hectares

4 Describe the proposed development

bungalow and store for poultry keeper

5 What is the applicant's interest in the land or buildings ? (Owner, Tenant, Prospective Purchaser etc.)

Tenant

6 Does the applicant own or control any adjoining land or buildings?

No

If YES, edge in blue on the location or site plans.

7 State present use of the site or buildings or state last previous use and the date last used

agricultural

8 Indicate whether the proposal involves:

New Building(s) — yes
Alteration or Extension to building(s)
Construction of new access to highway — yes
Alteration of access to highway
Change of Use
Other Operations

9 Indicate which ONE of the following the application is for:

yes — OUTLINE planning permission (for erection of a building(s) only)*
APPROVAL of reserved matters (Give ref. no. of outline permission)**
FULL planning permission (includes CHANGE OF USE and CONVERSIONS)
RENEWAL of temporary/previous permission (Give previous ref. no.)
REMOVAL OF CONDITION. Give condition no. ☐ permission no.

*   For outline permission, ring any of the following for which approval is sought now:

SITING   DESIGN   EXTERNAL APPEARANCE   MEANS OF ACCESS   LANDSCAPING

**   State any of the above reserved matters NOT applied for:

10 Give details of proposed means of:

Surface water disposal   soakaway

Foul sewage disposal   to main in adjoining
                        land
Water supply

11 List plans submitted:

location and site plans

12 State manufacturer,
type and colour of
ALL external wall   all reseved matters
and roof materials

13 Further information will be required for the following development:

				Tick the correct box to indicate that you have filled out the relevant extra form
Offices ☐	Industry ☐	Shopping ☐	Warehousing ☐	
Farm Buildings ☐	Farm Dwellings ☐	Waste Disposal ☐	Mineral Extraction ☐	

14 If the applicant

-owns all of the site or buildings, then complete Certificate A and the Agricultural Holdings Certificate
-owns none or part of the site, then complete Certificate B and the Agricultural Holdings Certificate
-does not know who owns any part of the site, refer to the GUIDANCE NOTES for further advice

15 CERTIFICATE A**

I certify that at the beginning of the period 21 days ending with the date of the accompanying application, nobody except the applicant, was the owner ** of any part of the land to which the application relates

SIGNED   *On behalf of   Date

─────────────────────────── OR ───────────────────────────

CERTIFICATE B**

I certify that I have/The applicant has* given the required notice to everyone else who, at the beginning of the 21 days ending with the date of the accompanying application, was the owner of any part of the land to which the application relates as listed below.

Owners name	Address at which notice was served.	Date notice served.
Lord Septon	The Castle, Septon	1.10.93

SIGNED   F GILES   *On behalf of   Date 1.10.93

* See GUIDANCE NOTES   ** Delete if not applicable

16 AGRICULTURAL HOLDINGS CERTIFICATE

Whichever is appropriate of the following alternatives must form part of Certificates A,B,C and D. If the applicant is the sole agricultural tenant he/she must delete the first alternative and insert "not applicable" as the information required by the second alternative.

*None of the land to which the application/appeal** relates, is, or is part of, an agricultural holding.*
**"I have/The applicant has/The appellant has* given the requisite notice to every person other than my/him/herself* who, on the day 21 days before the date of the application/appeal* was a tenant of an agricultural holding on all or part of the land to which the application/appeal* relates, as follows:-

Tenant's name	Address at which notice was served.	Date notice served.
J. Baldric	Septon Farm, Mildmay	1.10.93

SIGNED   *On behalf of   Date 1.10.93

* See GUIDANCE NOTES   ** Delete if not applicable

17 I/We hereby apply for permission to carry out the development described in this application and on the accompanying plans.

SIGNED   MR. F GILES   *On behalf of   Date 1.10.93

This Form is reproduced with the kind permission of North Wiltshire District Council, Monkton Park, Chippenham, Wiltshire, SN15 1ER.

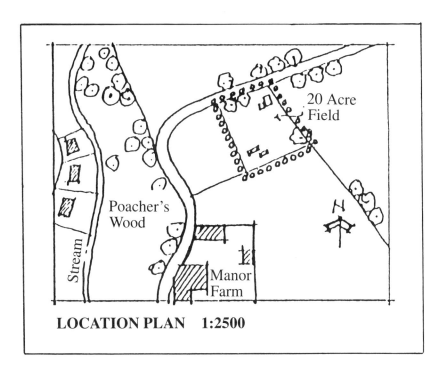

Figure 5.2. Illustrative example: landscaping plan showing proposed bungalow and store on a poultry farm (not to scale).
Key: ⭕⭕⭕⭕⭕ site boundary (shown in red on architect's drawings).

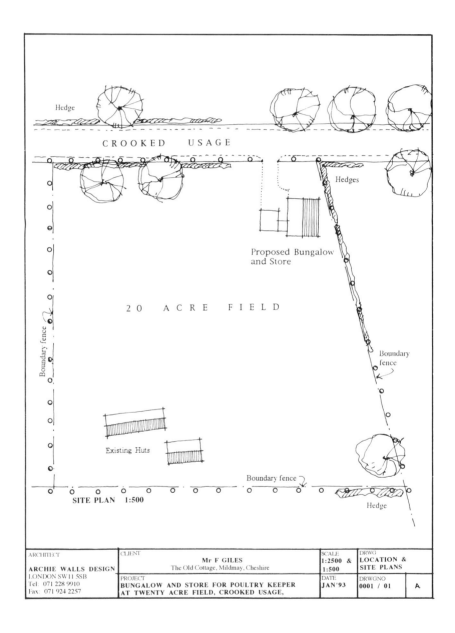

Figure 5.2, *cont.*

NORTH COUNTRY DISTRICT COUNCIL

Reference No: NC 1234

Decision Notice

TOWN & COUNTRY PLANNING ACT 1990

Outline Planning Application

Drawing No./Date Stamped:

The Council as Local Planning Authority REFUSES planning permission for the following development for the reason(s) set out in the schedule below:—

Proposal: Erection of a bungalow and store for poultry keeper.

Location: Twenty Acre Field, Crooked Usage, Mildmay, Cheshire.

REASON(S) FOR REFUSAL

1 The proposals are contrary to policy AONB1 of the adopted Local Plan which seeks to prevent new dwellings in the open countryside unless such dwellings are essential to meet the needs of agriculture or forestry.
2 The need for an agricultural dwelling has not been established in this case.

Informative:

In view of the location within an AONB, the Council consider an outline application is not acceptable since the Local Planning Authority is unable to assess the design and impact of the proposals.

Determined 1st January 1994   for DISTRICT PLANNING
                                                           OFFICER

(ATTENTION IS DRAWN TO THE NOTES ATTACHED)

The Planning Inspectorate

An Executive Agency in the Department of the Environment and the Welsh Office

PLANNING APPEAL TO THE SECRETARY OF STATE
TOWN AND COUNTRY PLANNING ACT 1990
TOWN AND COUNTRY PLANNING GENERAL DEVELOPMENT ORDER

The appeal must reach the Inspectorate within 6 months of the date of the Notice of the Local Planning Authority's decision, or within 6 months of the date by which they should have decided the application.

A. INFORMATION ABOUT THE APPELLANT(S)

Full name: MR. F GILES

Address   THE OLD COTTAGE, MILDMAY, CHESHIRE

Postcode
Failure to provide the post code may cause delays in processing your appeal.

Daytime Telephone number   Reference

Agent's name (if any) SMITH & JONES

Agent's Address   134 NEWTOWN ROAD, NEWTOWN

Postcode   N43 12AP
Failure to provide the post code may cause delays in processing your appeal.

Daytime Telephone number 081-550 1233   Reference   3/GUN

B. DETAILS OF THE APPEAL

Name of the Local Planning Authority (LPA)   North Country Borough Council

Description of the development

Bungalow and store for poultry keeper

Address of the site Twenty Acre Field, Crooked Usage, Mildmay, Cheshire

Postcode
Failure to provide the post codee, if any, may cause delays in processing your appeal.

National Grid Reference (see key on OS map for instructions).
Grid Letters: Grid Numbers
eg TQ: 298407

Date and reference no. of the application in respect of which you are appealing.   NC 1234   1.10.93

Date of LPA notice of decision (if any).   1.1.94

(REV 1994)

C. THE APPEAL

THIS APPEAL IS AGAINST the decision of the LPA:-   (✔)

1. to *refuse/~~grant subject to conditions~~, planning permission for the development described in Section B.   ☑

2. to *refuse/grant subject to conditions, approval of the matters reserved under an outline planning permission.   ☐

3. to refuse to approve any matter (other than those mentioned in 2 above) required by a condition on a planning permission.   ☐

Or the failure of the LPA:-

4. to give notice of their decision within the appropriate period on an application for permission or approval.   ☐

*Delete as appropriate

D. PROCEDURE

1a. Do you agree to the written procedure? (ie an exchange of written statements with the LPA and a visit to the site by an Inspector). If yes, please tick opposite and answer question 1b below.   ☐

1b. Tick if the whole site can clearly be seen from a road or other public land. (An unaccompanied site visit will be arranged if the Inspector can adequately view the site from public land).   ☐

OR

2. Do you wish to appear before and be heard by an Inspector? If yes, please tick.   ✔

3. If the LPA agree and the Inspectorate considers your appeal suitable, do you wish to proceed by way of a hearing rather than a local inquiry? If yes, please tick.

E. SUPPORTING DOCUMENTS

A copy of each of the following should be enclosed with this form.

1. The application submitted to the LPA;   ✔

2. Any Article 12(A) certificate (site ownership details) submitted to the LPA;   ✔

3. Plans, drawings and documents forming part of the application submitted to the LPA;   ✔

4. The LPA's decision notice (if any);   ✔

5. Other relevant correspondence with the LPA - Please identify the correspondence by date or otherwise
....

6. A plan showing the site in red, in relation to two named roads (preferably on an extract from the relevant 1:10,000 OS map)   ✔

Copies of the following should also be enclosed, if appropriate:

7. If the appeal concerns reserved matters, the relevant outline application, plans submitted and the permission;   ☐

8. Any plans, drawings and documents sent to the LPA but which do not form part of the submitted application (eg drawings for illustrative purposes);   ☐

9. Additional plans or drawings relating to the application but not previously seen by the LPA. Please number them clearly and list the numbers here:...   ☐

2

F. APPEAL CERTIFICATION

IMPORTANT: THE ACCOMPANYING GUIDANCE NOTES SHOULD BE READ BEFORE THE APPROPRIATE CERTIFICATE IS COMPLETED.

SITE OWNERSHIP CERTIFICATES

PLEASE DELETE INAPPROPRIATE WORDING WHERE INDICATED (*) AND STRIKE OUT INAPPLICABLE CERTIFICATE

CERTIFICATE A

I certify that:
On the day 21 days before the date of this appeal nobody, except the appellant, was the owner (see Note (i) of the Guidance Notes) of any part of the land to which the appeal relates.

OR

CERTIFICATE B

I certify that:
I have/The appellant has* given the requisite notice to everyone else who, on the day 21 days before the date of this appeal, was the owner (see Note (i) of the Guidance Notes) of any part of the land to which the appeal relates, as listed below.

Owner's Name	Address at which notice was served	Date on which notice was served
Lord Septon	The Castle, Septon	3.3.94

Signed Smith & Jones   (on behalf of) MR. F GILES

Name (in capitals) SMITH & JONES   Date 3.3.94

AGRICULTURAL HOLDINGS CERTIFICATE (TO BE COMPLETED IN ALL CASES)

* None of the land to which the appeal relates is, or is part of, an agricultural holding.

OR

* I have/The appellant has given the requisite notice to every person other than my/him/her* self who, on the day 21 days before the date of the appeal was a tenant of an agricultural holding on all or part of the land to which the appeal relates, as follows:-

Tenant's Name	Address at which notice was served	Date on which notice was served
J Baldric	Septon Farm, Mildmay	3.3.94

*Delete as appropriate. If the appellant is the sole agricultural tenant the first alternative should be deleted and "not applicable" should be inserted below the second alternative.

Signed Smith & Jones   (on behalf of) MR. F GILES

Name (in capitals) SMITH & JONES   Date 3.3.94

3

G. GROUNDS OF APPEAL If the written procedure is requested, the appellant's FULL STATEMENT OF CASE **MUST** be made - otherwise the appeal may be invalid. If the written procedure has not been requested, a brief outline of the appellant's case should be made here.

Please see attached sheet

continue on a separate sheet if necessary

PLEASE SIGN BELOW

I confirm that a copy of this appeal form and any supporting documents not previously seen by the LPA has been sent to them. I undertake that any future documents submitted in connection with this appeal will also be copied to the LPA at the same time.

Signed _____ Smith & Jones _____ (on behalf of) _____ F. GILES _____

Name (in capitals) SMITH & JONES _____ Date 3.3.94 _____

CHECKLIST

- This form signed and fully completed.

- Any relevant documents listed at Section E enclosed.

- Full grounds of appeal/outline of case set out at Section G.

- Relevant ownership certificate A, B, C or D completed and signed.

- Agricultural Holdings Certificate completed and signed.

Send one copy of the appeal form with all the supporting documents to:

The Planning Inspectorate
Tollgate House
Houlton Street
Bristol BS2 9DJ

A copy of the appeal form **must** be sent to the LPA at the address from which the decision on the application (or any acknowledgements, etc) was received, enclosing only copies of those documents not previously seen by the LPA.

Cdf 106170/6/B09955 10m 9/93 DTP

GROUNDS OF APPEAL

1. The proposals comply with policy AONB1 of the Local Plan. The dwelling is required for agricultural purposes.

    The existing business has been operating for some years but has increasingly been subject to vandalism and theft. New MAFF guidelines indicate that once poultry increases as envisaged, on site supervision will be essential.

2. The site lies in a depression and is well screened by trees and shrubs. The impact of a modest bungalow such as is proposed will be negligible and this is not a case where full details are required at the planning permission stage.

    All elements can be satisfactorily controlled by the Council at the approval of reserved matters stage.

Informal Hearing

Appellant's Documents

1. Photographs of site
2. Photomontage showing effects of bungalow
3. Illustrative drawings of bungalow
4. Landscaping proposals
5. Audited accounts
6. MAFF poultry guidelines

Local authority's documents
1. Development plan
2. Statement by Council's agricultural adviser

Chapter 6

Public Inquiry Procedure

6.1 Introduction

A public inquiry normally takes place because the appellant has chosen this procedure. However, it can also come about because the local authority or the Inspectorate have decided that the appeal ought to be dealt with by public inquiry. In rare cases the Secretary of State may decide that the appeal is not to be dealt with by an inspector but that he will decide it himself and in those circumstances also a public inquiry may be held. The procedure for those cases is described in Chapter 10, but much of the information in this chapter is also relevant.

A number of key points have to be decided at the outset: first, the appeal team must be finalised. A witness should not be asked to undertake the advocate's role as well. Next, the question of who is to present the case must be resolved. There are no rights of audience at a public inquiry. The advocate can be a barrister, a solicitor, a professional in a related field or someone without any qualifications at all. However, planning is a specialised area: if an appeal is worth pursuing at public inquiry, it should be done with experienced practitioners.

6.1.1 Preparation

The issues should be fully explored with the other parties, defining the approach and presenting a case closely tailored to the issues. Thorough and timely preparation is the order of the day. Appeals are often won and lost before the inquiry opens. Not to use the pre-inquiry period intensely and practically is to throw away the advantages of the procedure and expose oneself to a prepared opponent!

A timetable of team meetings (including counsel if instructed) should be set up. Such meetings may usefully be held after receipt of the local authority's statement of case to consider the appellant's; a few weeks later to consider first draft proofs; immediately before exchange of proofs to finalise them; immediately after exchange of proofs to consider additional matters; immediately before the opening of inquiry to mark up proofs and consider the thrust of cross-examination. The earlier the inquiry date is fixed, the earlier this programme of meetings can be set up. With a large team and busy people, such meetings can be difficult to arrange.

The lawyer on the appeal team often holds a pivotal role. Each expert naturally sees things from his own area of expertise. Someone independent needs to bring a sense of shape and priority to the developing case. There needs to be an arbiter on such matters as when an issue should be conceded or withdrawn, when evidence is not developing satisfactorily or to time, when a witness proves not to be the right one for the task in hand.

Preparing properly for a planning inquiry is time-consuming. An experienced assistant to keep meetings, proofs and queries under control will be useful for an inquiry of any size.

6.1.2   Burden of proof

There is, strictly speaking, no burden of proof in a planning appeal (*Pye (Oxford) Estates Ltd v Wychavon District Council and Secretary of State for the Environment* [1982] JPL 575). Inevitably a public inquiry centres on the reasons for refusal, challenged by the appellant and defended by the local authority. The inspector's job is to consider the evidence and points made to him in order to reach a conclusion as to whether there are sound reasons for refusal.

6.2   Procedure

The procedure is governed by the Inspector Rules which came into force on 30 September 1992, revoking the previous rules of 1988. Any appeal still outstanding which was lodged before 30 September 1992 and which has not yet been determined will proceed under the current rules with the modifications set out in r 22(ii).

The procedure covers all appeals under s 78 of the Act, eg ordinary planning appeals and also listed building consent appeals and conservation area consent appeals. Where the appeal is to be decided by the Secretary of State, the Secretary of State Rules will apply (see Chapter 10).

The rules are now dealt with in detail. It is also important to see the individual rules in the context of the inquiry procedure as a whole, and Figure 6.1 indicates the sequence of events. They are as follows:

- The appeal is lodged and the Inspectorate advise of the 'relevant date' from which time periods laid down in the procedure run.
- The local authority serves its statement of case and list of documents (usually within six weeks of the relevant date).
- Three weeks later the appellant serves his statement of case.
- The date and venue for the inquiry are fixed.
- Any other parties who wish to appear may also be required to serve a statement of case.
- For a major inquiry a pre-inquiry meeting may be held.
- At least three weeks before the date of the inquiry, all parties who have served statements of case exchange written proofs of evidence with their accompanying documents (if these have not already been disclosed to the other parties). A summary of the proof of evidence is also served at the same time if the main proof is more than 1500 words long.

Inquiry Procedure

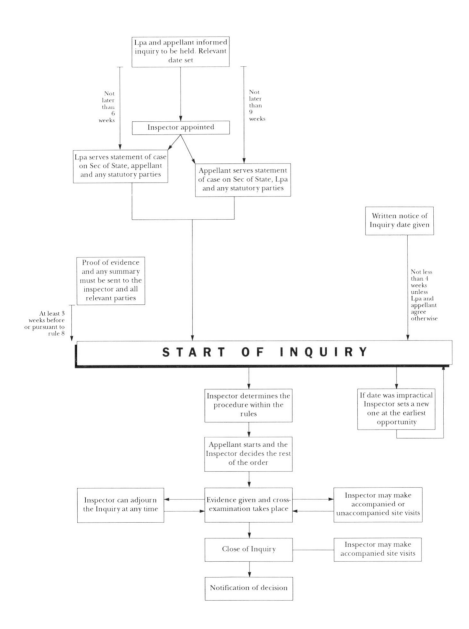

Figure 6.1. Public inquiries: sequence of events.

Although the 1988 Rules have been superseded, the circular which accompanied them (Circular 10/88) remains relevant. A more recent circular (24/92) draws attention to changes in the rules and also contains a useful annex relating to good practice at planning inquiries.

6.2.1   Pre-inquiry objectives

Paragraph 7 of Circular 10/88 draws attention to the fact that effective use of the period before the inquiry opens can make a crucial contribution to the speed and efficiency of the inquiry proceedings themselves.

> Early exchanges of information before the inquiry can help the inspector and the parties to identify the principal issues on which the inquiry should concentrate thus avoiding needless discussion of matters which are not relevant or can be resolved in advance. At a local inquiry there should be no place for surprise tactics.

The Rules do not themselves contain any sanctions for non-compliance but para 30 of the Guide to Good Practice at Planning Inquiries annexed to Circular 24/92 makes it clear that a party who fails to comply with the rules and causes other parties to incur extra expense as a result may lay themselves open to an award of costs on the basis of unreasonable behaviour.

Thus the principal objective of the rules is to make the inquiry process at all stages as efficient and effective as possible while impairing neither the fairness nor the impartiality of the proceedings, nor the ability of the participants to make representations which are relevant to the decision. This objective is to be achieved by ensuring a more effective use of the pre-inquiry period by the early exchange of information and by establishing timetables for the various steps.

The rules govern the procedure from the lodging of the appeal to issue of the decision letter in such a way that the issues can be first defined between the parties and then examined by the exchange of evidence and cross-examination so that the inspector has all the necessary information to reach an informed decision. The rules are also designed to ensure that third parties are able to play their part and that no one is taken by surprise at the hearing. While the planning inquiry procedure may appear adversarial, it must always be borne clearly in mind that co-operation is the order of the day. There is no place in the pre-inquiry system for attempts to score points by delaying the handing over of relevant information, refusing to co-operate with reasonable requests and trying to get some vague 'advantage' by the late introduction of evidence.

The inspector will want to see on the first day of the inquiry that all the evidence has been properly exchanged and discussed between the parties, so that the presentation of the case to him can be as focused and succinct as possible.

6.2.2   Major inquiries

For major inquiries, specific advice is contained in a Code of Practice annexed to Circular 10/88. The code supplements the relevant rules. The parties will be notified of a decision to deal with the appeal as a major inquiry and informed of the steps required. The purpose is to handle efficiently the large number of interested parties. A statement of issues will be issued and a system of registration of participants, pre-inquiry meetings and formal exchange of information initiated.

6.2.3   The Mirai Networks case

The case of *Mirai Networks Limited v Secretary of State for the Environment and Three Rivers District Council* [1994] JPL 337 illustrates what can happen where the rules are not adhered to. The applicants alleged that two conditions attached to a planning permission were invalid as a matter of law. This contention was rejected by the inspector on appeal and the applicants applied under s 288 to quash the decision. The first limb of challenge related to procedural matters. Three Rivers District Council had failed to serve a statement of case within the time limits. Indeed a document which was intended to be a statement of case emerged on the first day of the inquiry. Counsel for the appellant naturally sought an adjournment. The inspector, anxious to proceed with the appeal, agreed that the planning officer should be called first so that the appellant could know the case he had to meet, despite the opposition of the appellant. The inspector's decision, therefore, was contrary to r 15 which allows the appellant to put his case first unless he agrees otherwise.

This decision of the inspector did not mollify the appellant who continued to seek an adjournment which was finally agreed to by the inspector. Sir Graham Eyre QC, sitting as a deputy judge, noted somewhat wryly that it was difficult to see substantial prejudice to the appellant since his proof of evidence ran to over 160 pages, excluding plans. He thought it was clear that they had understood the case the local authority were adopting. In this particular case, the High Court did not interfere with the inspector's handling of the case.

6.3   The rules

In this section the rules will be considered in the order in which they appear and are followed by a commentary.

6.3.1   Application of rules

The rules will apply to any local inquiry held in England and Wales determined by an inspector which relates:

(1) to an appeal to the Secretary of State in relation to planning permission under s 78 of the Act and public inquiries where the inspector is to determine the appeal;

(2) to an appeal to the Secretary of State in relation to listed building consent under s 20 of the Planning (Listed Buildings and Conservation Areas) Act or conservation area consent under s 20 as applied by s 74(3) of that Act.

The same procedure applies to these appeals as to planning appeals. Specific listed building and conservation area consent aspects are dealt with in Chapter 13.

6.4   The relevant date/initial notifications

Once an appeal is lodged and it is clear that an inquiry is to be held, r 4 requires the Inspectorate to send out a notice informing both parties that an inquiry is to be held and stating in the notice the 'relevant date' for that particular appeal. This date is crucial for it is from it that all subsequent time periods are calculated. The parties will also see the name and telephone numbers of the case officer assigned to the appeal. It is advisable to keep in touch with the case officer and let him or her know immediately of any difficulties. The help of case officers can be invaluable; they usually have experience of a particular procedural problem and can advise on how it can be overcome.

The local authority take the first step by returning to the Inspectorate a questionnaire indicating points such as whether the building is listed, whether there are any other associated appeals and, most importantly, details of the 'statutory parties' who have made representations. 'Statutory party' means a person mentioned in para 1(b)(i) of art 22A of the GDO whose representations the inspector is required by para (3) of that article to take into account and such a person whose representations the local authority were required, by para (1) of that article, to take into account in determining the application occasioning the appeal.

The second category will comprise owners or agricultural tenants of the land concerned in the application. They will have been notified at the time of the original application by the applicant and a certificate signed indicating that this had been done. Similar notification is given on the lodging of the appeal. These parties are directly affected by the appeal and have a right to participate fully in the appeal process. They are particularly important because the inspector is under the same obligation as the local authority to consider their representations before reaching a decision in accordance with art 22A of the GDO.

In the same way the Secretary of State must as soon as practical inform the appellant and the local authority of the name and address of any 'statutory party' who has made representations directly to him. In practice, copies of the representations will be sent.

Difficulties may arise where a person has purchased a neighbouring property after the application has been dealt with. That person will not have made representations at the application stage and will not therefore fall within the scope of this rule. The local authority are not required to notify such a person even if they are aware of the changed circumstances (*Robson v Secretary of State for the Environment ex p Tynedale District Council and* Troldahl [1993] JPL 938).

On some occasions the local authority's decision may have been in response to views of other bodies. In these cases r 4 requires the local authority to notify the body concerned as soon as possible after the relevant date. Unless this has already been done, the person or body concerned is required to give the local authority a written statement of the reasons for the direction or the view they have taken. This is necessary to enable a local authority to frame the next important step in the proceedings, the statement of case.

This rule may come into play where the Secretary of State has issued a direction to the local authority restricting the grant of planning permission for which application was made. Such cases have recently arisen in respect of routes safeguarded for road or railway schemes or where the decision has strategic implications. The rule is also relevant where the Secretary of State or any other Minister of the Crown or government department or any body falling within r 11(i)(c) has expressed a view that the application should not be granted either wholly or in part or should be granted only subject to conditions. This situation would arise if the development proposed was considered to have implications of national security or to affect a licensed airport.

The following bodies are set out in r 11(i)(c):

- the county or district council;
- a national park committee;
- a joint planning board;
- an urban development corporation or an enterprise zone or authority;
- the Broads Authority or a Housing Action Trust.

Finally, the rule comes into play where any authority or person consulted in pursuance of a development order has made representations to the local planning authority about the application. Article 18 of the GDO contains lists of various bodies who are to be consulted in cases where the development is likely to affect their own function or where they have a particular input to make to the local authority's decision. Such consultations are obviously of particular significance where environmental statements are produced and specialist bodies have responded.

The local authority is responsible for contacting these bodies so that they can provide a written statement to be incorporated in the statement of case. However, it would be shortsighted of an appellant not to ensure that such bodies are alerted immediately so that the statement of case properly reflects their views. If such a body is inadvertently not notified, considerable delay and additional work may arise if its views have to be taken into account at a later stage. While the appellant has no responsibility for ensuring that this rule is complied with, he will normally have sought copies of the representations or views which have a bearing on the local authority's decision-making process.

The local authority will, in many cases, have consulted more widely than is strictly required, as suggested by the Secretary of State (particularly in Circular 22/88, Appendix C). They may also have received representations from interested members of the public and adjoining land owners notified through the normal publicity procedures at the application stage.

It is normal that all such parties are notified of the appeal if they have made representations at the application stage. Such parties may not have a right to appear (see r 11). The distinction is that for those parties who make representations and are strictly within the rules, their views are required to be taken into account before the inspector makes his decision. This distinction, however, may be more illusory than real. The inspector will make his decision based on all relevant information available to him. The purpose of this rule is simply to ensure that all those who are caught within the compulsory consultation procedure and who do make representations are properly notified of the inquiry.

Dealing with all such representations is an important part of preparing for the inquiry and is dealt with in Chapter 9.

6.5   Identity of inspector

Rule 5 requires that every person entitled to appear at the inquiry is notified of the name of the inspector. Where the inspector is changed and it is not practical to notify the new appointment before the opening of the inquiry, the inspector is required to announce his name and his appointment at the opening of the inquiry. The identity of the inspector may be of interest to the parties who may wish to obtain information on the previous type of appeals he has dealt with and how he has handled various issues. It is possible to obtain computer printouts of appeal decisions by an inspector from COMPASS, the Computerised Planning and Appeals Service, whose address is given in the section, Useful Information, at the front of this book. This may give valuable background information.

Notification of the inspector is given quite early in the appeal procedure. However, in relation particularly to smaller inquiries, the identity of the inspector assigned to a case may change as the Inspectorate adjust their detailed timetabling nearer the time of the inquiry.

6.6   Statements of case and lists of documents

Once all the preliminary information has been received, r 6 requires the local authority to serve their statement of case within six weeks of the relevant date. The statement of case must be served on the Secretary of State, the appellant and any statutory parties as defined above. Where r 4(2) applies (eg where some other body has given a direction or expressed a view or made representations), the local authority must include such information in their statement. In the case of a direction given by the Secretary of State, the statement of case must include the direction and reasons for it. Where there are any views expressed or representations made on which the local authority intend to rely in their submissions to the inquiry, they must include these in their statement of case and supply a copy of their statement to the person or bodies concerned.

6.6.1   Structuring the statement of case

The statement of case must cover all the relevant topics fully and include full particulars of the case to be put forward at the inquiry including the technical data upon which the parties wish to rely (Circular 24/92, Annex, para 5).

The writing of a statement of case is straightforward in some cases and difficult in others. It will not always be possible to include *full* particulars of *all* topics. Additional issues will arise to be dealt with in the course of the pre-inquiry preparation. However data, methodology and assumptions should wherever possible be included.

The broad line of the argument should be fixed by the local authority's statement of case. The appellant can be relatively confident that once he has received this document he knows all the issues in contention. He should not be lulled into a sense of complacency: the local authority may put in extra work as a result of receiving the appellant's statement of case.

If the local authority cannot produce their statement of case within the six weeks allowed by the rules, there is little to be gained by refusing a reasonable extension of time. The appellant should ensure, when agreeing an extension of time, that he in turn is granted the normal three weeks after receipt of the local authority's statement to respond. The Inspectorate should be kept informed.

If the local authority are unable or unwilling to submit their statement of case within a reasonable time, it may be possible to refer this to the inspector. The better course is to press on with the appeal hearing. In some cases there is no statement of case from the local authority before the hearing. The appellant's remedy lies in an application for costs on the basis that the appellant has been put to additional expense because, not knowing the local authority's case in detail, he has had to put additional work into preparing for all eventualities (see Chapter 11 on costs).

A list of documents on which the local authority are relying must also be attached. The right to add further documents is often included at the end of the list of documents. Rule 6(5) requires the local authority to send the appellant a copy of any document in the list or of any relevant part of any document as soon as practical, if this is required.

The appellant is required to serve his statement of case on the Secretary of State and the local authority not later than nine weeks after the 'relevant date'. The requirement as to content is the same as for the local authority's statement of case. This should be dealt with in the same way as the grounds of appeal: the local authority's statement of case should be dealt with point by point and any additional matters which the appellant believes are relevant should be added. The list of documents which should be annexed to the statement of case should properly reflect the evidence to be called. Similar rules apply to the list of documents in the appellant's statement of case as to the local authority's list, ie the local authority can require a copy of any document.

Both statements of case must be served four weeks before the date fixed for the inquiry (r 6(4)). This overrides the time periods given above. It may be important if an early date is offered for an inquiry which will telescope the procedure. Both statements of case may need to be served simultaneously, allowing very little time before proofs have to be exchanged three weeks before the inquiry. It is possible to agree a later date for exchange of proofs, but this will curtail the time available to deal with incoming proofs before the opening of the inquiry. In a straightforward case, a party may prefer an early hearing date (resulting in an early decision) to the sieving process of the procedure itself. Fixing an inquiry date is a delicate business and is dealt with in para 6.10.

If any part of the statement of case is unclear, either party can request clarification. It is an important part of the appeal process that the parties keep in touch with each other and work through the issues in a constructive way. Once the statements of case and the lists of documents have been exchanged and any necessary copies of the documents received and examined, both parties will be well placed to take stock of the issues to be dealt with at the inquiry. It is at this stage that the appellant will know what further work needs to be done to prepare the evidence for his own case and to counter the local authority's. This is often the best time for technical experts from either side to meet and agree what evidence needs to be presented to deal with the issues and to agree base data and methodology, even if they cannot agree the conclusions.

It will often be at this stage that one of the parties becomes aware that certain issues cannot or ought not to be disputed. Both parties should reconsider their position in the light of the statements of case and the documents. If the appellant considers that any of the reasons for refusal as carried forward in the statement of case of the local authority cannot be justified by evidence, a letter should be written inviting the local authority to withdraw that element. If they refuse, it will document the fact if a later application for costs is made. Likewise, as the appellant takes stock of his own position, he may wish to concentrate on certain issues and agree others in order to limit the matters and issues at the inquiry. Such a change in position should immediately be made clear to the local authority. It goes without saying that letters documenting any such changes should be copied to the Inspectorate.

From the appellant's point of view it is important that this pre-inquiry procedure is used to re-evaluate his case. Alternative ways of dealing with the planning problems by negotiation with the local authority should not be overlooked, even while preparation for the inquiry takes place.

6.6.2   Position of third parties

Rule 6(6) enables the inspector to require any other person who has notified his intention to appear at the inquiry to serve a statement of case within four weeks of being so required and to provide any other information that is required. The Secretary of State has indicated (Circular 10/88, para 27) that this power is intended to be used selectively and normally only for more important inquiries where bodies such as national amenity societies may play a major role.

Provision is also made for such statements to be exchanged and for inspection and copying of documents. This may be an important provision. Bodies who are required to be consulted by the local authority will have been dealt with earlier. Other third parties such as resident associations or amenity bodies who may wish to take part in the appeal procedure will be covered by this rule. This enables such third parties to be drawn into the pre-inquiry procedure to ensure that their case is fully articulated to the other parties so that the matters raised can be dealt with. Parties who have served statements of case have a right to appear at the inquiry.

From the appellant's point of view this may prove difficult. When dealing with an established body there may be no difficulty in obtaining such a statement in advance, but it may be onerous for voluntary bodies with few resources but who wish to turn up and express their views at the inquiry. But it is useful and time saving to know in advance what such bodies wish to say. An appellant may consider requesting the inspector to require them to serve a statement of case and such further information as is required.

A decision will have to be taken as to whether it is counterproductive to require these objectors to produce a statement of case in advance. In many cases what objectors have to say will be well known and the appellant may feel that he is prepared to deal with their arguments at the inquiry itself.

6.7 Inspector's statement of issues and pre-inquiry meetings

Rule 7 enables an inspector, not later than 12 weeks after the relevant date, to serve on the appellant, the local authority and any statutory party a written statement of the matters about which he particularly wishes to be informed and to hold a pre-inquiry meeting, when he considers it desirable, on two weeks' notice. A pre-inquiry meeting is defined in r 2 as a meeting held before an inquiry to consider what may be done with a view to securing that the inquiry is conducted efficiently and expeditiously.

Neither a statement of issues nor a pre-inquiry meeting is usually needed for smaller inquiries. The procedure is activated by the inspector but there may be cases where the local authority or the appellant may see advantages in asking for either or both of these matters to be dealt with. In major inquiries it will certainly be helpful to have both the pre-inquiry meeting and guidance from the inspector on the issues. The procedure for this is dealt with in the guidance for major inquiries in Circular 10/88, Annex 1.

It may be useful to ask for a pre-inquiry meeting if there is real difficulty in preparing the case. If there is a lack of co-operation between the parties, the inspector may be prepared to hold a pre-inquiry meeting and to identify the issues which should be covered. This could be the case even in relatively low-key inquiries where one party is raising issues which the other party considers irrelevant or where the rules have not been complied with. It may also be useful where there is a great deal of public interest and the parties wish to channel public participation and to request statements of case in accordance with r 6.

One important function of a pre-inquiry meeting is to bring the parties together in advance of the inquiry. This may be useful in enabling the appellant to meet objectors in a formal situation and clarify their views, even if no formal order is made for statements of case and proofs of evidence to be exchanged. From the objectors' point of view, a pre-inquiry meeting or an agreed statement from the inspector of the matters about which he particularly wishes to be informed may be useful in focusing their work and avoiding preparing evidence on matters which are not considered important by the inspector.

Pre-inquiry meetings can be a useful forum for bringing under control inquiries which show signs of becoming unmanageable because of the number of parties who wish to be heard and because of the wide range of issues in dispute. If a pre-inquiry meeting is held and the inspector issues instructions as to how representations are to be made, third parties who are notified but who fail to appear at that meeting and identify their position may find themselves in difficulties at the inquiry itself.

6.7.1   Witness summons

This is also the time to consider asking the inspector for a witness summons to compel a witness to attend. The inspector can issue a summons by virtue of s 250 of the Local Government Act 1972 which is applied to planning inquiries by s 282 of the Town and Country Planning Act 1990. Witness summonses are extremely unusual in public inquiries relating to planning permission, although more common in enforcement notice appeals. An inspector has a discretion as to whether to issue a witness summons. He will therefore wish to be persuaded that it is essential and proper for the witness to be called. A witness summons is ill advised in most circumstances for the following reasons. Firstly, one usually has an unwilling witness. Exceptionally, the reasons for requiring the summons are purely technical (police officers often require a witness summons before attending on any private proceedings). Secondly, one will not know in advance what a witness is going to say, which is a major disadvantage. It is a well-established principle of advocacy that no advocate asks a question to which he does not already know the answer. To require an unwilling witness to attend is the equivalent of firing a loose cannon. It usually has no place in a public inquiry into a planning application where professional witnesses will be dealing with planning issues and relevant information within a party's knowledge given by willing witnesses.

Appellants are sometimes aggrieved at what may or may not be said in local authority meetings or at meetings with officers. They wish formal evidence to be called and for the elected members or the officers who attended the meetings to be called on these points. Usually this is a mistake. Only in the most exceptional case, where perhaps members have refused an application for what are clearly non-planning reasons and against officers' advice, should this be even considered. The inspector will have his mind firmly fixed on the planning merits. He is reaching his decision as if the application had been made to him in the first place. What may or may not have been said at an earlier stage will be largely peripheral and may distract the inspector from the merits of the case.

The question of witness summons of professionals was discussed in *Seyfang v G D Searle & Co and Another* (1973) 1 QB 148. A witness summons may be considered in cases where evidence to be given is a question of fact and the evidence is essential to the case. It may be used where a document is essential, its contents are known and its production can properly be required, or where the witness indicates his willingness but does not wish to be seen voluntarily to be taking sides. Finally, a witness summons is appropriate to enable a public servant of some kind to be called, ie police and social workers (if it is proper for them to be called).

A witness summons is inappropriate where the evidence is not absolutely essential and the issue could be dealt with in a more appropriate way. It is unsuitable in cases which do not involve questions of fact, *ie* questions of policy or opinion. Expert witnesses cannot usually be required to give evidence. It should not be used for witnesses who are employees or members of the local authority or persons similarly connected with the appellant, or where a witness might feel personally exposed and drawn in to someone else's dispute or open to retribution of some kind or where the interpretation of facts is involved.

It is not always easy to disentangle questions of fact from questions of opinion. Whether brick making was taking place when a witness inspected the site is a question of fact. Whether that activity required planning permission is *not* a question of fact.

Before a witness summons is requested the following questions should be considered. What if unwilling witnesses fail to turn up despite a summons? What if they answer 'I don't know' to every question? What if, having had the information prised out of him, the witness then goes on to show the client in an unattractive light? Whether or not it is relevant, mud has a habit of sticking. Careful thought, then, is needed before compelling a witness to attend and give evidence.

6.8 Inquiry timetable

Rule 8 enables the inspector to set a timetable tailored for a particular case. This will enable the larger inquiry to be properly structured. Issues are dealt with in a logical order which is understood by all the parties. Inquiries may be divided up into topic-based sections or site-specific sections.

6.9 Notification of appointment of assessor

Assessors are experts on separate matters who sit with the inspector and advise him as to the issues within their competence. For most planning inquiries there will be no need for an assessor. Rule 9 provides for an assessor to be appointed if the need is apparent. The appeal may raise technical issues, such as civil engineering matters, on which an assessor can assist the inspector. The appointment of an assessor can be raised at the pre-inquiry meeting if it has not already been raised or discarded. For the appellant, it may be a double-edged sword. In cases where an environmental statement has been presented and issues of pollution control arise, there may be a difficult boundary between land use planning matters and evidence which is more properly the preserve of the Health and Safety Executive or other bodies under licensing regimes. Government advice in PPGs indicates that planning should not normally duplicate the function of other regulatory regimes, but the appointment of an assessor may mean that detailed technical evidence will be produced at the planning appeal stage and may alter the character of the evidence to be presented. On the other hand, in a technical case, an assessor may enable the inspector to deal with the planning merits more effectively.

If an assessor is appointed under this rule, there is nothing the parties can do about it. The real question is whether, since assessors are rarely appointed, an appellant or the local authority wishes to ask for an assessor to be appointed.

The decision on the appeal will rest with the inspector. The assessor will only advise him.

6.10   Date and notification of the inquiry

Rule 10 requires the Secretary of State to hold an inquiry not less than 20 weeks after the relevant date unless he considers it is impractical, in which case he shall hold it as soon as is practical. Four weeks' written notice is required.

This is one of the most important rules. The Secretary of State has clearly indicated that he wishes to expedite appeal hearings and inquiry dates are now fixed as soon as possible. The rules are amplified by Circulars 18/86 and 24/92. Each principal party will only be permitted one refusal of a date offered. The period for negotiating dates will normally be limited to one month. Once a date has been fixed, it will be changed only for exceptional reasons. Unavailability of counsel or witnesses is not considered 'exceptional circumstances'. Recently there has been a move to curtail even further the room for negotiation and to fix dates as early as possible. This will undoubtedly improve the time taken to handle appeals and enable the Inspectorate to organise the inspectors' timetables effectively.

It is vital for the appellant to be proactive and agree a date for the inquiry as soon as possible, and fixing the date of the inquiry is absolutely crucial for him. Professional advisers will already be involved and it will be essential to have a date which does not conflict with the availability of advocates and witnesses. It is frustrating for the appellant to discover that an inquiry date has been imposed which does not suit either his advocate or his witnesses. It is possible to contest the imposition of a date, either at the beginning of the inquiry or by requiring a pre-inquiry meeting with the inspector at which dates can be discussed. Once a date is imposed, urgent action is required if it does not suit the appellant.

The local authority may be more relaxed as regards dates because advocate and witnesses may be in their permanent employ. However, there may be constraints on the venue. Most public inquiries are held at town halls or satellite public buildings and these can be booked up for other functions. The local council offices will usually be made available free of charge. However, a local authority may not have a venue available at the time that the appellant wishes the public inquiry to be heard. The appellant may therefore consider reaching agreement with the local authority on a suitable venue for the inquiry (perhaps at a local hotel) and on how the costs are to be defrayed.

6.10.1   Time estimate

The estimated length of the public inquiry will have an effect on the arrangements made for the attendance of witnesses and the availability of a venue. As soon as the appeal has been lodged, a realistic assessment of the number of witnesses from both sides and the time needed to hear the evidence should be made. The estimate should err on the side of caution. It is preferable to have an inquiry finish a day early than to find that insufficient time has been allowed. If the latter happens, the inquiry is likely to be adjourned until some future date when all parties are available. If there are a number of witnesses and a busy inspector, it may be several months before the inquiry can be resumed.

6.10.2   Best practice for fixing dates

The best practice is for the appellant to contact the local authority at a very early stage in order to discuss how long the inquiry will take, the most sensible venue for the inquiry and dates where the venue is available for the periods involved and which meet both parties' requirements. If both parties indicate that they have agreed on the length of the inquiry, the venue and the dates, the Inspectorate will do their best to make an inspector available. Once the date has been fixed, both sides should consider 'housekeeping' arrangements. Will a photocopier and fax machine be available, and separate rooms with telephones for the inspector and each team? Can tea and coffee be supplied? Where can sandwiches be obtained for lunch? In addition, the appellant will want to consider overnight accommodation for the team assembling the evening before the inquiry. It is efficient to have the whole team staying at a local hotel, with a conference room reserved for them.

6.10.3   Site notices and other publicity

Rule 10(5) requires the local authority to publicise the inquiry as required by the inspector, ie by newspaper advertisement, by serving notice on third parties or by posting a notice near the land. A letter is normally sent to those who have made representations.

Where the land is under the control of the appellant, he is required to fix a site notice either to the land or some object on or near the land (in such a manner as to be readily visible to and be legible by members of the public); he must not remove the notice or cause it to be removed for such a period before the inquiry as the Secretary of State may specify. The Inspectorate will usually send the appellant a site notice to be displayed for 14 days before the inquiry. If there are any changes, ie the inspector's name or the venue has changed, a revised site notice will be sent by the Inspectorate.

This is an important provision from the appellant's point of view and should be given careful attention. The thrust of the rule is that all those who may be interested shall be aware of the public inquiry. Consideration should be given as to where the notices should be affixed and how many there should be. If they are likely to be subject to vandalism, the notice should be regularly inspected and replaced as necessary. It is difficult if a third party comes forward, claiming that there was no notice. The appellant should ensure that he is in a position at the opening of the inquiry to produce a witness who will state that the notices were put up and regularly inspected.

6.11   Appearances at inquiries

Apart from the appellant and the local authority, r 11 provides that the following bodies are entitled to appear at the inquiry if the land is in their area and they are not the local planning authority:

- county or district council;
- national park committee;
- joint planning board;
- urban development corporation;
- enterprise zone;
- Broads Authority;
- Housing Action Trust;
- the development corporation or the Commission for the New Towns and its successor if the land is within their area;
- a statutory party, parish or community council if representations were made to the local planning authority;
- any other person who has served a notice of case in accordance with r 6(6).

Those bodies who have an interest in the inquiry will, in accordance with the rules, have already made representations. One difficulty arises out of r 11(2), which states that 'Nothing in paragraph (1) shall prevent the inspector from permitting any other person to appear at an inquiry and such permission shall not be unreasonably withheld'. This means in effect that any objector can appear and by virtue of r 11(3) may be represented by counsel, solicitor or any other person.

Inspectors are increasingly taking control of the procedure and ensuring that time is not wasted. Nevertheless, both the local authority and the appellant should bear in mind that considerable latitude will be extended at a public inquiry to individuals, particularly those appearing in person. It is to the appellant's advantage to prepare his case so that third party objections have been met and to ensure that he is not seen to be preventing these parties from expressing their views. The likelihood is that, in view of the wording of this rule, the inspector will hear any person who wishes to be heard except in the most exceptional circumstances, for example if a person is rude and disruptive.

6.12   Representatives of government departments and other authorities at the inquiry

Rule 12 relates to situations where directions have been given by the Secretary of State or another minister or government department or where any of the bodies falling within r 11(1)(c) (see 6.11) has expressed a view which the local authority has included in its statement of case and on which it intends to rely in accordance with r 6(1).

The appellant can apply in writing to the inspector for a representative of that body to attend at the inquiry. This must be done no later than two weeks before the date of the inquiry. A person attending in this capacity is required to state the reasons for the direction or expressed view, to give evidence and be subject to cross-examination to the same extent as any other witness. However, he does not have to answer any questions which, in the opinion of the inspector, are directed to the merits of government policy. From the government's point of view this is a sensible restriction, preventing public inquiries being used as an opportunity to challenge government policy which the inspector is bound, where relevant, to take into account.

6.13   Ability of the inspector to act in place of the Secretary of State

By virtue of r 13, an inspector can act in place of the Secretary of State under the following rules:

- *Rule 6(6)–6(8)*: requiring any other person who wishes to appear at the inquiry to serve a statement of case; supplying such a person with a copy of the other statements of case and information as to who is to receive a copy of his statement of case; requiring any person who has served a statement of case to provide further information as specified.
- *Rule 10*: date and notification of the inquiry.
- *Rule 12(1)–12(2)*: making representatives of government departments, etc available for the inquiry;
- *Rule 20*: allowing further time for the steps required by these rules.

In practice, the Inspectorate will see that correspondence is dealt with appropriately by forwarding correspondence to the inspector as required and ensuring that any decisions to be taken by the Secretary of State are taken by an appropriate civil servant after consulting with the parties and the inspector.

6.14   Exchange of proofs of evidence

Rule 14 sets out the procedure for the advance exchange of proofs of evidence and summaries. All those appearing at the inquiry have to provide a written copy of the evidence which they intend to call, and a summary if that evidence is more than 1,500 words, at least three weeks before the inquiry or in accordance with the timetable if the inspector has arranged one. This applies to the appellant, local authority, a statutory party or a person who has served a statement of case because he has notified the inspector that he intends to appear. Summaries are often exchanged on the morning of the inquiry itself and are thus completely up to date. This may be particularly helpful for members of the public attending the inquiry.

Conditions to be put forward if planning permission is granted may be included as part of the evidence. It will always be possible to alter them. For some cases, however, it is difficult to frame conditions at this stage and they may be better discussed between the parties towards the end of the appeal hearing.

Where a summary is submitted because of the length of the proof, the rule provides that only the summary shall be read at the inquiry unless the inspector permits or requires otherwise. The proof of evidence and summary (if required) must be sent to the other parties and to the inspector together with relevant documents or parts of documents unless they have already been exchanged at an earlier stage with the statement of case.

The local authority is required to afford to any person who so requests a reasonable opportunity to inspect and, where practical, take copies of any documents sent to or by them in accordance with this rule. This means that members of the public who are not directly involved may see the proofs and summaries and underlying documents as they become available.

The written exchange of proofs and summaries is the cornerstone of the procedure. It is designed to facilitate public participation in the inquiry process, to save time at the inquiry and to avoid any party being taken by surprise. This will not only save time (because normally only summaries will be read) but it has an important effect on the preparation for the inquiry. The procedure is usually that one party will usually contact the other immediately before proofs are due to be exchanged to ascertain whether the other party's proofs are available. It may be a little paranoid but there is a view that it is only right that if one makes one's evidence available to the other side they should do the same simultaneously. Otherwise they might have the opportunity of reading the incoming proof and rewriting their own evidence in the light of that proof. Sometimes some but not all of the proofs are available. It is suggested that if, for instance, the planning proofs are ready, these should be exchanged but other proofs (eg highway evidence) should be sent only when the other side's highway evidence is available.

In any event, the inspector should receive his copies on time despite the fact that the other side's evidence is not available. Indeed, sending proofs to the inspector on time will not only comply with the rules but also enable him to consider carefully your case. The reality is that for most cases it will be too late for the other side to restructure their evidence if they have missed a point.

It will be possible at the inquiry to amplify the summary and to deal with any additional points arising directly out of the other side's evidence. This rule penalises the ill-prepared participant and gives enormous advantage to the participant who has prepared his case properly and in good time.

The advance exchange of evidence affords a last opportunity for the parties to meet and deal with the issues before the hearing. Consideration should be given as soon as proofs are exchanged to fine-tuning evidential matters and presentation. Cross-examination points can be prepared. Any conditions to be imposed should planning permission be granted can be discussed and agreed, if this is not premature.

The inspector's aim is to gather the information he needs to make a decision on the planning merits. Both from his own point of view and from that of members of the public, he will want to avoid wasting time during the inquiry on sterile discussions as to how information should be presented.

6.15   Procedure at inquiry

Rule 15(1) makes it clear that, except as set down in the rules, the inspector determines the procedure. Unless the inspector (with the consent of the applicant) determines otherwise, the appellant begins and has the right of final reply. Others entitled or permitted to appear are heard as the inspector determines.

6.15.1   The usual order

The inspector will open the inquiry by introducing himself and identifying the appeal. He will ask if there are members of the public who wish to speak and deal with the formalities: circulation of attendance list, site notice, notice of appeal hearing to third parties and checking the relevant drawings and other documents. Advocates should have the necessary papers and information to hand. A poor impression is given if the parties are not sure which are the right drawings.

The inspector will then finish by asking who appears for the appellant. The appellant's advocate rises, gives his name and status, who he represents and the name and qualifications of his witnesses. The inspector will already have copies of proofs of evidence. The local authority go through the same procedure. Inspectors are usually addressed as 'sir' or 'madam', but omission of this formal address is not serious, provided that politeness and attention are not neglected.

The appellant's advocate then introduces his case and calls his witnesses. The opening address should be as brief as possible unless a tactical decision has been made that the nature of the case requires a full introduction. The inspector wants to hear the evidence, not the advocate's view of the evidence.

Each witness will read his written evidence or his summary (in whole or in part). The inspector will usually indicate whether a document is to be read. It is always advisable to have spare copies of proofs available for members of the public. An advocate may ask his witness to read certain key passages from the proof if this is essential. The witness will be given the opportunity to add to his proof in the light of matters which may have arisen since it was written and particularly in response to matters raised in the local authority's proof (which he will have received after preparing his own).

The local authority advocate will have an opportunity of asking questions and testing the evidence. The inspector may ask one or two questions himself. The appellant's advocate will then have an opportunity of re-examining his witness to deal with any matters raised in the cross-examination.

Once the appellant has called all his witnesses, the local authority will call their witnesses. They do not have the right to make an opening address. Their witnesses will be examined in chief, cross-examined and re-examined in exactly the same way as the appellant's witnesses. When all witnesses have been called, the inspector usually allows third parties and members of the public to speak although he may arrange for such people to be heard earlier if appropriate.

The local authority will then make their closing submissions which will be followed by the appellant's closing submissions. Before formally closing the inquiry, the inspector will arrange for a site inspection and hear any application for costs.

The order of witnesses at the inquiry is subject to the inspector's discretion and witnesses are sometimes slotted in out of order with the agreement of all parties. This may occur if a third party objector has taken a day off work and wishes to be heard on that day or perhaps a professional witness unexpectedly has other commitments.

6.15.2   Taking of evidence

A person who is entitled to appear is also entitled to call evidence and the appellant, the local authority and a statutory party are entitled to cross-examine. Otherwise the calling of evidence and cross-examination is at the inspector's discretion. The inspector takes his own notes and each party should assign a person specifically to take notes in order to clarify any point which arises later. This is particularly important during cross-examination. Advocates will take their own notes as well.

Rule 15(4) allows the inspector to refuse to hear evidence or to allow cross-examination which he considers to be irrelevant or repetitious but any person wishing to give such evidence may do so in writing before the close of the inquiry.

6.15.3   Proofs of evidence, summaries and additional evidence

Where a summary has been exchanged, the usual rule is that it is read at the inquiry. This is because r 15(5) states that the full proof of evidence is treated as tendered in evidence under r 15(5). This means that the whole proof is formally before the inspector and the advocate can raise any additional points upon it that he wishes to and, further, that the proof of evidence itself is available for cross-examination purposes. The cross-examining advocate is not restricted to cross-examining on the summary alone; he is at liberty to cross-examine on the proof of evidence as if the witness had in fact read it to the inquiry.

It is possible to rely on the summary alone (r 15(5)). This would prevent cross-examination on the full proof of evidence. It is difficult to see where this could be of advantage. If there is something incorrect in the proof of evidence which needs to be withdrawn or is superseded by later evidence, the straightforward course of action will be the best. The paragraph should either be withdrawn or amended. The inspector will, in any event, have read the full proof of evidence but will bear the revised circumstances in mind. The other side will also have seen the full proof of evidence, and if there is an inaccuracy or error, they will be able to tease it out from cross-examination of the summary.

There may be cases where wholly new matters come into play at a late stage. If it is necessary to completely revamp the case, it is better to do so in a straightforward way by withdrawing most proofs and summaries and issuing revised proofs and summaries as quickly as possible, accepting any cost burden which may flow from this. For those dealing with their first inquiry the Annex to Circular 24/92, 'Good Practice at Planning Inquiries', should be studied carefully.

Rule 15 goes on to recognise that supplementary proofs of evidence may need to be submitted either shortly before or even at the inquiry as a result of evidence brought forward by the main exchange of proofs. However, para 38 of Circular 24/92 makes it clear that the Department do not wish to encourage such a practice and there is a risk of an award of costs if an adjournment results. If a supplementary proof contains more than 1,500 words, it must be accompanied by a summary.

In most cases all that will be required will be for a witness to deal orally with the new evidence when he gives evidence. In technical cases it may be wise to have a brief supplemental text available so that it can be handed in. The inspector, however, has a discretion to exclude evidence which has not been exchanged in advance. In practice, he is unlikely to exclude evidence if it is relevant to his decision but he might grant an adjournment at the expense of the party calling the new evidence if a substantially new point is raised.

Rule 15(8) allows an inspector to permit any person to alter or add to a statement of case but he is entitled to give any other person an adequate opportunity of considering any fresh matter or document. Any adjournment so required or additional expense caused at the last minute may be subject to a costs penalty.

6.15.4 Circulation of information

The inspector may order that any person appearing at the inquiry may take or obtain copies of documentary evidence open to public inspection. Since co-operation underpins the public inquiry system, it will be unwise to refuse a person appearing at the inquiry a copy of a document either before or during the inquiry. Additionally, it is customary to have further copies of summaries available so that members of the public who are attending the inquiry can follow the proceedings.

6.15.5 Evidence on oath

The inspector is enabled by s 250 of the Local Government Act 1972 to hear evidence on oath. This is almost never necessary in planning inquiries and it is counterproductive to demand it. If there is a question as to the credibility of witnesses, it is better to expose it in cross-examination or by bringing unassailable contradictory evidence rather than by directly questioning the veracity of witnesses. In enforcement inquiries evidence on oath is more common. This is partly because there is often conflicting evidence as to facts and partly because of the possibility of criminal sanctions as a result of enforcement proceedings.

6.15.6   Leading questions

While planning inquiries do not operate under strict rules of evidence, it is accepted that an advocate should not ask leading questions of his witness, either in examination in chief or in re-examination. A leading question is a question which contains within itself the answer required. The question, 'Will this development, in your opinion, make a positive contribution to the character and appearance of the Conservation Area?' would be a leading question. The right way to put this question is, 'What, in your opinion, will be the effect of the development?'

The reason why leading questions can be challenged is that they contain the answer sought, and no one can be sure that the witness, if left properly to consider an unprompted answer, would have answered in the same way. Leading questions are permissible, however, where evidence is not in dispute or on common ground, such as the name and address of the witness or the description of the site. In cross-examination, it is permissible to ask leading questions.

It is important that witnesses as well as advocates are aware of the rules of evidence in so far as they apply to planning inquiries. Although inspectors tend to be lenient, answers to inappropriate leading questions may be discredited.

6.15.7   Examination in chief

Examination in chief will have been prepared in conjunction with the witness. It is useful for proofs to be marked to show at what point additional oral material is to be introduced; any supplementary proof should also be introduced at an appropriate point. With the exchange of proofs in writing, examination in chief should be completed as quickly as possible, without going over ground which is already apparent from the proofs.

6.15.8   Cross-examination

Cross-examination is a critical area and one of the most difficult to control in respect of courtesy and consideration. At no stage should advocates resort to discourtesy, impatience, sarcasm or the like. It inevitably reflects badly on the questioner and it seems unwise to rely on the inspector to disassociate the advocate from the case.

If preparation has been thorough, the areas for cross-examination of each witness will have been identified in advance and discussed with the relevant witness on the team. The advocate should ensure he is properly briefed, since once the cross-examination has begun, all decisions on what to ask (and when to stop) must lie with him. He has been chosen for his skill and judgment, and it is usually dangerous to interfere. If pressed, he may put a question despite his better judgment, which might prove to be one question too many.

It is perfectly proper for suggestions to be forwarded to the advocate (usually on pieces of paper) for consideration as cross-examination proceeds. Members of the team, and the client in particular, may feel that questions have not been put that might have been or that certain points have not been adequately pressed. It is courteous for the advocate to check with his team that nothing has been omitted before sitting down again.

The cross-examination of third party witnesses requires a fine touch. If the ground has been carefully prepared and representations have been dealt with specifically in the proofs of evidence, no cross-examination will be necessary. This is the safest course. Third parties may have put their case badly as a result of their inexperience but will have their attention focused by a question in cross-examination and deliver evidence which they did not bring out in their evidence in chief. There may be occasions when a witness can clarify questions of fact or where, if he was a signatory to a petition which has been proved by the evidence to be wholly unfounded, this can be confirmed. Usually, the best response to such witness is, 'No questions, Sir'.

The same advice may be valid as regards third party witnesses called by the appellant in support of his case. Taking them beyond their proofs is fraught with danger which does not arise with professional witnesses who understand the rules and the case they are presenting.

6.16　Re-examination

Re-examination of one's own witnesses is restricted to matters arising from cross-examination. It is not an opportunity to embark on areas overlooked in evidence in chief. There is a view that if one's witness has conceded ground in cross-examination, the point is emphasised by going back in re-examination. It may be safer, at any rate for the advocate new to planning inquiries, to restrict re-examination to correcting errors or statements out of context made under cross-examination. Other responses may be best dealt with in closing submissions.

6.17　Written representations

The inspector is empowered by r 15(10) to take into account written representations or evidence or any other document received before the inquiry opens or during the inquiry, provided he discloses it at the inquiry. As a result the inspector will take care both at the opening of the inquiry and during it to ensure that all representations have been properly circulated.

6.18　Absences

Rule 15(9) permits the inspector to proceed with an inquiry in the absence of any person entitled to appear at it. Unless there has been some administrative oversight, it is usually an unrepresented appellant, rather than the local authority, who fails to appear on the appointed day. If the appellant does not appear, it is for the local authority to make representations to the inspector as to whether they wish him to proceed or for the matter to be adjourned. It is generally wise to make contact with the appellant to discover the reasons for his non-appearance. Is this the result of an oversight, or does he intend to withdraw the appeal?

Because the inspector stands in the same place as the local authority originally and will make his decision in accordance with the evidence he hears, it is quite possible for an inspector to hear the local authority's evidence in the absence of the appellant and still decide to grant the appeal.

6.19   Adjournments

The inspector is permitted at any time to adjourn the inquiry (r 15(11)). This usually happens if insufficient time has been booked to finish the inquiry or if it is crucial to hear a particular witness and he is not available on that day. If an adjournment is caused by the unreasonable behaviour of one party, the other party may claim the additional costs incurred.

6.20   Closing submissions

Closing submissions are made first by the local authority. The appellant has the last word. The local authority will not have had the opportunity to introduce their case and will therefore be running through the issues and the evidence, drawing the strands together for the first time.

The inspector may allow a short adjournment for closing speeches to be prepared. If he does not suggest it and it is not possible to time proceedings appropriately (eg to take an early lunch break), there is no reason why the advocate should not ask.

Brief skeleton arguments may be handed out in writing to assist the parties and the inspector. Closing submissions should be as short as possible but deal adequately with the issues and the evidence. Traditionally closing speeches are not interrupted, even if the opponent's submissions seem to depart from the evidence as one heard it. It is unwise for an advocate to bore and delay the inspector, who will have heard the evidence and no doubt formed his own views.

6.21   Site inspection

Rule 16(1) permits an inspector to make an unaccompanied site inspection before or during an inquiry without giving notice. On opening the inquiry, he will very often indicate that he has visited the site to gain a preliminary impression of the site and its situation. It is always prudent, therefore, to ensure that the site notices are posted on the site, and that a site under the control of the appellant is not being used so as to prejudice evidence to be given at the inquiry.

Before closing the inquiry, the inspector will normally arrange a time for an accompanied site visit in accordance with r 16(2). The appellant, the local authority and any statutory party are entitled to accompany him. Lawyers do not, by tradition, attend site visits. A question may arise as to how many other interested parties, such as neighbours, are also allowed to accompany the inspector. It is suggested that the inspecting party should be as small as reasonably possible. If there are a large number of objectors, they should be asked to nominate one or two representatives to accompany the inspector. The site will normally be private land and often under the control of the appellant.

If it is necessary to go on private land to carry out the site inspection, the landowner should be consulted. It is important that no further evidence or arguments are presented to the inspector during a site inspection. The inspection is simply an opportunity to show the inspector aspects canvassed at the inquiry and to point out the location of a particular site of interest (*Hibernian Property Company Ltd v Secretary of State for the Environment* [1973] 27 PECR 197).

6.21.1   Appearance of fairness

It is important that the inspector should be seen to be acting fairly. For this reason those attending the site visit should ensure that there are no private discussions with the inspector or any behaviour which could lead a party to believe that there was an occasion for impropriety. For this reason, too, a representative of the appellant and the local authority should always be present throughout the site inspection. The inspector may on occasion not have a car available and need a lift to the site. It would be sensible to ensure that representatives of both the appellant and the local authority are present in the car at all times.

Finally, beware of having a drink with the inspector afterwards. The case of *Cotterell v Secretary of State for the Environment* [1991] 2 PLR 37 provides a salutary warning. Any conversations with the inspector should be in the presence of the other side. If the appellant feels that the post-mortem should take place in the nearest pub, it is best to do so as a team, excluding the inspector. It is probably also best for appellants not to be seen drinking with the local authority, as third parties might view it as collusion.

6.22   Post-inquiry matters

Letters of objection or support are sometimes received after the close of the inquiry. They are normally circulated and there is an opportunity to respond if required (r 17(2)). Another post-inquiry matter is for the assessor, if one has been appointed, to make his report to the inspector.

An inspector may cause an inquiry to be re-opened if new evidence is raised and he thinks it right to do so. He will then circulate a written statement on the matters on which he invites further representations. This is unusual in inspector inquiries (although more frequent in cases dealt with by the Secretary of State) and is covered by the rules.

6.23   The decision letter

All that remains is to wait patiently for the inspector's decision letter. By virtue of r 18 the letter will contain his reasons for allowing or dismissing the appeal. For a two-week appeal, the letter can take about three months. Efforts have recently been made to ensure the decision letters come through as quickly as possible.

Decision letters can be quite long, but the final paragraph at the end of the letter will contain either the words 'by virtue of the powers transferred to me I hereby allow this appeal . . .' or the words 'by virtue of the powers transferred to me I hereby dismiss this appeal . . .'. If the appeal decision is not satisfactory either as a whole or because conditions attached to the planning permission are not acceptable, then a High Court challenge is the only way forward. High Court challenges are dealt with in Chapter 12.

An appellant should not neglect to contact the local authority. It is surprising how often a decision unsatisfactory to the appellant is also unsatisfactory to the other party. A local authority may be prepared to accept a compromise to avoid a High Court challenge. This will involve submitting a new application.

Time for a High Court challenge is limited, and the letter should not be put to one side to be dealt with later. The possibility of challenge should be considered and decided on within the week following receipt of the decision letter (although the statutory time for lodging the papers is longer). The possibility of challenge should also be borne in mind if implementation may occur within the six-week period.

6.24   Procedure following High Court challenge

Where a decision is quashed by the High Court, r 19 provides for the Secretary of State to send a written statement of the matters in respect of which he requires further representations, allowing three weeks for parties to make representations or to ask for the inquiry to be re-opened. He may direct that the inquiry shall be re-opened and if he does so the direction takes effect in accordance with r 10. The procedure thus begins anew.

6.25   Allowing further time

Rule 20 permits the Secretary of State (or the inspector) to allow further time for taking any of the steps required by the rules. There is no formal sanction for failing to keep to the time limits set out in these rules nor does the passing of a time limit preclude further steps being taken.

If parties have difficulty complying with the rules in any particular respect, they should contact each another and the Inspectorate. Proofs of evidence are sometimes exchanged a few days late, in some cases only a few days before the inquiry.

The purpose of these rules is to ensure an orderly and prompt exchange of information and clarification of the issues. If the parties have simply agreed to certain delays, they should notify the Inspectorate but it is unlikely that the inspector himself will intervene. Due to difficulties in staffing, some local authorities can be very late in preparing their statements of case and proofs of evidence. The usual recourse is to seek costs because the delay has involved additional expenditure.

However, if the rules cannot be complied with, the party concerned may contact the inspector and ask formally for additional time to be granted. It is suggested that this formality should be complied with more often than is generally done at present. In effect, where the inspector has granted an extension of time, because of the way this rule is framed, the document only becomes due on the expiry of the time allowed. Providing, therefore, the step is complied with within the additional time allowed, it is unlikely that any award of costs can be sought simply for the failure to comply with the rules in that particular respect.

Section 79(6A) of the Act provides that if the appellant is responsible for undue delay, the Secretary of State may give him notice that the appeal will be dismissed unless he takes certain steps within the time specified. This change, which practitioners should note, was introduced by the Planning and Compensation Act 1991 and is the equivalent of being struck out. Any such notice must of course receive immediate attention. The provision does not apply in reverse. If the local authority fail to comply with the rules, the appellant's normal remedy will lie in an award of costs.

6.26 Service of notices by post

Rule 21 simply states that notices or documents may be sent by post. Where documents are sent to the local authority or professional party, service by post is the normal arrangement. Exchange of proofs of evidence by hand or by courier is also frequent. Where time is crucial, or where a party may wish to establish beyond doubt that a document has been received, it may be sent by hand, courier or fax. If an inquiry is to start on a Tuesday, it may be vital to ensure that the other side receives an important document on the Friday before the inquiry so that they have time to prepare a response. This is better than leaving it until the day before the inquiry (ie the Monday). Likewise it is well to avoid all questions by unrepresented third parties as to whether they did or did not receive certain documents. Care should be taken to ensure that receipt is documented. Recorded delivery or personal service may be indicated.

Worked Example

SMITH & JONES

Solicitors, Davis House, 134 Newtown Road, Newtown N43 12AP

Tel 0181 500 0000   Fax 0181 050 0000

The Director of Planning   1-6-93
Red Forest Borough Council
Council Offices
Red Forest

Dear Sir

EUROPA ELECTRONICS, SMITH FARM, STRAIT LANE, RED FOREST

We enclose an application form, completed Certificate A and Part II and the required fee completed for the above development. We enclose the following plans:

(1) site plan with the application site edged in red and adjoining land owned by the applicant edged in blue and location plans.

(2) Proposed plan and elevations.

This extension is urgently required for the purposes of the business and we would be grateful if you would process it as soon as possible. It will result in the creation of an additional 20 jobs which are sorely needed in the area.

Yours faithfully

SMITH AND JONES

Please read the *GUIDANCE NOTES* before completing this form

APPLICATION FOR PLANNING PERMISSION

Send at least four copies (preferably five) of the application forms and the same number of each set of plans together with the correct fee to:

CHIEF PLANNING OFFICER
RED FOREST BOROUGH COUNCIL
LONDON

Application No. □□□■□□□□

1 Name and address of APPLICANT

EUROPA ELECTRONICS
SMITH FARM, STRAIT LANE, REDFOREST

Post Code

Telephone No.

2 Name and address of AGENT (if any)

SMITH & JONES
134 NEWTOWN ROAD, NEWTOWN

Post Code N43 12AP

Telephone No. 081–550 1234

3 Full address or Location of Site

Land adjacent to Smith Farm, Strait Lane, Redforest known as Keeper's Cottage

Post Code

Site Area 1.6 Acres/Hectares

4 Describe the proposed development

Demolition of house, erection of extension to existing factory and use of adjacent land as storage.

5 What is the applicant's interest in the land or buildings ? (Owner, Tenant, Prospective Purchaser etc.)

owner

6 Does the applicant own or control any adjoining land or buildings?

Yes, Smith Farm adjacent

If YES, edge in blue on the location or site plans.

7 State present use of the site or buildings or state last previous use and the date last used

Caretaker's accommodation for adjacent factory unit

8 Indicate whether the proposal involves:

New Building(s)	yes
Alteration or Extension to building(s)	no
Construction of new access to highway	no
Alteration of access to highway	no
Change of Use	yes
Other Operations	

9 Indicate which ONE of the following the application is for:

no	OUTLINE planning permission (for erection of a building(s) only)*
	APPROVAL of reserved matters (Give ref. no. of outline permission)**
yes	FULL planning permission (includes CHANGE OF USE and CONVERSIONS)
	RENEWAL of temporary/previous permission (Give previous ref. no.)
	REMOVAL OF CONDITION. Give condition no. □ permission no:

*   For outline permission, ring any of the following for which approval is sought now:

SITING   DESIGN   EXTERNAL APPEARANCE   MEANS OF ACCESS   LANDSCAPING

**   State any of the above reserved matters NOT applied for:

10 Give details of proposed means of:

Surface water disposal

Foul sewage disposal

Water supply   as existing

11 List plans submitted:

12 State manufacturer, type and colour of ALL external wall and roof materials

All to be approved by local planning authority

13 Further information will be required for the following development:

Offices ☐ Industry ☐ Shopping ☐ Warehousing ☐
Farm Buildings ☐ Farm Dwellings ☐ Waste Disposal ☐ Mineral Extraction ☐

Tick the correct box to indicate that you have filled out the relevant extra form

14 If the applicant

-owns all of the site or buildings, then complete Certificate A and the Agricultural Holdings Certificate
-owns none or part of the site, then complete Certificate B and the Agricultural Holdings Certificate
-does not know who owns any part of the site, refer to the GUIDANCE NOTES for further advice

15 CERTIFICATE A**

I certify that at the beginning of the period 21 days ending with the date of the accompanying application, nobody except the applicant, was the owner ** of any part of the land to which the application relates

SIGNED Smith & Jones   *On behalf of Europa Electronics   Date 1.6.93

─────OR─────

CERTIFICATE B**

I certify that I have/The applicant has* given the required notice to everyone else who, at the beginning of the 21 days ending with the date of the accompanying application, was the owner of any part of the land to which the application relates as listed below.

Owners name   Address at which notice was served.   Date notice served.

SIGNED   *On behalf of   Date

* See GUIDANCE NOTES   ** Delete if not applicable

16 AGRICULTURAL HOLDINGS CERTIFICATE

Whichever is appropriate of the following alternatives must form part of Certificates A,B,C and D. If the applicant is the sole agricultural tenant he/she must delete the first alternative and insert 'not applicable' as the information required by the second alternative.

*None of the land to which the application/appeal** relates, is, or is part of, an agricultural holding.
**I have/The applicant has/The appellant has* given the requisite notice to every person other than my/him/herself* who, on the day 21 days before the date of the application/appeal* was a tenant of an agricultural holding on all or part of the land to which the application/appeal* relates, as follows:-

Tenant's name   Address at which notice was served.   Date notice served.

SIGNED Smith & Jones   *On behalf of Europa Electronics   Date 1.6.93

* See GUIDANCE NOTES   ** Delete if not applicable

17 I/We hereby apply for permission to carry out the development described in this application and on the accompanying plans.

SIGNED Smith & Jones   *On behalf of Europa Electronics   Date 1.6.93

This Form has been reproduced with the kind permission of North Wiltshire District Council, Monkton Park, Chippenham, Wiltshire, SN15 1ER.

PA2a(R)

APPLICATION FOR PLANNING PERMISSION

(Extra Form for INDUSTRIAL or WAREHOUSING Applications)

Send at least four completed copies of the application forms (preferably five) and the same number of each set of plans together with the correct fee to:

CHIEF PLANNING OFFICER

REDFOREST BOROUGH COUNCIL

LONDON

1 If the application is for an industrial process or research development, give a description of the processes, the type of machinery to be used and the end products.

Manufacture of electronic components and equipment

2 Is the application related to an existing or proposed use nearby? If so, please describe the relationship.

Yes, extension of existing factory

3 What is the existing and proposed gross floor area (in square metres) of all buildings related to the application?

(1) How much industrial floor space is included in the above figure?
(2) How much warehousing or storage space is included in the above figure?
(3) How much office, retail or other floor space (used in connection with either of the above uses) is included in the above figure?

	Existing	Proposed
	150 sq m	500 sq m
(1)	none	500 sq m
(2)	none	none
(3)	none	none

4 How many staff will be employed on the site as a result of the development?

22

How many will be new staff?

5 Indicate on your plans the parking and/or garaging of vehicles required by staff and visitors. If no or limited provision to be made, indicate what other arrangements will be made.

employees car parking accommodated on existing site; loading and unloading areas shown

6 What is the nature, volume and proposed means of disposal of any trade effluents or refuse.

as existing

7 Will the proposal involve the production, storage or handling of notifiable quantities of hazardous material? If so, please specify type and quantity.

No

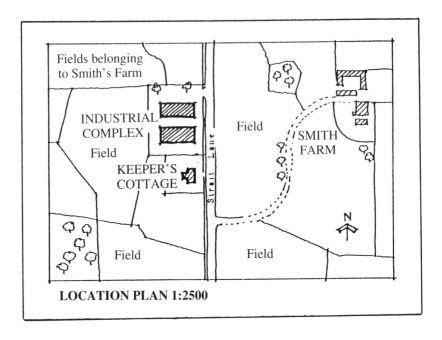

Figure 6.2. Illustrative example: landscaping plan for a proposed extension to a factory (not to scale).
Key: ○ ○ ○ ○ ○ site boundary (shown in red on architect's drawings).
+ + + + + boundary of adjacent land owned by the applicant (shown in blue on architect's drawings).

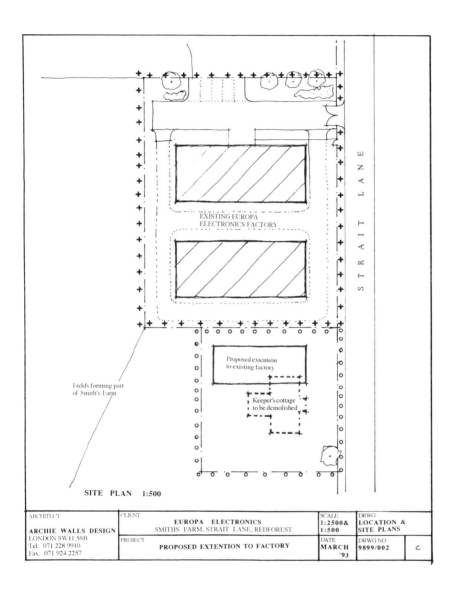

SITE PLAN 1:500

ARCHITECT	CLIENT		SCALE	DRWG
ARCHIE WALLS DESIGN	**EUROPA ELECTRONICS** SMITHS FARM, STRAIT LANE, REDFOREST		**1:2500&** **1:500**	**LOCATION &** **SITE PLANS**
LONDON SW11 5SB Tel: 071 228 9910 Fax: 071 924 2257	PROJECT	**PROPOSED EXTENTION TO FACTORY**	DATE **MARCH** **'93**	DRWG.NO. **9899/002**

Figure 6.2, *cont.*

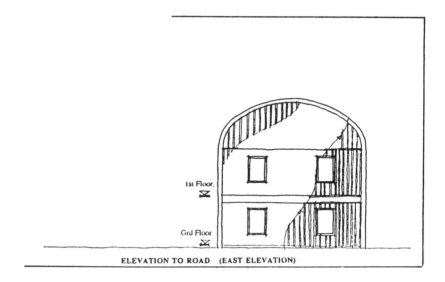

Figure 6.2, *cont.*

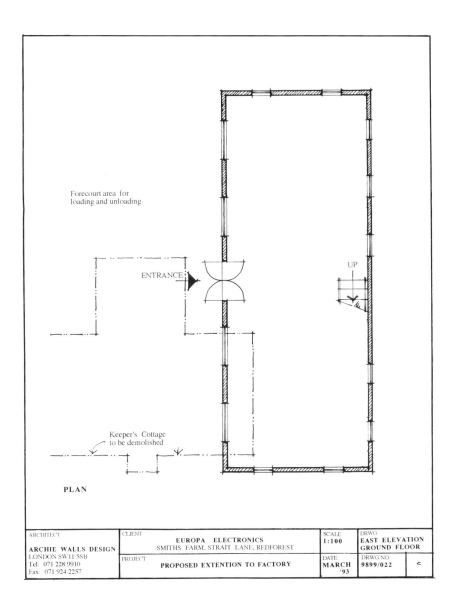

Forecourt area for
loading and unloading

ENTRANCE

UP

Keeper's Cottage
to be demolished

PLAN

ARCHITECT	CLIENT		SCALE	DRWG
ARCHIE WALLS DESIGN	**EUROPA ELECTRONICS** SMITHS FARM, STRAIT LANE, REDFOREST		**1:100**	**EAST ELEVATION** **GROUND FLOOR**
LONDON SW11 5SB Tel: 071 228 9910 Fax: 071 924 2257	PROJECT **PROPOSED EXTENTION TO FACTORY**		DATE **MARCH '93**	DRWG.NO 9899/022 ⊆

Figure 6.2, *cont.*

RED FOREST BOROUGH COUNCIL

This matter is being dealt with by: Department of Planning
                                                    and Transportation
Mr. A. N. Body   Red Forest Borough Council
                                                    London

My reference: Your reference:
AB/CD/1   SJ/JS/1   Director: Mr. A. Body
                                                    Fax: 081-xxx xxxx

Smith & Jones
Newtown Road   Tel: 081-xxx xxxx
Newtown   Date: 1st November 1993
N43 12AP

Dear Sirs,
TOWN AND COUNTRY PLANNING ACT 1990
REFUSAL OF PERMISSION TO DEVELOP

The Council has considered your application and refuses to permit the development referred to below as shown on the plans submitted.

Your attention is drawn to the enclosed Statement of Applicant's Rights.

SCHEDULE

Application Date: 1.6.93   Date Rec'd: 4.6.93

Registered No: RF 1234/83   Plan Nos: A1 & A2

Address: Land adjacent to Smith Farm, Strait Land, Red Forest known as Keeper's Cottage.

Proposal: Demolition of house; erection of extension to existing factory and use of adjacent land as storage.

See next page for reason for refusal.

Yours faithfully

DIRECTOR OF PLANNING AND TRANSPORTATION

Reasons for refusal:

1. The proposed development is contrary to Policy GB1 of the adopted Red Forest UDP and would form an alien intrusion into the metropolitan green belt.

2. The development would serve to extend the boundary of the present built up area into open land alongside the highway and is likely to make adjacent areas of the green belt less defensible against further encroachment.

3. The proposals involve the loss of a dwellinghouse contrary to policy H1 of the adopted Red Forest UDP.

4. The proposals would result in an intensification of industrial use and would cause unacceptable additional traffic on the local road network.

5. The proposals would adversely affect the residential amenity of existing houses along Strait Lane.

The Planning Inspectorate

An Executive Agency in the Department of the Environment and the Welsh Office

FOR OFFICIAL USE ONLY

Date received

PLANNING APPEAL TO THE SECRETARY OF STATE
TOWN AND COUNTRY PLANNING ACT 1990
TOWN AND COUNTRY PLANNING GENERAL DEVELOPMENT ORDER

The appeal must reach the Inspectorate within 6 months of the date of the Notice of the Local Planning Authority's decision, or within 6 months of the date by which they should have decided the application.

A. INFORMATION ABOUT THE APPELLANT(S)

Full name: EUROPA ELECTRONICS

Address   SMITH FARM, STRAIT LANE, REDFOREST

Postcode

Failure to provide the post code may cause delays in processing your appeal.

Daytime Telephone number   Reference

Agent's name (if any) SMITH & JONES

Agent's Address   134 NEWTOWN ROAD, NEWTOWN

Postcode   N43 6AP

Failure to provide the post code may cause delays in processing your appeal.

Daytime Telephone number   081-922 1234   Reference   1/GUN

B. DETAILS OF THE APPEAL

Name of the Local Planning Authority (LPA) RED FOREST BOROUGH COUNCIL

Description of the development

Demolition of house, erection of extension to existing factory and use of adjacent land as storage.

Address of the site land adjacent to Smith Farm, Strait Lane, Redforest, known as Keeper's Cottage

National Grid Reference (see key on OS map for instructions). Grid Letters: Grid Numbers eg TQ: 298407

Postcode

Failure to provide the post codee, if any, may cause delays in processing your appeal.

Date and reference no. of the application in respect of which you are appealing.   RF 1234/93   1.6.93

Date of LPA notice of decision (if any).   1.11.93

1

(REV 1994)

C. THE APPEAL

THIS APPEAL IS AGAINST the decision of the LPA:- (✔)

1. to *refuse/~~grant subject to conditions~~, planning permission for the development described in Section B. ✔

2. to *refuse/grant subject to conditions, approval of the matters reserved under an outline planning permission.

3. to refuse to approve any matter (other than those mentioned in 2 above) required by a condition on a planning permission.

Or the failure of the LPA:-

4. to give notice of their decision within the appropriate period on an application for permission or approval.

*Delete as appropriate

D. PROCEDURE

1a. Do you agree to the written procedure? (ie an exchange of written statements with the LPA and a visit to the site by an Inspector). If yes, please tick opposite and answer question 1b below.

1b. Tick if the whole site can clearly be seen from a road or other public land. (An unaccompanied site visit will be arranged if the Inspector can adequately view the site from public land).

OR

2. Do you wish to appear before and be heard by an Inspector? If yes, please tick. ✔

3. If the LPA agree and the Inspectorate considers your appeal suitable, do you wish to proceed by way of a hearing rather than a local inquiry? If yes, please tick.

E. SUPPORTING DOCUMENTS

A copy of each of the following should be enclosed with this form.

1. The application submitted to the LPA; ✔

2. Any Article 12(A) certificate (site ownership details) submitted to the LPA; ✔

3. Plans, drawings and documents forming part of the application submitted to the LPA; ✔

4. The LPA's decision notice (if any); ✔

5. Other relevant correspondence with the LPA - Please identify the correspondence by date or otherwise

6. A plan showing the site in red, in relation to two named roads (preferably on an extract from the relevant 1:10,000 OS map) ✔

Copies of the following should also be enclosed, if appropriate:

7. If the appeal concerns reserved matters, the relevant outline application, plans submitted and the permission;

8. Any plans, drawings and documents sent to the LPA but which do not form part of the submitted application (eg drawings for illustrative purposes);

9. Additional plans or drawings relating to the application but not previously seen by the LPA. Please number them clearly and list the numbers here:

F. APPEAL CERTIFICATION

IMPORTANT: THE ACCOMPANYING GUIDANCE NOTES SHOULD BE READ BEFORE THE APPROPRIATE CERTIFICATE IS COMPLETED.

SITE OWNERSHIP CERTIFICATES

PLEASE DELETE INAPPROPRIATE WORDING WHERE INDICATED (*) AND STRIKE OUT INAPPLICABLE CERTIFICATE

CERTIFICATE A

I certify that:
On the day 21 days before the date of this appeal nobody, except the appellant, was the owner (*see Note (i) of the Guidance Notes)* of any part of the land to which the appeal relates.

OR

CERTIFICATE B

I certify that:
I have/The appellant has* given the requisite notice to everyone else who, on the day 21 days before the date of this appeal, was the owner (*see Note (i) of the Guidance Notes)* of any part of the land to which the appeal relates, as listed below.

Owner's Name	Address at which notice was served	Date on which notice was served

Signed _____ Smith & Jones _____ (on behalf of) EUROPA ELECTRONICS

Name (in capitals) SMITH & JONES _____ Date 15.3.94

AGRICULTURAL HOLDINGS CERTIFICATE (TO BE COMPLETED IN ALL CASES)

* None of the land to which the appeal relates is, or is part of, an agricultural holding.

OR

* I have/The appellant has given the requisite notice to every person other than my/him/her* self who, on the day 21 days before the date of the appeal was a tenant of an agricultural holding on all or part of the land to which the appeal relates, as follows:-

Tenant's Name	Address at which notice was served	Date on which notice was served

*Delete as appropriate. If the appellant is the sole agricultural tenant the first alternative should be deleted and "not applicable" should be inserted below the second alternative.

Signed _____ Smith & Jones _____ (on behalf of) EUROPA ELECTRONICS

Name (in capitals) SMITH & JONES _____ Date 15.3.94

3

G. GROUNDS OF APPEAL If the written procedure is requested, the appellant's FULL STATEMENT OF CASE **MUST** be made - otherwise the appeal may be invalid. If the written procedure has not been requested, a brief outline of the appellant's case should be made here.

Please see attached sheet

continue on a separate sheet if necessary

PLEASE SIGN BELOW

I confirm that a copy of this appeal form and any supporting documents not previously seen by the LPA has been sent to them. I undertake that any future documents submitted in connection with this appeal will also be copied to the LPA at the same time.

Signed _____ Smith & Jones _____ (on behalf of) _ EUROPA ELECTRONICS _

Name (in capitals) __ SMITH & JONES _____ Date _ 15.3.94 _

CHECKLIST

- This form signed and fully completed.

- Any relevant documents listed at Section E enclosed.

- Full grounds of appeal/outline of case set out at Section G.

- Relevant ownership certificate A, B, C or D completed and signed.

- Agricultural Holdings Certificate completed and signed.

Send one copy of the appeal form with all the supporting documents to:

> The Planning Inspectorate
> Tollgate House
> Houlton Street
> Bristol BS2 9DJ

A copy of the appeal form **must** be sent to the LPA at the address from which the decision on the application (or any acknowledgements, etc) was received, enclosing only copies of those documents not previously seen by the LPA.

4

Cdf 106170/6/B09955 10m 9/93 DTP

This Form is Crown Copyright and is reproduced by kind permission of the Planning Inspectorate, Houlton Street, Bristol B52 9DJ.

GROUNDS OF APPEAL

1.   The proposed development is acceptable as an exception to the policy of restraint in the green belt as set out in policy GB1.

2.   The development will not be visible from the road and is within an area already used for industrial development and will not form an alien intrusion into the metropolitan green belt.

3.   The site of the development is a special case as it is an extension to an existing industrial unit. There is therefore no precedent and it will not affect the green belt boundary.

4.   Keeper's Cottage has never formed part of the housing stock of the area since it has always been occupied as tied accommodation for the caretaker of the factory unit. There will therefore be no loss to the housing stock of the area by its demolition and it is against such a loss of housing stock that council policy H1 is directed.

5.   Because of the nature of the electronic components being made, there will be no significant additional traffic, nor will there be any intensification of any industrial use since the new building is needed primarily to replace substandard facilities in existing buildings.

6.   There will be no increase in traffic or noise and the building is well screened from the road. It will not therefore adversely affect the residential amenity along Strait Lane.

LOCAL AUTHORITY STATEMENT OF CASE

1. The land lies within the metropolitan green belt where there is a strong presumption against further development except in the limited circumstances set out in policy GB1. This development does not fall within any of the exceptions to the policy and is therefore unacceptable.
2. The proposal will result in the loss of a dwellinghouse contrary to policy H1 which seeks to protect the stock of dwellinghouses in the area where there is a shortfall to meet demand, particularly in respect of family properties.
3. The proposals will result in an intensification of industrial activity which will inevitably lead to additional traffic along Strait Lane which will detrimentally affect the amenity of existing residential occupiers along Strait Lane.
4. The proposals represent an alien intrusion of built form into the green belt, replacing a traditionally built detached cottage standing in substantial grounds with a modern industrial unit. This represents not only an extension of the built-up area within the green belt but the encroachment will mean that the green belt boundary will be less defensible in the future.
5. The extension of this factory, which is located at a distance from any public transport, will encourage traffic movements and is contrary to the local plan and central government policies.

LIST OF DOCUMENTS

1. Adopted Unitary Development Plan
2. Annual Housing Report 1993
3. PPG2, green belts
4. This Common Inheritance and Sustainable Development

APPELLANT'S STATEMENT OF CASE

1. It is acknowledged that the site lies within the metropolitan green belt. However, the business has been established at this location for at least 50 years and the proposals are for a modest extension to the existing site. As such, it does not amount to new development within the green belt.

2. The development itself will be well screened from the road and will hardly be visible.

3. The extension is needed to meet modern manufacturing requirements. The company has looked for alternative sites within a five-mile radius. This is the maximum which is believed possible in order to retain the existing skilled workforce. No suitable site is available.

4. The dwellinghouse on the site has been used as a caretaker's house since the factory started. It has never been occupied as a separate residential unit and there is therefore no loss of general housing stock by its demolition. The grounds have always been used in association with the adjacent industrial unit.

5. The increase in traffic along Strait Lane will be minimal, if any occurs at all. The products are not bulky but high in value. While the company anticipates increasing production with the new facility, both incoming materials and the outgoing products should normally be accommodated within existing traffic movements.

6. The appellant denies that an undesirable precedent will be set which will make it more difficult to defend the green belt policies in future. The circumstances of this case are exceptional.

7. The council has given insufficient weight to the importance of increasing employment and government policy and development plan policies which should guide planning decisions. This is particularly important in the countryside where there are very few jobs in traditional countryside sectors such as agriculture. This is resulting in local people moving away to find employment and pressure for many houses to be turned into commuter homes or weekend cottages which do not meet the needs of the rural community and are detrimental to community life.

List of documents

1. Annual Report of Europa Electronics
2. Traffic report
3. Landscaping proposals (Figure 6.2)
4. Letters from local chamber of commerce and parish council
5. Government and local policies

SUMMARY OF PROOF OF EVIDENCE OF THE APPELLANT'S PLANNER

1. My name is Geoffrey Green. I am a partner in the firm of Blanc & Blanc. I am a fellow of the Royal Town Planning Institute and fellow of the RICS.

2. Two years ago my firm was instructed to find an alternative site for Europa Electronics but despite extensive marketing we were unable to do so.

    Six months ago I was instructed by Europa Electronics to consider the alternative of expansion of the present business on to the site of Keeper's Cottage.

3. Keeper's Cottage lies along Strait Lane and is bounded on one side by the existing Europa factory and on the other side by woodland forming part of the extensive grounds of the adjacent house, Millionaires Row. However, there are no dwellinghouses within 500 metres of the appeal premises. Keeper's Cottage is a pleasant vernacular Victorian building. To the rear of the house there is a small area of garden with a washing line. This is, however, within the very high security perimeter fencing of Europa Electronics. There is an access gate in front of Keeper's Cottage but this was locked when I inspected. There is no physical separation between what was presumed to be the grounds of Keeper's Cottage and the factory unit adjacent.

4. Keeper's Cottage lies within the metropolitan green belt where restrictive policies operate in respect of new developments, both at government level and as incorporated in the Red Forest UDP.

    It is accepted that exceptional reasons are required to override the presumption against development within the green belt but I believe that there are exceptional reasons in this case for such development to be permitted.

5. The proposals are for an extension to an existing factory which will be virtually invisible from the road.

6. No precedent will be set because such isolated established industrial units in the metropolitan green belt are very rare. Within the area of Red Forest District Council I have found only two other industrial units placed as isolated development in the open countryside. One of these units is vacant, the owner having gone into liquidation, and the other is occupied by a small-scale toy maker.

7. Whilst it is true that there will be an additional building within the green belt if these proposals are permitted, the existing building will have been demolished and there will be no real intensification of industrial activity because of the nature of the business.

8. The history of Keeper's Cottage, as explained by Mr. Smith leads me

to the view that Keeper's Cottage was in fact incorporated into the industrial unit before 1st July 1947 when development control began. The only live issue is therefore the erection of the industrial building.

9. As Mr. Smith has explained, no additional traffic will be created by this development and there will be no damage to the amenity of residential owners along Strait Lane who are in any event too far away to be influenced by any change.

10. It is accepted that the factory is located at a distance from public transport and in a situation where under present policies new industrial development would be discouraged. However, in this case the Company's evidence that there will be no additional traffic and the circumstances which require a new building outweigh any possible damage to the Government's policies on sustainable development.

11. The Council resist the loss of a dwellinghouse but for the reasons I have already given Keeper's Cottage has not been part of the housing stock of the area. It has never been available for purchase or letting on the market and has always been ancillary to the industrial unit. In these circumstances there is no loss of a dwellinghouse.

12. The appellant has given very careful consideration to the aesthetic appearance of the development. I do not believe that the proposals will adversely affect the visual appearance of Strait Lane.

13. The Council have wholly failed to give adequate weight to their own policies for the encouragement of employment generating uses generally and in particular in rural areas. They have also failed to give due weight to their own policies which seek to enhance industrial uses as against service uses.

14. The proposal will harm no interest of acknowledged importance and indeed will contribute to the local environment and I would urge the Inspector to allow this appeal.

SUMMARY OF PROOF OF JOHN SMITH
THE MANAGING DIRECTOR OF EUROPA ELECTRONICS

1. I am the managing director of Europa Electronics, a position I have occupied for 15 years. Before that I was research director of the company for 10 years. I have a degree in electronic engineering and a diploma in business management.

2. Europa Engineering was established on this site at least 50 years ago by my father. It is well known to be at the forefront of development of components and equipment. A very substantial proportion of our products are exported, particularly to Europe. Out of a total sales last year of £10 million, 60 per cent went to Europe and 10 per cent elsewhere in the world.

3. The company has successfully managed to weather the recession and has not laid off any staff. Indeed we have recently increased our staff. The new extension is urgently needed for two reasons. Firstly, because we need a modern airtight building to meet the latest manufacturing specifications. While we have been able to maintain standards in the existing old buildings, it is becoming extremely difficult in some areas of our work. Secondly, we have recently obtained a very substantial new order from a European company and we will need the additional capacity in order to fulfil this order. Twenty new jobs will be created.

4. During this time, Keeper's Cottage has always been used as an annex to the main site. It has always been occupied by a caretaker, certainly during the time I have been with the company. Apart from the immediate area of the house, the grounds have been used as was necessary for storage of materials, finished products and other matters in association with the factory. Modern security methods mean that it is no longer necessary to have a caretaker on site because we are able to maintain better security using a security patrol on shift work and modern security systems. In fact the caretaker position has been redundant for some time and the cottage is at present occupied by Mr Daly who was a caretaker here for a number of years but retired two years ago. Arrangements have been made with him to leave the accommodation if planning permission is received.

5. We have looked for an alternative site. Our area of search was a radius of five miles from the present site. The workforce is skilled and experienced with a very low turnover in staff. Indeed I believe the success of this business is due primarily to the quality of the staff.

6. Eighteen months ago we engaged a local firm of surveyors, Messrs Blanc & Blanc, to find an alternative site. They have been unable to do so. The Council have also been approached recently but their Economic Development Office has also been unable to locate a suitable site.

7.   The extension sought is essential to the future of this firm and if it is not granted we shall lose our competitive edge and will no doubt join many other firms who have ceased trading as a result of a combination of difficult market conditions and a requirement to invest and upgrade. We have always been willing to invest in the firm, both in equipment and buildings and in respect of training of staff. I trust that this firm will be permitted to thrive on this site and continue making its contribution to the local and national economy.

LOCAL AUTHORITY SUMMARY OF PROOF OF EVIDENCE

1. My name is Ronald Archibald. I am a chartered planner employed by Red Forest Borough Council and have been employed by the council for 20 years.

2. It is a prime thrust of Red Forest Borough UDP that the metropolitan green belt should be preserved. The policies are set out in the supporting papers.

3. The proposals meet none of the criteria for exceptions to policy GB1: they are not related to agricultural use nor the use of an institutional building in the open countryside. It is the council's position that there can be no justification at all for permitting an additional industrial unit in the green belt which falls outside such policies.

4. The council is particularly concerned at the proposed demolition of Keeper's Cottage. Although this is not listed, it is certainly of listable quality, being a very good example of Victorian flint and brimstone construction. The building is not in a good state of repair as the company have failed to maintain it adequately over many years but it could be repaired at a reasonable cost and provides a type of house which council policy H1 seeks to protect. The council views it as particularly important to protect these buildings in the vicinity of non-conforming industrial uses in the green belt to form a barrier to further encroachment.

5. There is a considerable shortfall in housing of the type represented by Keeper's Cottage in the area. The housing supply figures are contained in annex 1.

6. The industrial activity represented by the enlargement of this factory will inevitably lead to additional traffic and additional noise and disturbance for residential occupiers along Strait Lane. The proposed buildings will be clearly visible from Strait Lane despite landscaping and represent an industrial building which will clearly be seen as alien in the wooded setting.

7. The council accept that there will be some additional jobs. However, the number of additional jobs is very small and in no way justifies this substantial industrial development in the green belt.

8. The Inspector is asked to support the very high priority which both the government and the local authority accord to preserving the green belt and to dismiss this appeal.

Chapter 7

Planning Conditions in the Appeal Context

7.1   Introduction

The ability to attach conditions to a planning permission to overcome a planning objection is usually considered when resubmitting an application; when considering conditions attached to an existing consent and whether they should be amended; and, most commonly in the appeal context, in the presentation of the appeal itself. Whatever the appeal route chosen, at some stage the appellant will be required to produce a list of conditions, agreed with the local authority if possible. These are submitted to the inspector for his consideration. Planning obligations perform a similar role in enabling planning objections to be overcome. The distinction between conditions and planning obligations must be clearly identified in order to exploit the advantages of each in the appeal process.

   This chapter deals with the nature and scope of conditions, distinguishing conditions from planning obligations and the use of conditions in the appeal context. Mineral conditions have a separate section (para 7.14) because of the special nature of conditions attached to mineral consents. A decision letter incorporating a number of conditions appears at the end of this chapter.

   Circular 1/85 contains current government advice on conditions and includes a useful annex of model conditions.

7.2   Legal nature of planning conditions

Section 70 of the Town and Country Planning Act 1990 authorises local authorities to grant planning permission either unconditionally or subject to such conditions as they think fit; both the Secretary of State and an inspector are in the same position. Section 72 of the Act amplifies the powers of s 70 in relation to land under the control of the applicant, but outside the application boundary. This section also authorises temporary permissions and removal of works together with reinstatement of the site at the end of the temporary period.

   If conditions are to overcome planning objections effectively so that a planning permission can be granted, it is essential that they are both legal and enforceable.

The power in s 70 is expressed in very wide terms, ie 'such conditions as they think fit'. However, such power must be exercised in accordance with public law principles in general, as established by the courts. The leading case is that of *Newbury District Council v Secretary of State for the Environment* [1981] AC 578.

Public law limitations on the power to impose conditions can be analysed as follows: a condition is imposed as part of a planning function and as such must be imposed for a *planning* purpose, not some ulterior purpose, however worthwhile. In *R v Hillingdon London Borough Council ex p Royco Homes* (1974) 1 QB 720 a condition requiring a house to be first occupied by a person on the council's housing waiting list was held to be unlawful. In effect, the council was trying to forward its housing responsibilities using the planning system. Secondly, conditions should fairly and reasonably relate to the permitted development. In the *Newbury* case, the local authority had taken the opportunity when granting temporary permission for change of use of two existing aircraft hangars to require their removal after the end of the temporary period. They would thus achieve the laudable planning objective of removing an eyesore. This was held to be illegal because it did not relate to the change of use itself. It did fulfil a planning purpose and would have been accepted under the preceding paragraph.

A condition must not be 'unreasonable' in the public law sense. The test here is that of '*Wednesbury* unreasonable' (see *Associated Provincial Picture Houses v Wednesbury Corporation* [1948] 1 KB 223) as opposed to use of the word 'unreasonable' in its ordinary English meaning. In other words, the condition must be so unreasonable that no reasonable planning authority could have imposed it. Thus it is not a question of carefully weighing up the planning merits.

A planning condition may not lawfully require the payment of money or other consideration by the developer because the section does not authorise such payments. This means that planning obligations must be used to deal with financial payments.

Planning is not normally concerned with the ownership of land. No ownership of land is required to lodge an application or an appeal. However, there is a danger that a land owner could find himself saddled with a condition relating to his land of which he was entirely unaware because it was outside the application boundary and no formal notice under s 66 was served on him, either when the application was made or the appeal lodged. Moreover, since the planning permission does not override private property rights, the developer would be unable to ensure that that condition was effective, thus rendering the condition incapable of being fulfilled. A condition, therefore, that requires works on land that is not within the application site *and* is not within the control of the appellant will normally be unlawful. If a condition is so uncertain as to be incapable of enforcement it will probably be unlawful.

7.3   Review of condition on its merits

Once it has been ascertained that an existing or proposed condition is lawful, it is necessary to consider whether the condition is justified on its merits on planning grounds. An inspector on appeal will weigh up the merits of conditions. Circular 1/85 gives advice both to local authorities determining applications and to inspectors on appeal as to how conditions should be approached.

Six tests are set out in para 11 of Circular 1/85. Conditions should only be imposed where they are necessary, relevant to planning and to the development, enforceable, precise, and reasonable in all other aspects.

7.3.1   Necessity

The test as set out in Circular 1/85 is whether planning permission would have to be refused if that condition were not imposed. As a matter of practice this test is not always strictly applied. If a condition gives comfort to one of the parties and is not otherwise objectionable it may be sensible to suggest it at some stage.The local authority might be concerned about archaeological remains and yet not have any firm evidence. In these circumstances it would be very difficult for them to refuse planning permission without a condition in respect of archaeological investigation but nonetheless it may be sensible to include such a condition.

7.3.2   Relevance to planning

This is similar to the *Newbury* test. It does throw up difficulty, particularly in the social housing field. In *Royco Homes* a condition requiring units to be made available for people on the council's housing waiting list was held to be relevant to the council's housing function, not its planning functions. A planning condition should also not be used to duplicate other controls, for instance, building regulations, fire regulations or advertisement regulations.

7.3.3   Relevance to the development to be permitted

This is the test which the condition failed in the *Newbury* case. It is sometimes extremely difficult to decide whether in a particular case a condition fairly and reasonably relates to the development to be permitted. If there is real doubt it may be better to consider using a planning obligation to achieve the objective.

7.3.4   Enforceability

This means that the condition is sufficiently clear for both the local authority and the developer to know when it has been breached. Once both parties are clear that it has been breached, can the local authority effectively deal with the breach, ie will the developer be in control of the land at the relevant time? Does it require an intrusive policing role for many years? A condition prohibiting more than five people living in a flat would fall into that category.

7.3.5 Precision

Insufficient care is often given as to whether the condition as worded will indeed work. A condition which requires council approval of a particular aspect before a certain date will be dangerous for the developer as it leaves the council entirely in control. Likewise, since it is the local authority who is imposing the condition, it cannot seek to leave any decision to a third party. For instance drainage works may be the concern of the National Rivers Authority. If so the condition will have to read 'that drainage works shall be approved by the local authority' even if the words 'after consultation with the National Rivers Authority' are included. It is the local authority who must take responsibility for approving or not approving any consent.

7.3.6 Reasonableness in all other respects

Circular 1/85 appears to take the test beyond the issue of *Wednesbury* unreasonableness (ie so unreasonable that no local authority properly considering the case could impose the condition) by considering whether as a matter of policy it is reasonable. This is quite a different test and much broader in its application. This is the final planning test: a condition having met all the preceding tests must finally, as a matter of planning law, be 'reasonable' in the ordinary sense of the word.

Circular 1/85 thus imposes broader tests than the courts have laid down as a matter of statutory interpretation alone. This was illustrated recently by the court in a case concerning a *Grampian* condition (see para 7.7). Paragraph 33 of Circular 1/85 advises that a negatively worded condition (ie that development shall not be begun until a given point) must meet a stricter test 'whether there are at least reasonable prospects of the action in question being performed'. In *British Railways Board v Secretary of State for the Environment and Others* [1994] EG 15 it was held that this gloss was not necessary as a matter of law and that a condition not meeting the strict test was a valid condition and a material consideration. The Secretary of State promptly issued a press release stating that whether strictly required as a matter of statutory interpretation or not, he will continue to uphold the gloss as a matter of policy. The policy is itself a material consideration.

7.4 Doubtful conditions

Doubtful conditions are dangerous for two reasons. Firstly, if there is any doubt as to whether they are effective (either because they are invalid as a matter of law or because they are contrary to government policy), an inspector is unlikely to accept the condition. Secondly, if a condition is challenged and found to be unlawful, the decision itself is likely to be quashed and remitted to the decision-maker. He will then have to consider whether planning permission can properly be granted without the invalid condition or whether permission ought to be refused. In many cases the very reasons which made a planning condition necessary in the first place will mean that planning permission cannot be granted without it.

7.5   Distinguishing conditions from limitations on planning permission

The description of the development given as part of an application for planning permission sometimes operates to limit the scope of development in much the same way as a condition. The usual rule is set out in s 75(3) of the Act. If no purpose is specified in a grant of planning permission, the permission is construed as including permission to use the building for the purpose for which it was designed. 'Designed' in this sense means 'intended' rather than 'architecturally designed' (*Harding v Secretary of State for the Environment and Bridgnorth District Council* [1984] JPL 503). Thus an application for the erection of an 'artist's studio' will limit the use to that particular use unless a change of use is subsequently authorised.

An application for planning permission for 'an office building with 50 car parking spaces' will operate in a similar way to a condition in requiring 50 car parking spaces to be provided. However once the car parking spaces are provided, failure to continue to make them available will not be a breach of planning control unless what has occurred is development requiring planning permission. This is often not the case. A condition is therefore usually imposed requiring car parking areas to be made available for car parking. Breach of such a condition is enforceable by the local authority as a breach of planning control. There is, however, some room for ambiguity. Development described as 'offices for Great Britain plc' will not be limited to that company unless there is a personal condition attached to the planning permission. If, therefore, a feature of the description has consequences beyond the immediate implementation, consideration should be given to incorporating a condition on the consent.

7.6   Types of condition

7.6.1   Conditions affecting land outside the application site

Conditions affecting land outside the application site are normally only acceptable where the applicant controls the land. Additionally, because a condition carries with it an implied planning permission for the use or the works required, such permission would escape the usual notification procedures. However it should be remembered that a planning permission does not give any private property law rights, ie planning permission does not give any powers to any person to carry out development unless he owns the land or has secured the agreement of all owners. Private property rights such as rights of way and rights of light are unaffected by the grant of planning permission.

The meaning of 'control' is a question of fact and degree and does not require ownership. What is needed is for the applicant to be able to say that the condition can be complied with. Since such conditions are governed by s 72 of the Act, a condition must be imposed 'for the purposes of or in connection with the development'. In other words, if a condition relates to land outside the application site, it must bear a close relationship to the development itself. If this causes difficulties and it is necessary to restrict the use of land outside the application site or carry out work outside the application site, it may be better to use a *Grampian* condition which will bite even though it relates to land outside the application site.

7.7   *Grampian* conditions

A *Grampian* condition is a condition which prevents development beginning or some other event occurring before a pre-condition is satisfied, eg the permitted development shall not be occupied until the highway works as set out in the application have been completed to the reasonable satisfaction of the local planning authority. This condition was held to be lawful in the case of *Grampian Regional Council v City of Aberdeen District Council* 47 P&CR 633, hence the name of this type of condition.

In *Kingsley Lewis Stretch v Secretary of State for the Environment and North West Leicestershire District Council* CA 19 May 1993, road improvements were required for access to a proposed bungalow. The inspector found that this was the only issue in the way of a grant of permission but found there was no reasonable expectation that the necessary road improvements would be carried out. He therefore refused planning permission. The Court of Appeal agreed with the inspector that the imposition of a condition which is beyond the power of the applicant to carry out or which had no reasonable prospect of being fulfilled would not be a reasonable condition and upheld for refusal of planning permission.

The House of Lords has recently held in the case of *British Railways Board v Secretary of State for the Environment and Others* [1994] EG 107 that the gloss placed on such conditions in Circular 1/85 (ie that there is a reasonable prospect of the pre-condition being fulfilled within the time limit of the planning permission) is not required as a matter of law. The Circular 1/85 gloss was drawn from a Court of Appeal judgment in the case of *Jones v Secretary of State for Wales* (1974) 28 P&CR 28 which was overruled by the House of Lords in the *British Railways Board* case. The Secretary of State responded in a press release on 28 January 1994 that he intended to maintain as a matter of policy that for negative conditions to be imposed there should be at least reasonable prospects of the action in question being performed within the time limit imposed by the planning permission. The Secretary of State thus imposes a policy requirement which in practice limits the scope of such conditions and is more stringent than that required by statute.

Inspectors are following this advice, as is illustrated by the following excerpt from a decision letter dated 14 March 1994 in respect of appeal reference T/APP/H1515/A/93/226294/P7.

> In principle, therefore, I regard condition 1 [relating to highway improvements] as drafted as necessary in order to solve a particular planning problem arising from the proposal. Turning to the second issue, I note the legal submissions which were made to me about *Grampian*-type conditions. In particular, I note that in *British*

Railways Board v SOSE and *Hounslow LBC* the House of Lords held that there was not an automatic legal bar against the use of negative conditions where there appeared to be no reasonable prospect of the action in question being carried out within the time limit imposed by the planning permission. Nevertheless, this judgement does not prevent the Secretary of State (or an Inspector) from applying the 'reasonable prospects test' as a matter of policy. Thus, for a negative condition to be imposed, there should normally be at least a reasonable prospect of the action in question being carried out before the putative permission lapses.

In these circumstances, and recalling what I was told at the inquiry, I have concluded that there is no reasonable prospect of works being forthcoming from any provider — whether the appellant, the local authority, the two parties acting in concert, or any third party. As I mention above, it would therefore be contrary to the Secretary of State's normal policy to impose a negative condition requiring them. This being the case, and despite the merits of the proposals, not least the prospect of securing a new use for a prominent vacant site, I see no alternative but to dismiss the appeal and refuse outline planning permission.

The disadvantage to the developer of the most common form of *Grampian* condition is that he has to satisfy the pre-condition before beginning the development. If the pre-condition involves substantial operations such as infrastructure improvements this will in effect be front-loading the expenditure. A better wording may be that the development authorised by the planning permission shall not be *occupied* until a pre-condition is met. This will delay the time when the expenditure has to be incurred. In any event, the developer should ensure that he has all necessary consents before accepting such a condition. If he does not he may be unable to carry out the development despite the grant of planning permission.

7.8 Time limits

Sections 91 and 92 of the Act require a condition to be imposed in respect of the commencement of development or submission of reserved matters within a specified period. In the case of full planning permission this is normally five years. In addition a condition may be imposed regulating how long development once implemented shall be allowed to continue. Section 72 of the Act allows the imposition of such temporary permissions and authorises the imposition of a condition requiring removal of any buildings or works authorised by the permission.

The general advice in Circular 1/85 is that a temporary condition should be used only sparingly and usually where it is necessary to have a project up and running in order to properly evaluate its effects. This may be the case with a non-conforming use to evaluate whether it is detrimental to residential neighbours. It may also be the case with an application for the stationing of a caravan for a new agricultural unit. In the latter case it may be necessary to allow the agricultural operation to function for two or three years before finally assessing its viability. Circular 1/85 also advises that it is very rarely appropriate to grant temporary planning permission for a permanent building unless the building is genuinely required for a limited time. This may be the case for an exhibition building or a sports facility.

7.8.1   Infrastructure conditions

A model condition requiring a scheme of drainage to be approved by the local authority prior to the commencement of drainage is set out in Circular 1/85. However, since the advent of the Water Industry Act 1991 there must be a question as to whether this should not be dealt with directly by the water/sewerage undertaker concerned. Such a condition may be simply storing up trouble for the future if there is a disagreement as to capacity of the system and what works are needed. A pragmatic decision as to the real position should be taken before accepting or refusing such conditions.

In many cases, details of off-site highway works may be better dealt with by an agreement under the Highways Act rather than by a condition, although there may be a *Grampian* condition to tie the works into the development sequence.

7.9   Common conditions (extracted from Circular 1/85)

7.9.1   Outline permission

For outline permission, time limits must be imposed by virtue of ss 91 and 92 of the Act.

(a) Approval of details of the siting, design and external appearance of the building(s), the means of access thereto and the landscaping of the site (hereinafter called 'the reserved matters') shall be obtained from the local planning authority [delete any matters not reserved on original application].
(b) Application for approval of reserved matters shall be made to the local planning authority before the expiration of three years from the date of this permission.
(c) The development hereby permitted shall be begun either before the expiration of five years from the date of this permission or before the expiration of [two] years from the date of approval of the last of the reserved matters to be approved, whichever is the later.

7.9.2   Detailed planning permission

The development permitted shall be begun before the expiration of [five] years from the date of this permission.

7.9.3   Landscaping

(a) No development shall take place until there has been submitted to and approved by the local planning authority a scheme of landscaping which shall include indications of all existing trees and hedgerows on the land, and details of any to be retained, together with measures for their protection in the course of development.
(b) All planting, seeding or turfing shall be carried out in the first planting and seeding seasons following the occupation of the buildings or the completion of the development, whichever is the sooner and any trees or plants which within a period of five years from the completion of the development die, are removed or become seriously damaged shall be replaced in the next planting

season with others of similar size and species, unless the local planning authority gives written consent to any variation.

7.9.4 Agricultural workers' condition

The occupation of the dwelling shall be limited to a person solely or mainly employed, or last employed, in the locality in agriculture as defined in s 336 of the Town and County Planning Act 1990, or in forestry, or a dependant of such a person residing with him or her, or a widow or widower of such a person.

7.9.5 Archaeology

The developer shall afford access at all reasonable times to any archaeologist nominated by the local planning authority and shall allow him to observe the excavations and record items of interest he finds.

7.10 Unacceptable conditions

The following are examples of unacceptable conditions and are taken from Annex B to Circular 1/85:
(1) The development shall be completed within [five] years.
(2) No advertisements shall be displayed in the site.
(3) Land fronting the highway shall be made available for future road widening.
(4) A layby shall be constructed and assigned to the highway authority.
(5) Flats or dwellings shall not be occupied by more than [ten] people.
(6) The site shall be kept clean and tidy at all times.
(7) A shop window display shall be maintained in an attractive condition.
(8) Forty acres of open space shall be provided for public use before the development is occupied.
(9) The first opportunity to buy houses to be given to local people.

Each of these conditions fails to meet one or more of the tests.

7.11 Exclusion of Use Classes Order and permitted development rights

Both the Use Classes Order and the GDO give rights to carry out development which would otherwise require express planning permission without such a consent. This is done in the case of the Use Classes Order by stating that development within the use class is not development and in the case of the GDO by specifying certain types of operation which would normally require planning permission are permitted development for which no application needs to be made providing they fall within certain restrictions. It is this provision which enables individual houses to be extended within certain limits without planning permission.

In some circumstances it may be desirable to exclude these provisions and such a condition is lawful provided it meets the ordinary tests. A relevant case is *The City of London Corporation v Secretary of State for the Environment* (1972) 23 P&CR 169. However, as Sir Douglas Frank stated in *Carpet Decor (Guildford) Ltd v Secretary of State for the Environment and Guildford Borough Council* [1982] (JPL 806), if it was desired to exclude the Use Classes Order or the GDO the condition should state this in unequivocal terms. In the absence of such a condition it must be assumed that those orders will have effect by operation of law.

7.12 Distinguishing conditions from planning obligations

Planning conditions were felt in the past to be weaker than planning obligations. However, since 1991 failure to comply with a condition may be an offence. The local authority also have powers to issue an enforcement notice or seek an injunction. The perception is therefore less justified now. It remains true that a planning obligation will enable a local authority to enforce an agreement by injunction or by entering land themselves to carry out the work. They do not need to comply with the requirements of the enforcement notice procedure nor, at any rate in the short term, are planning obligations open to appeal to the Secretary of State.

However, it is now clear that planning obligations are wider in scope than conditions in a number of ways, despite the earlier view that the same rules applied. (See *Good and Another v Epping Forest District Council* CA 5 Nov 1993, para 8.)

Certain matters are better dealt with by condition, including changes of use or works to be carried out on the application site or within land controlled by the applicant. Temporary consents falling within the established rules, matters of detail (such as landscaping, materials and means of enclosure) and matters which can effectively be dealt with by a negative condition are also suitable candidates for planning conditions.

However, where restrictions need to be imposed and work carried out on land the applicant does not own or control and where a *Grampian* condition may not be sufficiently flexible, planning obligations are a more suitable option. Provided that the applicant can require the owner of the land to execute a planning obligation, quite complicated provisions can be made. Similarly, where payments of money are required, a planning obligation is suitable since this cannot be covered by condition attached to planning permission.

Other circumstances are those where ongoing obligations of a positive or 'housekeeping' nature are involved. Housekeeping provisions, ie recurrent obligations which need monitoring and enforcement, are not normally suitable for conditions. A planning obligation may be used where complex co-operation is required between two parties who each have obligations to perform. If a *Grampian* condition is relied on, there may be a real risk that no agreement on the detailed scheme will be possible. For large applications where complex phasing and consent procedures are required, a planning obligation may form a more flexible method of controlling the development. Finally, where land is to be dedicated or made available to the public or where the issues to be dealt with do not meet the *Newbury* or Circular 1/85 tests but nonetheless fall within the broader test for planning obligations, the obligation route should be selected.

7.13   Practical approach to choosing how issue is to be dealt with

The following sequence may serve as a checklist:
- Is the point at issue a material consideration which will affect the decision and therefore needs to be dealt with as part of the appeal process?
- Does it fall squarely within the ambit of planning conditions, either positive or negative (*Grampian*)? If so, use a condition.
- If the matter is not beyond attack as a condition (bearing in mind that if there is doubt the condition will not achieve its objective), does the applicant own the land involved? Can he procure that the land owner will enter into a planning obligation to cover the points? If the answer to this is yes, consider whether it falls within proper ambit of a planning obligation.
- If the answer to both questions is no, consider alternative strategies. For example, can the planning application be properly amended to remove the difficulty and will the local authority agree to this?

7.14   Mineral workings

Because of the special nature of mineral working, additional powers, contained in Sched 5 to the Act, may be exercised to impose conditions. Every planning permission for the winning and working of minerals is automatically subject to a condition limiting its life. This contrasts with the ordinary position on planning permissions where a condition gives a period within which the development must be begun but does not deal with the time during which it can be carried out. New permissions will be issued subject to a condition that development must cease not later than 60 years from the date of permission, although there is discretion to impose a different period if this can be justified (this is currently under review).

After-care conditions can be imposed on a minerals consent, requiring steps to be taken for restoration to use for agriculture, forestry or amenities. Schedule 5 also defines the 'after-care period' as a period of five years after the restoration has been completed in accordance with the restoration condition. A special mechanism for enforcing restoration and after-care conditions in a mineral consent is the express provision in para 6 of Sched 5 that a person who complies with an after-care condition but who has not himself exploited the minerals is entitled to recover his expenses against the person who last carried out such operations. As mineral consents cover a long period, an injunction may be an inadequate remedy. The person who was responsible for the mineral abstraction and who failed to comply with the restoration and after-care conditions may be out of reach.

As a matter of practice, it may be appropriate to offer a planning obligation incorporating a bond to ensure that the obligation of restoration and after-care will run with the land and bind successive owners. In this way inspectors on appeal can be satisfied that if planning permission is granted, restoration and after-care have been secured by a practical scheme by means of a legally binding agreement which will run with the land.

THE PLANNING INSPECTORATE

Messrs. Denton Hall
5 Chancery Lane
Clifford's Inn
London EC4A 1BU   5th November 1994

Dear Sirs

TOWN AND COUNTRY PLANNING ACT 1990, SECTION 78 AND
SCHEDULE 6
APPEAL BY MR AND MRS J ALEXANDER

1.   I have been appointed by the Secretary of State for the Environment to
determine the above mentioned appeal. This appeal is against the decision of
the Riverside Borough Council to refuse planning permission for alterations to
an access ramp in association with the construction of a steel and cast iron
staircase in the basement lightwell and the formation of a new doorway at Flat
3 Victoria Court, Riverside. I have considered the representations made by you
and by the Council, and also those made by interested persons. I have also
considered those representations made directly by interested persons to the
Council which have been forwarded to me. I inspected the site on 12 September
1994.

2.   From my inspection of the site and its surroundings and the written
representations made, I consider the principal issues in this case to be the effect
of the proposals on the residential amenities that occupants of the building could
reasonably expect to enjoy, and the effect on the listed building and the
conservation area.

3.   Victoria Court is a Grade II listed building within the East Quay
Conservation Area and is described in the listing schedule as a large purpose-
built block of mansion flats erected 1890-C1900. It appears to be mainly in
residential use with some office accommodation. Flat 3 is situated at basement
level at the south east corner of the building and, according to the
representations, has in the past been used by maintenance staff. It has been
converted to offices and is at present unoccupied.

4.   At present the only access to Flat 3 is from a narrow courtyard/lightwell
by way of a short metal staircase from the upper basement level. From that
level there is an internal service staircase and a service elevator connecting to
the ground floor entrance lobby, and an external concrete ramp between the
face of the building and the pavement retaining wall which leads from the upper
basement to a gate in the railings alongside the pavement. The gate is fitted
with a lock and the ramp appears to be used as a means of access to the upper
basement, as a tradesmens entrance and for the collection of refuse.

5.   Your clients propose to cut back the end of the concrete ramp, erect a new staircase from the end of the ramp to the basement level, and construct a new door in an existing window opening in order to provide a direct external access to Flat 3 from the pavement. This would necessitate repositioning the gate to provide access to both the proposed staircase and the ramp.

6.   Dealing first with the effect of the proposals on residential amenities, the Riverside District Plan seeks to improve the quality of the residential environment. In this instance the flat most directly affected would be Flat 5 which is situated at ground floor level immediately above Flat 3. Windows of the flat facing east over the existing ramp and the site of the proposed new staircase are just over 1 metre from the back of the pavement and are double glazed; those in the vicinity of the ramp are protected by metal grills and bars.

7.   In dealing with the noise and disturbance that might occur as a consequence of the use of the proposed staircase I have had regard to the uses suggested. The use of Flat 3 as an office would be likely to lead to an increase in pedestrian activity. The Council consider that ten people would work in the office and the staircase would additionally be used by visitors. I accept that high heels on a metal staircase, the noise of the gate and door shutting, and voices could be heard. However, in view of the amelioration measures suggested including the prevention of air and structure-borne noise and the use of resilient pads and neoprene bearings, and the general level of noise in this location very close to a relatively busy street, I do not consider that those noises would be unduly disturbing. In so far as people using the proposed staircase would not use the ramp and the internal courtyard/lightwell and metal stair, there could well be a reduction in noise and disturbance at those locations.

8.   The residential use of Flat 3 would be likely to give rise to less use than commercial premises during the week, but there would be week-end and some night time use. Although the background noise levels would be lower at such times I consider that the noise of residents on the proposed staircase would be no greater than noise on the ramp, and as the use of the internal courtyard would be diminished there would be a reduction in noise in that location.

9.   If the premises were used for maintenance purposes the use of the stair would not be likely to give rise to significantly greater noise and disturbance than the use of the ramp and the internal courtyard.

10.   Turning to considerations of privacy and security the existing access gate to the ramp is opposite an area of wall between two windows of Flat 5. The repositioned gate would be directly opposite one of the windows. However, pedestrians on the pavement can at present look directly into the window at a distance of approximately 1 metre, people on the ramp at present pass directly in front of the window, and the cutting back of the ramp would increase the distance between the edge of the ramp and the window to the south, thus reducing overlooking of that window. The rake of the proposed staircase would preclude direct overlooking of the windows of Flat 5. Any additional shadowing

due to movements at the access gate would be momentary. I also consider that the use of the proposed staircase would not result in a significant increase in security risks. Bearing in mind its location and that of Flat 5, I consider that the proposed development would not detract to an unacceptable degree from the residential amenities that occupants of the building could reasonably expect to enjoy, and would not undermine the policies of the Council which seek to improve the quality of the residential environment.

11.   Turning finally to listed building and conservation area considerations, section 66(1) of the Planning (Listed Buildings and Conservation Areas) Act 1990 requires special regard to be had to the desirability of preserving a listed building or its setting or any features of special architectural or historic interest it possess when considering whether to grant planning permission, and section 72(1) of that Act requires special attention to be paid to the desirability of preserving or enhancing the character or appearance of conservation areas.

12.   I have noted that Listed Building Consent has been granted for the works. In my view, provided that the new works matched the existing detailing as far as possible, the repositioning of the gate, the erection of a metal staircase, and the insertion of a door in the basement would be of very minor significance, and would not detract from the special character of the listed building or its setting. Staircases leading down to basements are not an unusual feature in the area and although the proposed development would not enhance the character or appearance of the conservation area, it would cause no harm and the character and appearance of the conservation area would therefore be preserved.

13.   The Council and others are concerned that a precedent should not be set, but I consider the Council has sufficient powers to prevent harmful development. I have noted the conditions suggested by the Council and I have included those that I consider to be reasonable and necessary to secure the satisfactory development of the site, the protection of the listed building, and the amelioration of the potentially harmful effects of noise. In that regard, bearing in mind the advice contained in paragraph 62 of Circular 1/85, I am satisfied that a condition relating to the maintenance of closure and buffer devices is warranted.

14.   I have taken account of the objections of the Victoria Court Residents Association, the Riverside Association, the occupier of Flat 5, and those of other residents. I have also taken account of all the other matters raised but they do not outweigh the considerations that have led me to my decision.

15.   For the above reasons, and in exercise of powers transferred to me, I hereby allow this appeal and grant planning permission for alterations to an access ramp in association with the construction of a steel and cast iron staircase in the basement lightwell and the formation of a new doorway at Flat 3 Victoria Court, Riverside in accordance with the terms of the application (No 900780) dated 13 February 1993 (as amended) and the amended plans (Drawing No 8941/02) submitted therewith, subject to the following conditions:

(i)   The development hereby permitted shall be begun before the expiration of 5 years from the date of this letter.

(ii) Detailed drawings of the railings, staircase (including details of measures to reduce airborne and structure-borne noise), and doorway, to a scale of 1:20 and 1:5 shall be submitted to and approved by the local planning authority before work is commenced on the relevant part of the development.

(iii) The gate at pavement level and the door at basement level shall be fitted with closure and buffer devices and those devices shall thereafter be maintained in working order.

(iv) All new external work and finishes and work of making good shall match adjacent original work and finishes except where indicated otherwise in the details approved in accordance with condition 2.

(v)   Except as may be agreed with the local planning authority, building work to implement the development hereby permitted shall not take place except between 0800 and 1800 hours on Mondays to Fridays, and 0800 to 1300 hours on Saturdays. No building works shall take place on Sundays or Bank Holidays.

16.   An applicant for any consent, agreement or approval required by a condition of this permission has a statutory right of appeal to the Secretary of State if consent, agreement or approval is refused or granted conditionally or if the authority fail to give notice of their decision within the prescribed period. The developer's attention is drawn to the enclosed note relating to the requirements of the Building Regulations 1991 with respect to access for disabled people.

17.   This letter does not convey any approval or consent which may be required under any enactment, bye-law, order or regulation other than section 57 of the Town and Country Planning Act 1990.

Yours faithfully,

J S SMITH

Inspector

Chapter 8

Planning Obligations in the Appeal Context

8.1 Introduction

Many planning agreements have been made between the local planning authority and owners of land regarding the use of land under s 52 of the 1971 Town and Country Planning Act and its predecessors and under its successor, s 106 of the 1990 Planning Act. However, from 5 October 1991 a revised s 106 came into force introducing a new concept, that of the 'planning obligation'. The new planning obligation comes in two forms: a deed between the local authority and parties interested in the land concerned and a unilateral obligation which the landowner can execute without assistance from the local authority. In this chapter, the term 'planning agreement' refers to the former type, and 'unilateral obligation' to the latter. The term 'planning obligation' includes both. This chapter explains when, in the context of appeals, planning agreements and unilateral obligations may be helpful and just what these documents are. Finally it deals with drafting points.

DoE Circular 16/91 gives advice in connection with planning obligations and sample deeds are also included at the end of this chapter. These worked examples are given for illustrative purposes only and are not intended to be used as precedents. A planning obligation needs to be tailored to the particular circumstances and requirements of the party for whom one is acting.

8.2 When to use a planning obligation

Planning obligations arise in the context of appeals in the following ways:
(1) As part of the strategy when an appeal is lodged and at the same time a revised application is submitted to the local authority. A planning obligation can be used to overcome certain objections which cannot be dealt with satisfactorily in any other way.
(2) In the course of an appeal, to lay on the table the developer's offer in a legally binding form to deal with points where the local authority and the developer cannot agree on exactly what is appropriate.
(3) During the course of an inquiry or immediately afterwards, to deal with a matter which has emerged, or the importance of which has been emphasised by the inquiry proceedings. The developer will wish to make

sure that there is a legally binding solution which the inspector can take into account in reaching his decision.

Negotiations with the local authority during the course of consideration of a planning application and evaluation of the reasons for refusal should enable an appellant to form a clear view of objections which can be overcome either by way of a planning obligation or by offering conditions (which are dealt with in Chapter 7). If a matter falls within the proper ambit of conditions, it is nearly always preferable to invite the inspector to impose a suitable condition in accordance with the advice given in para B6 of Annex B of DoE Circular 16/91. This may be of some importance because it is easier to obtain a variation of a condition than a planning obligation.

If, however, what is contemplated falls outside the legitimate scope of a condition, or if there is doubt, then consideration should be given to whether the matter can be dealt with by a planning obligation. The ambit of planning obligations is limited by the words of the statute and by policy. It is possible that some matters cannot be dealt with either by conditions or by planning obligations.

8.2.1 Planning agreements

The use of a planning agreement to overcome objections to an application, or to make certain that the developer will do what he has offered to do, will often have been discussed with the local authority during the processing of the application. In some cases there may even be a draft which has been agreed in many respects. It will often be the case that such an agreement is offered at the application stage on the basis that it will be withdrawn if the applicant is forced down the appeal route.

A local authority's objection to the proposal may not lie in the area to be dealt with by a planning obligation. The parties may, for example, have agreed that a riverside walk should be provided but the local authority may have refused the application because of unacceptable traffic implications. In these circumstances, many local authorities are prepared to negotiate and enter into a planning agreement even though the proposals as a whole are unacceptable and they are defending that position at appeal. If the local authority can be persuaded to adopt this course of action it is certainly preferable from the appellant's point of view. Both parties are able to say to the inspector that they agree on these matters, if on nothing else.

8.2.2 Unilateral obligation

In many cases, however, it is not possible to agree a legal agreement with the local planning authority. There may in fact be no basis for agreement between the local authority and the appellant as to what should properly be in such an agreement. Alternatively, the local authority, having refused the application, may be unwilling to negotiate and execute such a deed. In these cases a unilateral obligation offers a solution. The statute is so framed that a landowner can execute a deed without the local authority's co-operation in such a form that it will be binding on him and run with the land.

In the appeal context, therefore, a unilateral obligation overcomes the problem of an unco-operative local authority. Previously an inspector may have been constrained to refuse permission in the absence of a legally binding document. The Secretary of State has no power to enter into agreements under this section of the Act.

What the inspector does not want at the inquiry is a discussion as to the validity of the document itself. It is therefore suggested that once a draft of the unilateral obligation has been prepared, it should be submitted to the local authority with a request for their comments. It is perfectly legitimate at a public inquiry to ask a local authority witness for his views on a unilateral obligation. If the authority agree with it as a document they should say so. They should point out where they do not agree, and the reasons for that disagreement. Such a document should if possible be executed before the end of the inquiry so that it may be formally submitted during the inquiry. If this is not possible, because it has been drafted in the light of events which have occurred during the inquiry, then before the close of the inquiry the inspector should be given a clear indication of the contents and the timescale within which the obligation will be forwarded. A copy must be sent to the local authority who will register it as a local land charge.

8.2.3 Other legislation

There may be matters which should be dealt with under other legislation. Off-site highway works will often be dealt with by agreements under the Highways Act 1980. Agreements required for the provision of water and sewerage facilities are also often dealt with under the powers of the relevant water company or water and sewerage company under the Water Industry Act 1991.

8.3 What are planning obligations?

A planning obligation is a deed made under s 106 of the Town and Country Planning Act 1990. The outstanding feature of the provisions, as brought in by the Planning and Compensation Act 1991, is that the co-operation of the local authority is no longer required: an obligation can be unilateral on the side of the developer. There are two important characteristics of a planning obligation. Firstly, the covenants will run with the land and bind successors in title irrespective of the usual land law limitations on the enforceability of such positive and negative covenants, and secondly, an obligation must be made as a deed either between the local planning authority and the landowner, or by the landowner alone.

Section 106 of the Act states that:

> 106. (1)   Any person interested in land in the area of a local planning authority may, by agreement or otherwise, enter into an obligation (referred to in this section and sections 106A and 106B as 'a planning obligation'), enforceable to the extent mentioned in subsection (3)—

(a)   restricting the development or use of the land in any specified way;
(b)   requiring specified operations or activities to be carried out in, on, under or over the land;
(c)   requiring the land to be used in any specified way; or
(d)   requiring a sum or sums to be paid to the authority on a specified date or dates or periodically.
(2)   A planning obligation may—
(a)   be unconditional or subject to conditions;
(b)   impose any restriction or requirement mentioned in subsection (1)(a) to (c) either indefinitely or for such period or periods as may be specified; and
(c)   if it requires a sum or sums to be paid, require the payment of a specified amount or an amount determined in accordance with the instrument by which the obligation is entered into and, if it requires the payment of periodical sums, require them to be paid indefinitely or for a specified period.

8.4   Who can execute a planning obligation?

Both the local authority and 'any person interested in the land' can execute a planning obligation. The expression 'person interested in the land' was brought forward from earlier legislation. There is some academic doubt as to whether the word 'interested' should be interpreted in the normal land law sense or whether the word can have a wider everyday meaning which would include, for instance, a prospective developer. These issues were canvassed in *Jones v Secretary of State for Wales* (1974) 28 P&CR 280 and *Pennine Raceway Limited v Kirklees Metropolitan Council (No 1)* [1983] QB 382. This is of little practical significance because it will be essential that the obligation captures successors in title and this will only be the case if the person entering into it has a legal interest. Local authorities and an inspector on appeal will need to be satisfied that the person making the covenant does have a sufficient legal interest. Title will be required to be deduced in the normal way. The deed will then be registered as a local land charge. Some local authorities will require such deeds to be registered with the Land Registry against the title of the land.

8.5   What can be included and what cannot

Two points should be considered here. Does the deed comply with s 106 as a matter of statutory interpretation? And are the covenants of such a nature that they ought to be taken into account in making the decision? In other words, are they material considerations? If so, are the local authority empowered to execute the agreement?

8.5.1   The first test: within the scope of s 106

Section 106(1)(a)–(d) of the Act specifies what can be included. An obligation may restrict the development or use of land in any specified way. It may require specified operations or activities to be carried out on the land, require the land to be used in any specified way or require sums to be paid to the authority. This contrasts with the much more limited scope of conditions.

Care must be taken to consider each covenant separately to ensure that provisions fall squarely within the words of the Act and that all the required formalities have been complied with. The Act makes no reference to the transfer of land. In *Wimpy Homes Holdings Ltd v Secretary of State for the Environment* a unilateral obligation contained a provision that certain open space land should be transferred to the planning authority. The authority considered the commuted maintenance sum inadequate and took High Court proceedings to quash the inspector's decision which had taken the unilateral obligation into account. The court held that an obligation to transfer land was not permitted by the section.

8.5.2   Conditions and planning obligations

In the case of *Good and Another v Epping Forest District Council* [1994] 27 EG 135 the local authority had attached an agricultural condition to a new dwelling. They had also backed this up with a planning agreement in the same terms but including a covenant that the house should not be sold separately from the farm land.

A challenge was made on the basis that the local authority's ability to make planning agreements was limited to matters which could have been dealt with as conditions.

This was robustly rejected on the basis that if this was so it was difficult to see what purpose planning agreements could achieve.

Matters which make a condition unlawful may also make terms of a planning obligation such that they should not be taken into account. What is clear is that the ambit of planning obligations is wider than that of conditions. The fact that it may be advantageous to a local authority to enforce a matter by way of planning agreement is not itself sufficient to make it unlawful.

8.5.3   The second test: are the covenants material considerations?

The balancing of material considerations and the excluding of those that are non-material lies at the heart of the decision-making process. It is crucial that a decision-maker determines whether a planning obligation is a material consideration for his decision or not. If it is, he must take it into consideration. If it is not, he must not, under any circumstances, take it into consideration.

What is at issue here is whether the obligation is to be taken into account by the decision-maker. The weight such a material consideration may be given in balancing out adverse factors in any particular case is a matter for the decision-maker. Once the hurdle of materiality is overcome and the decision-maker takes the obligation into consideration, he may decide that in the particular circumstances it weighs very little against other factors. The courts are most reluctant to interfere with such an exercise of judgment and discretion: this second step will be very difficult to challenge.

Particular problems are thrown up by planning obligations because of the power under s 106 to covenant to make payments of money. Such contributions are a fertile ground for disagreement.

Because the courts are much less likely to intervene in a challenge based on the weight accorded to a material issue, attention has focused on the question of whether an issue is a material consideration or should have been discarded entirely. The latter is a question which the courts will review. The starting point for the interpretation of a material consideration for the purpose of s 70(2) of the Act is the *Newbury* case. Although that case concerned a condition the same principles will hold true for a planning obligation. The test of materiality is threefold:

(1) The agreement must serve a planning purpose.
(2) It must fairly and reasonably relate to the permitted development.
(3) It should not be perverse.

With regard to the first test, there is normally little difficulty in establishing whether the obligation fulfils a planning purpose. An example of the kind of topic which causes difficulties is that of social housing. A condition relating to occupation by persons on a council waiting list was held unlawful in *Royco Homes* (see para 7.2).

Two cases illustrate the difficulties of the second test, particularly as to the validity of developer offers which go beyond what is strictly necessary to enable the development to proceed. In the recent case of *R v Plymouth City Council et al ex parte Plymouth and South Devon Co-operative Society* [1993] JPL 538, the local authority resolved to grant planning permission for two superstores, one proposed by Tesco and one by Sainsbury. The local authority resolved to approve each application providing that a planning obligation was executed to provide for certain items which were not part of the development applied for and which the respective developers had offered.

Sainsbury offered to contribute to the enhancement of the river Plym and Plymouth Road and to contribute towards the provision of a creche, park and ride and £1 million for industrial development. Within the application site, but not included in its application, it would provide a tourist information centre, an art gallery display and a birdwatching hide. Tesco's package was also comprehensive. The company offered to provide park and ride facilities and a wildlife habitat outside the site, to contribute towards the provision of childcare facilities and an art competition and to provide a sculpture within the site.

The Co-op's application for a store had been deferred at the committee meeting where the committee resolved to grant the Tesco and the Sainsbury stores, subject to a planning obligation. The Co-op began proceedings for judicial review on the grounds that the local authority had acted unlawfully in taking into account immaterial considerations, ie the community benefits. Reliance was placed on the gloss to the *Newbury* rules set out in government policy in para B7 of Circular 16/91, ie that a planning obligation must pass a test of necessity to be material. The decision-maker must be able to say that without the benefits planning permission should be refused. This was not the case with these two applications. The local authority's decision was upheld. Thus at the initial materiality stage, the court rejected government advice which imposed an additional test.

Government advice was also tested in the case of *Tesco Stores Limited v Secretary of State for the Environment, West Oxfordshire District Council and*

Tarmac Provincial Properties Ltd [1994] EGGS 103. Tesco had applied for planning permission to erect a store in Witney in Oxfordshire. Witney suffers traffic problems, with only one bridge across the river Windrush which flows through the centre of the town. The problem has been recognised for some years and the local plan provides for a new road with a new river crossing to be provided. This is known as the West End Link. At the local plan inquiry the inspector judged that funding for this was most unlikely to come from the highway authority and recommended that the policy in favour of the Link should be preceded by a paragraph indicating the local authority's intention to negotiate funding or a major contribution before a superstore went ahead.

Both Tesco and Tarmac (in conjunction with Sainsbury) put in applications for superstores. These came before the Secretary of State (one by way of an appeal and one by way of call-in). Tesco was willing to fund the whole cost (£6.6 million) of the Link. They argued that the contribution was necessary because without it there would be a lack of highway capacity. The inspector found that the relationship between the highway improvement and the store was 'tenuous', partly because of the distance from the store and partly because the development would not generate a great deal more traffic than the uses of the site already permitted. She found that there was little to choose between the competing sites but on balance recommended that the Tesco application be granted and the Tarmac appeal refused.

The Secretary of State in his decision letter did not accept this recommendation and relied on his own policy set out in Circular 16/91 that the Link was not necessary to enable the superstore proposals to go ahead or otherwise so directly related to the development that the development ought not to be permitted without it. He did not accept the inspector's conclusion that there was a difference between the requirement for a contribution to be made, which would be the case if the link was needed in order for the development to proceed, and an offer freely made by a developer. She had formed the view that it would be perverse to refuse such benefit. The Secretary of State stated that it would be unreasonable to seek even a partial contribution from developers towards the costs of the Link in connection with proposals currently before him. He considered the offer of funding, since it failed the tests of Circular 16/91, as falling to be treated neither as a reason for granting planning permission to Tesco or for dismissing either of the other appeals. However, in the following paragraph the Secretary of State did hedge his bets. He stated that if he was wrong then he would take into account only a small part of the contribution and in the context of the proposals it would not affect his decision. He therefore allowed Tarmac's appeal and refused permission for the Tesco store.

This decision was challenged by Tesco under s 288 of the Act on the basis that the Secretary of State had failed to take into account a material consideration when he decided that Tesco's offer could not be treated as a reason for granting permission. The Secretary of State had erred in applying the tests he had himself set out in Circular 16/91. He had applied a test of necessity which was not the correct test of materiality as a matter of law.

At first instance the challenge was successful and the Secretary of State's decision quashed. The judge held that the test of necessity was not appropriate where an offer from a proposed developer is under consideration: the Secretary of State had introduced glosses on the *Newbury* test which he should not have done. The correct test was whether the West End Link *fairly and reasonably related to the development* in accordance with the *Newbury* test and not whether it was necessary and related in scale to the benefit which the proposed development would derive from the facilities to be provided, which is the Circular 16/91 gloss. On the traffic figures, the development would derive very little benefit from the link but the judge held that the obligation did fairly and reasonably relate to the development. Accordingly he quashed the Secretary of State's decision.

Tarmac, on seeing their planning permission disappear, appealed to the Court of Appeal. The Secretary of State and Tarmac contended that the Secretary of State had not in fact treated the offer of funding as immaterial or applied the wrong test. He had simply attached no weight to the offer as in all the circumstances he was entitled to do. This was accepted by the Court of Appeal who did not consider it important how a planning obligation came into being, ie whether it was required or offered.

The final result is unfortunate. The legal position on materiality as established by the courts does not match the tests set out by the government in Circular 16/91. The difficulty is that while the Secretary of State may as a matter of policy apply guidelines, he cannot as a matter of policy make a material consideration irrelevant or make a non-material consideration relevant. This is different from the situation which has arisen on *Grampian* conditions discussed in Chapter 7. Here the Secretary of State has indicated that as a matter of policy *Grampian* conditions will be subject to a test which goes beyond the *Newbury* tests. He is not saying that the *Newbury* tests are wrong, but that as a matter of policy he will reject conditions which do not meet his own policies.

The uncertainty puts practitioners in a difficult situation. It will be resolved in the future, either by the House of Lords changing rules in respect of planning obligations or the Secretary of State altering his advice. In the meantime, the best advice to practitioners in the appeal situation is to structure their planning obligations so that they comply with the circular.

8.6   Government advice: Circular 16/91

Circular 16/91 offers government advice on planning obligations, their contents and limitations. Paragraphs B8 and B9 set out the Secretary of State's views on the required tests.

> B8.   The test of the reasonableness of seeking a planning obligation from an applicant for planning permission depends on whether what is required:
> (1) is needed to enable the development to go ahead, for example the provision of adequate access or car parking; or
> (2) in the case of financial payment, will contribute to meeting the cost of providing such facilities in the near future; or

(3) is otherwise so directly related to the proposed development and to the use of the land after its completion, that the development ought not to be permitted without it, e.g. the provision, whether by the applicant or by the authority at the applicant's expense, of car parking in or near the development, of reasonable amounts of open space related to the development, or of social, educational, recreational, sporting or other community provision the need for which arises from the development; or

(4) is designed in the case of mixed development to secure an acceptable balance of uses; or to secure the implementation of local plan policies for a particular area or type of development [e.g. the inclusion of an element of affordable housing in a larger residential development]; or

(5) is intended to offset the loss of or impact on any amenity or resource present on the site prior to development, for example in the interests of nature conservation. The Department welcomes the initiatives taken by some developers in creating nature reserves, planting trees, establishing wildlife ponds and providing other nature conservation benefits. This echoes the Government's view in 'This Common Inheritance' (Cm 1200) that local authorities and developers should work together in the interest of preserving the natural environment.

Planning obligations can therefore relate to land, roads or buildings other than those covered by the planning permission, provided that there is a direct relationship between the two. But they should not be sought where this connection does not exist or is too remote to be considered reasonable.

B9.   If what is required passes one of the tests set out in the preceding paragraph, a further test has to be applied. This is whether the extent of what is required is fairly and reasonably related in scale and kind to the proposed development. Thus a developer may reasonably be expected to pay for or contribute to the cost of infrastructure which would not have been necessary but for his development, but his payments should be directly related in scale to the benefit which the proposed development will derive from the facilities to be provided. So, for example, a developer may reach agreement with an infrastructure undertaker to bring forward in time a project which is already programmed but is some years from implementation.

8.7   Planning obligation open to challenge

A challenge to a planning obligation which is tendered at an inquiry can cause difficulties, whether or not the inspector accepts the planning obligation as a material consideration. Either of the parties involved in the appeal or an aggrieved third party can make an application to the High Court under s 288 to set aside the decision on a point of law (see Chapter 12). Although the courts will strive to give effect to such obligations, the result of such a High Court hearing could be to quash the grant of the planning permission. Few developers will wish to begin a development until the issue of the planning permission is beyond doubt and such an application will therefore cause a considerable delay.

If the decision goes the other way and planning permission is refused because the inspector does not accept the planning obligation, the developer may wish to appeal himself to overturn the refusal. If the decision is quashed, there is a real possibility that an inquiry might have to be re-opened and considerable time will elapse even after the High Court decision before the new permission is issued or refused. Two to three years is not uncommon.

The costs factor should also be borne in mind. While in the planning procedure itself parties are normally expected to pay their own costs unless they behave unreasonably, once a matter is referred to the High Court the ordinary rules as to costs apply and a losing party will be almost always required to pay the winning party's costs in the usual way.

8.8   The nature and effect of planning obligations

Planning obligations are deeds with special properties as set out in s 106 of the Act. In some ways they operate as ordinary contracts, in others they do not. The most important property of a planning obligation is that it will run with the land in its entirety, although not all parts of the site are necessarily bound by every covenant. Thus the original parties and successors in title will be bound.

A party entering into a contract can only bind his own interests and successor interests. In the normal way this will not bind prior or superior interests. A tenant cannot bind the landlord without the landlord's agreement and a mortgagee entering into possession under a mortgage executed prior to a planning obligation will take free of it. In the normal way, an inspector or the local authority will require the agreement of superior and prior interests in order to ensure that the agreement will remain effective.

The obligation is required to conform to the provisions of s 106 (9) in order to be effective. These are mandatory requirements and failure to comply may well render the obligations ineffective.

Positive planning obligations run with the land as do negative covenants. They can be enforced by the local authority who do not need to own adjacent land which benefits from the covenants. Successors in title can thus find themselves bound in respect of onerous positive covenants to pay money or carry out work. No application to the Lands Tribunal to vary or release negative covenants in planning agreements made under the new provisions is possible (s 106A(10) of the Act), but future appeals to the Secretary of State are possible (s 106B of the Act). The local authority are in a privileged position as regards enforcement. They will be able to enforce an obligation against a covenanting party (unless the deed provides otherwise). They also have two further methods of enforcing a planning obligation: injunctions or carrying out the work in default. In respect of injunctions (s 106(5) of the Act) the position is not the same as that in ordinary contractual situations. There is clear authority that a local authority can use their powers to apply for an injunction without necessarily exhausting other remedies available. In other words in an appropriate case an injunction could be sought to enforce a planning obligation even though the breach might at the same time be a breach of the conditions attached to the planning permission which would entitle the local authority also to issue a breach of condition prosecution or an enforcement notice.

A local authority are not normally required to give an undertaking in damages for an interlocutory injunction (*Kirklees Metropolitan Borough Council v*

Wickes Building Supplies Ltd [1993] AC 227). Moreover, because the local authority are acting in the public interest the normal rules for assessing the balance of convenience on interlocutory injunctions do not apply, ie financial advantage or the status quo will not be used as a guideline. In a clear case of breach of a planning obligation, the local authority may obtain an injunction despite the fact that it may cause hardship to the landowner or developer.

The local authority also have power under s 106(6) of the Act to enter on to the land concerned to carry out the works required by a positive obligation and to recover the costs against any party against whom the obligation is enforceable. The power to charge such expenses against the land has not yet been brought into force and the Department of the Environment have indicated that they have no immediate plans to do so (Circular 16/91, para A10). However, the cost is recoverable as a civil debt. Local authorities have in the past been reluctant to enter land to carry out works under parallel powers in respect of enforcement notices and this power is therefore likely to be used sparingly. Local authorities have first to incur the expenditure out of their own budgets and then to defend the expenditure as reasonable if a claim for repayment is resisted. All in all, then, the provisions of a planning agreement should not be lightly entered into. Full consideration needs to be given to the total impact, since the local authority have ample powers to ensure compliance.

A planning obligation can be amended at any time by agreement between the parties. If agreement cannot be reached, planning obligations may be varied under s 106A and 106B after five years from the date of the deed (as currently prescribed) by a party to the deed or his successor in title making a formal application to the local authority. If this is refused, he may appeal to the Secretary of State for the Environment. As five years has not yet elapsed since the introduction of this provision, no deeds have been executed which meet the five-year threshold. There have been no applications and no appeals under this section but it is anticipated that these will be dealt with on planning grounds in the same way as a variation of condition.

8.9   Difference between planning agreements and unilateral obligations

Section 106 draws no clear distinction between planning agreements between the local authority and landowner and unilateral obligations. Both operate in the same way and both are subject to the same enforcement regime. In practice, however, one important distinction is that in a deed between the local authority and the landowner it is perfectly possible for both sides to make covenants. In a common situation, the owner would covenant to pay a sum of money to the local authority and the local authority would covenant to build and maintain certain public facilities. However, with a unilateral obligation only the landowner is covenanting and the local authority cannot have responsibilities and obligations foisted upon them by the landowner.

This can be dealt with by the landowner covenanting to do certain acts only after the local authority has done certain others. For example the landowner might covenant to pay a sum of money to the local authority only after it had erected the car parking and made it available for public use or on some other trigger event. This clearly has limitations. If what is involved is a complex scenario where real co-operation is required on both sides, it may be better to avoid an over-complex unilateral obligation open to argument that it will not work in practice. In these cases a *Grampian* condition (see para 7.7) prohibiting certain things until some trigger event occurs might be suitable. Or the landowner might make a negative covenant not to carry out the development until car parking arrangements have been agreed with the local authority. Care is needed, however, to avoid jumping out of the frying pan into the fire. The lawyers will be blamed if at a later stage the local authority has an effective way of holding up the development because of the drafting of the unilateral obligation.

8.10   Drafting points

Attention to detail in drafting is essential. Badly drafted agreements may effectively blight the land to which they relate or fail to achieve their purpose.

8.10.1   Parties

For a planning obligation, the enforcing party will nearly always be the local authority to whom the application was addressed. There may be occasions when both the county council and a district council will wish to be a party to an agreement or the county council rather than the district council. Great care should be taken in identifying who is to be the enforcing authority.

On the developer's side, the most important determining factor will be who is able effectively to bind the land. A local authority or an inspector is unlikely to accept a deed which will be ineffective to bind the land and thus incapable of binding successors in title. While there may therefore be academic argument as to the legal scope of the expression 'interested in land' in s 106 of the Act, for practical purposes all interests in the land will need to be caught by the deed. With freehold land not subject to mortgage, the freeholder alone need be a party to the deed. The local authority can be satisfied that even if it is subsequently mortgaged or a lease created, the inferior interests will be bound.

However, if the appellant holds a leasehold interest or the land is already subject to a mortgage, there may be a requirement for the freeholder to enter into the agreement as well as the leaseholder and to obtain a formal deed of postponement from the mortgagee if the latter does not actually enter into the deed. In most cases the freeholder will already have consented to the development under the terms of the lease and may believe that his freehold reversion will be enhanced by the development proposed. Mortgage companies are usually co-operative, particularly if the provisions do not contain onerous financial terms.

If the leaseholder alone executes the deed, the danger for the enforcing authority is that the obligations will bind the person who makes them and his successors in so far as his own interest and inferior interests are concerned but it will not bind other pre-existing interests nor superior interests. There is therefore always a risk that if the lease ceases to exist, perhaps because it is surrendered by the tenant or a prior mortgagee comes into possession, the obligations will cease to have any effect.

Difficulties can arise where a distant freeholder simply cannot be bothered to consider the proposals or take legal advice, even at the tenant's expense. If the provisions are relatively short term and the appellant is a residential leaseholder under a long lease, it may be thought that the chances of default are very small. However, rather than presenting an imperfect obligation at appeal, particularly if the local authority will not co-operate on their side, it may be better to deal with the situation by way of *Grampian* condition. This effectively prevents the development being either begun or occupied until certain things happen.

A further difficulty arises when the appellant has no interest in the land at all or, more likely, has a contract to buy the land subject to conditions, one of which may be the grant of planning permission or an option to purchase subject to similar conditions. The conditional contract itself will have to be examined. Has a beneficial interest passed? However, planners are not highly alert to the nicer points of land law, and many disputed contracts find their way to the courts.

The object of an obligation is to reassure the inspector that what the appellant has promised to do he will do. A planning obligation subject to any kind of doubt will not achieve its objective. This situation should be dealt with at the contractual stage by ensuring that the vendor will enter into the obligation if required to do so.

Occupiers under personal licences or even unlawful occupiers can pose difficulties. While their right to remain on the land may be tenuous, the enforcing authority will want to ensure that compliance will not be thwarted or made more difficult by such occupiers. A lawful occupier should ideally be a party to the deed, even where his interest is very short term. It may be possible to incorporate a requirement that the superior interest will see that such occupiers leave the site if they are unco-operative. Unlawful occupiers may also pose a practical problem, particularly if they are only occupying part of the site. This can also be dealt with by appropriate provisions within the sale document itself.

An up-to-date office copy entry may be required to assure the inspector that there are no subsequent entries which affect the title. Immediately on execution, a copy of a unilateral undertaking should be given to the local authority to register as a local land charge.

8.10.2   Recitals

Recitals merit careful attention. They should establish in clear terms the status of the parties and the planning purpose of the obligation. If the obligation fulfils a policy requirement of the development plan, this should be stated. The recitals should make it immediately clear that the provisions are both within the precise meaning of s 106 of the Act and 'reasonable', being in accordance with local policies and government advice.

8.10.3   Operational clauses

Section 106(9) of the Act includes a formal requirement that the obligation must be in the form of a deed and also identifies other requirements:

106(9) A planning obligation may not be entered into except by an instrument executed as a deed which—
(a) states that the obligation is a planning obligation for the purposes of this section;
(b) identifies the land in which the person entering into the obligation is interested;
(c) identifies the person entering into the obligation and states what his interest in the land is; and
(d) identifies the local planning authority by whom the obligation is enforceable.

The deed should comply strictly with this subsection so that there is no doubt that the formalities have been observed. This subsection also provides a useful checklist for those drafting the document.

8.10.4   Coming into effect

The provisions of the Law of Property (Miscellaneous Provisions) Act 1989 should be borne in mind during drafting. The document must be complete in itself and not come into effect prematurely. This will normally mean including a provision that it does not come into effect until it has been dated. It is also essential that the covenants in the deed do not come into effect unless planning permission is granted and implemented. There is seldom justification for allowing an obligation to come into effect before planning permission is granted, except perhaps where sums are to be paid for the local authority's legal fees in relation to the deed. However, in complex agreements there may be covenants which come into effect immediately, some effective on grant of planning permission and some effective on implementation. If a provision on coming into force is overlooked, restrictions may bite and sums of money become payable even though a developer had decided not to pursue the scheme, either because he has abandoned it altogether or because he has decided to apply for a new permission.

In some circumstances the local authority may feel that once the principle of a development is established on appeal, certain provisions should come into effect immediately, irrespective of whether a permission is implemented, if at all. Such a deed is onerous and rarely justifiable. It is possible that planning permission may be granted on appeal but subject to conditions which are unacceptable. If the obligation is subject to planning permission being issued and implemented, the developer has the choice as to whether to proceed or not. If it is subject only to the grant of planning permission, the developer could be saddled with an effective obligation and yet have a planning permission which he does not want to implement. This can be avoided by careful drafting, ie annexing conditions which *are* acceptable to the deed and defining them accordingly.

If it is necessary to accept an obligation dependent only on the grant of planning permission, the deed should not become effective until the six-week period allowable for application to the High Court has elapsed and any proceedings issued within this period have been dealt with. This can be achieved by defining 'the planning permission' as a valid planning permission and ensuring it covers all eventualities.

8.10.5   Miscellaneous drafting points

If substantial works are required, it may be necessary to include a bonding arrangement or to ensure that the development cannot be begun until satisfactory arrangements for the works to be carried out are in place. Consider this carefully – it will bind the land, resist if too large.

If there is more than one party on the landowning side, consideration should be given as to whether the covenants should be joint and several or whether liability should be restricted to the owner of each part of the land.

A planning obligation should include requirements as to notice and to the determination of disputes by an expert or arbitration as appropriate. If financial payments are included, consideration should be given to the VAT position, and the current Customs and Excise Statement of Practice may be referred to.

Finally, the position of the local authority as a public body should be borne in mind. They cannot fetter their discretion for the future and would have difficulty in agreeing not to exercise their powers.

8.10.6   Timing

Ideally, the planning obligation should be in final draft and submitted to the local authority for their comments well before the hearing or inquiry, whether or not the local authority are a party. In this way any particular points they raise can be dealt with and the draft amended if necessary. There is then no risk of falling into technical arguments at the hearing; the clauses which the local authority do not accept can be clearly identified and explained to the inspector. In practice this is not always possible. Work on drafting the obligation will continue during the course of the inquiry or hearing as the planning issues are developed. It is not unusual for an inspector to make it clear that he views some elements differently from the appellant or the local authority. In the course of evidence, particularly at public inquiries, concessions are made and difficulties exposed. In these cases it may not be possible to finalise or execute a planning obligation before the hearing.

Every effort should be made to finalise the deed before the close of the hearing so that its terms can be explained to the inspector and discussed. Even though the executed copy may not arrive until after the close of the hearing he can satisfy himself as to form and content. Before the close of the hearing inspectors should be given a clear indication of when the executed deed will be sent in. No changes should be made after the close of the hearing since this could be seen as prejudicial to either party and may result in the re-opening of the hearing. If changes cannot be avoided, they should be notified to the other side promptly and before sending the document in. If the changes are contentious, they may undermine the acceptability of the obligation.

Worked Example 1*

SECTION 106 AGREEMENT

This Deed is made on the Thirtieth day of May 1994 between East Loamshire District Council of the Town Hall New Town in East Loamshire (hereinafter called 'the Council') of the first part and Riverside House Limited whose registered office is at Smith Road London EC4 (hereinafter called 'the Company') of the second part

WHEREAS

(a) the Council is the local planning authority for the area within which the Company Land is situated;

(b) the Company has submitted an application for planning permission to the Council and has lodged an appeal under section 78 of the Town and Country Planning Act 1990 against the Council's refusal to grant the planning permission;

(c) the Council has entered into this deed to secure construction and dedication of the Riverside Walk in accordance with policy RW3 of the Council's adopted Local Plan in the event that the planning permission is granted on appeal;

(d) the Company is the freehold owner of the Company Land.

NOW THIS DEED WITNESSETH AS FOLLOWS:

1. DEFINITIONS

'the Company Land' means: the land edged in red on the plan annexed hereto

'the Planning Permission' means: the planning permission relating to the Company Land granted pursuant to the application submitted to the Council by the Company on 15 December 1993 and registered under reference number SL506

'the Riverside Walk' means: the works and specifications set out in Schedule One hereto

The expressions 'the Council' and 'the Company' shall include their respective successors in title and assigns.

2. Planning Obligation

This deed and the obligations herein are made pursuant to section 106 of the Town and Country Planning Act 1990 and

This Worked Example is primarily for illustrative purposes and should not be used as a precedent.

(a) the obligations are planning obligations for the purposes of the said section 106;

(b) the Company is interested in the Company Land as proprietor with absolute title registered at HM Land Registry under title number ELS1062;

(c) the obligations are undertaken by the Company in its capacity as freehold owner of the Company Land;

(d) the obligations undertaken by the Company in this deed shall be enforceable by the Council as local planning authority for the area of the Company Land.

3. CONDITIONAL UPON IMPLEMENTATION

It is hereby agreed and declared that the obligations under this deed will not have effect unless

(a) the planning permission shall have been granted; and

(b) the planning permission has been implemented by the carrying out of a material operation pursuant to section 56(4)(a) to (e) of the Town and Country Planning Act 1990.

4. Council Covenants

The Council hereby covenants with the Company that it will carry out and comply with its obligations set out herein and in the schedules hereto.

5. Company Obligations

The Company hereby covenants with the Council that it will carry out and comply with its obligations set out herein and in the schedules hereto.

6. General

(a) For the avoidance of doubt the provisions of this deed (other than those contained in this clause) shall not have any effect until this document has been dated.

(b) Covenants on behalf of the parties hereto to be observed and performed under this deed shall be treated as local land charges and registered at the Local Land Charges Registry for the purposes of the Local Land Charges Act 1975.

(c) Nothing in this deed shall prejudice or affect the rights powers duties and obligations of the Council in the exercise by it of its statutory functions.

(d) No person shall be liable in respect of a breach of any obligation after it has disposed of its entire interest in the land in respect of which such breach occurs PROVIDED THAT any such person shall remain liable in respect of any breach occurring prior to such disposal.

SCHEDULE ONE

THE RIVERSIDE WALK

[Plan and Specification]

SCHEDULE TWO

THE COMPANY OBLIGATIONS

1. The Company shall

   (a) construct the Riverside Walk at its own cost to the reasonable satisfaction of the Council;

   (b) upon receipt of a certificate from the Council in accordance with paragraph 1 of Schedule Three dedicate the Riverside Walk to the Council;

   (c) on receipt of the Council's certificate in accordance with (b) above pay to the Council the sum of £100,000 as a commuted maintenance payment for the Riverside Walk.

2. The Company shall not occupy or permit the occupation of the office building whose construction is authorised by the Planning Permission until the Riverside Walk has been dedicated in accordance with paragraph 1(b) above and the commuted sum has been paid in accordance with 1(c) above without the written consent of the Council.

SCHEDULE THREE

THE COUNCIL OBLIGATIONS

1. The Council shall at the Company's request inspect the Riverside Walk and issue a certificate that it has been completed in accordance with this deed such certificate not to be unreasonably refused or delayed.

2. Having issued the certificate in accordance with the preceding paragraph and upon receipt of the payment mentioned in paragraph (c) of Schedule Two the Council shall release the Company from any further liability of whatsoever nature in relation to the Riverside Walk.

IN WITNESS WHEREOF this deed has been duly executed as a deed

EXECUTED BY THE SAID COUNCIL
IN THE PRESENCE OF

THE COMMON SEAL OF RIVERSIDE HOUSE
LIMITED was hereunto affixed
in the presence of

Worked Example 2*

UNILATERAL OBLIGATION

UNDER SECTION 106

This Undertaking is made on 1 August 1994 by Riverside House Limited whose registered office is at Smith Road London EC4 (hereinafter called 'the Company') for the benefit of East Loamshire District Council (hereinafter called 'the Council') of the Town Hall New Town East Loamshire

WHEREAS

(a) the Council is the local planning authority for the area within which the Company Land is situated;

(b) the Company has submitted an application for the Planning Permission to the Council and has lodged an appeal under section 78 of the Town and Country Planning Act 1990 against the Council's refusal to grant the planning permission;

(c) the Council's adopted local plan contains a policy numbered RW3 requiring the formation of a Riverside Walk along the northern banks of the River Loam when adjacent redevelopment takes place and the Company acknowledges that it is necessary that the provision of the Riverside Walk should be secured in the event that Planning Permission is granted in the manner hereinafter appearing;

(d) the Company is the freehold owner of the Company Land and has resolved to give this undertaking to the Council.

NOW THIS DEED WITNESSETH AS FOLLOWS:

1. Definitions

'the Company Land' means: the land edged in red on the plan annexed hereto

'the planning permission' means: the planning permission relating to the Company Land granted pursuant to the application submitted to the Council by the Company on 15 December 1993 and registered under reference number SL506

'the Riverside Walk' means: the works and specifications set out in Schedule One hereto

The expressions 'the Council' and 'the Company' shall include their respective successors in title and assigns.

This Worked Example is primarily for illustrative purposes and should not be used as a precedent.

2. Planning Obligation

This deed and the obligations herein are made pursuant to section 106 of the Town and Country Planning Act 1990 and

    (a) the obligations are planning obligations for the purposes of the said section 106;

    (b) the Company is interested in the Company Land as proprietor with absolute title registered at HM Land Registry under title number ELS 1062;

    (c) the obligations are undertaken by the Company in its capacity as freehold owner of the Company Land;

    (d) the obligations undertaken by the Company in this undertaking shall be enforceable by the Council as local planning authority for the area of the Company Land.

3. CONDITIONAL UPON IMPLEMENTATION

It is hereby declared that the obligations under this deed will not have effect unless

    (a) the planning permission shall have been granted; and

    (b) the planning permission has been implemented by the carrying out of a material operation pursuant to section 56(4)(a) to (e) of the Town and Country Planning Act 1990.

4. Company Obligations

The Company hereby covenants with the Council that it will carry out and comply with its obligations set out herein and in Schedule Two hereto.

5. General

    (a) For the avoidance of doubt the provisions of this deed (other than those contained in this clause) shall not have any effect until this document has been dated.

    (b) Covenants on behalf of the Company to be observed and performed under this deed shall be treated as local land charges and registered at the Local Land Charges Registry for the purposes of the Local Land Charges Act 1975.

    (c) Nothing in this deed shall prejudice or affect the rights powers duties and obligations of the Council in the exercise by it of its statutory functions

    (d) No person shall be liable in respect of a breach of any obligation after it has disposed of its entire interest in the land in respect of which such breach occurs PROVIDED THAT any such person shall remain liable in respect of any breach occurring prior to such disposal.

SCHEDULE ONE

THE RIVERSIDE WALK

[Plan and specification]

SCHEDULE TWO

THE COMPANY OBLIGATIONS

1. The Company shall
    (a) construct the Riverside Walk within five years of the implementation
         of the planning permission in accordance with Clause 3(b) hereof at its
         own cost in accordance with the specification;
    (b) after the completion of the Riverside Walk in accordance with paragraph
         1(a) above dedicate the Riverside Walk to the Council for open space
         purposes within three months of being requested so to do by the Council;
    (c) within three months of the dedication in accordance with paragraph 1(b)
         above pay to the Council the sum of £100,000 as a commuted
         maintenance payment for the Riverside Walk.

IN WITNESS WHEREOF this deed has been duly executed

THE COMMON SEAL OF RIVERSIDE HOUSE
LIMITED was hereunto affixed
in the presence of

Chapter 9

Dealing with the Public

9.1 Introduction

While the local authority and the appellant are the main protagonists in a planning appeal, other people and bodies have an important role to play. A 'public inquiry' is, after all, an inquiry into the merits of proposals which the public have a right to attend. Experienced practitioners will know of cases where, unexpectedly, third parties have played a pivotal role. Whatever attention was given to this aspect at the planning application stage, it certainly needs close attention by planning professionals once an appeal is lodged. This is an area where inexperienced practitioners may fail to achieve the same level of expertise as in preparing the more technical aspects of the case.

The view is often taken that an appeal is in a way akin to a civil law suit and it is therefore wrong to seek to speak to or influence potential witnesses. This is not strictly true in a planning appeal which is an administrative process but care needs to be taken when dealing with third parties. This chapter sets out the role of third parties, whose rights must be respected at all times. It is important to bear in mind that the inspector will wish to hear the views of all those who have relevant information to give him.

Written representations, whether made within the written representation appeal procedure or as written submissions to the inspector to be considered as part of the hearing of an appeal, offer little scope for direct intervention. The appellant's best course is normally to deal with such representations in his own evidence. This chapter considers primarily cases where a hearing is held.

Witnesses at public inquiries are protected by the Witnesses (Public Inquiries) Protection Act 1892 which makes it an offence to threaten, punish, damage or injure or attempt the same in respect of evidence given or to be given. This Act was recently considered in the case of *Fulham Football Club v Cabra Estates* [1993] 1 PLR 29 where it was held that there was no objection of public policy to an agreement whereby a party to a commercial transaction covenanted not to give evidence at a public inquiry. Such an agreement, however, could not require false evidence to be given or render a witness summons ineffective.

9.2   Who may make representations?

Three main categories of people are considered in this chapter. The first covers those with certain legal interests in the appeal site (ie freeholders and leaseholders whose leases have more than seven years to run) and agricultural tenants. These people are 'statutory parties' and have a right to make representations and to appear at an inquiry. Whether the appellant owns the land or not, such people are directly affected by the proposals and in most cases have good local knowledge. The inspector is required by s 71 of the Act to take their views into account.

The second category comprises bodies and persons who have been consulted by the local authority and have made representations. In some cases individual local councillors may become involved independently of the formal local authority position. The category is a large catchall and includes local bodies such as the parish council and amenity associations, involving national organisations such as the Ramblers Association. It also includes more formal bodies such as English Nature, the Highway Authority, government departments, transport authorities, education authorities and the like. In any particular application, one or more may be important. The views of these parties are often incorporated into the local authority's case, and a great deal of weight will be accorded to their views. The inspector will wish to have the benefit of their specialist knowledge and general experience in reaching his decision.

The third category covers ordinary members of the public, ie neighbours and those who have simply heard about the appeal and wish to express their views.

9.2.1   General principles

A number of general principles will apply to all these representations. It is important to ensure that all the representations that were made to the local authority at the application stage have been collected. New representations may be made as a result of the appeal procedures and should be dealt with as they arise. It is important, however, to take stock of those who made representations at the planning stage.

If there are many representations, it may assist to produce summary sheets dividing the representations into categories and analysing them according to the issues raised. This will enable a preliminary analysis of what the issues are perceived to be and where the objections lie, and provide in a collated form information as to numbers of objectors according to issue. Figure 9.1 gives an example of a proposed development on a rural site (shown on the map) and a Schedule of representations, broken down by type of objection.

If petitions have been produced, signatures and addresses should be analysed and verified. It may be useful to assign objectors or those signing petitions a number and enter the address on a composite local map. This enables one to see at a glance the centres of opposition and whether they are likely to be affected by the proposals. If petitions are received both for and against the proposals, cross-check carefully, as people do not always read what they sign.

An appellant may be uneasy at having to deal with such representations, feeling that most people are objecting for the sake of it, with no planning reasons underpinning them. While it is true that strength of opposition does not mean that an application ought to be refused, the inspector will pay careful attention to what people say. It will certainly be counterproductive to attempt to belittle representations genuinely made by concerned individuals and bodies, whatever the appellant feels about their objective validity.

A separate section of evidence should deal specifically with representations, either individually or on an issue-by-issue basis. The inspector in his decision letter will catalogue the representations made to him by third parties and the weight he attaches to what they say. A careful appellant will take stock of the situation beforehand and deal with such representations systematically.

9.3   Negotiating with objectors

The inspector will deal with the appeal as he finds it on the day. If, therefore, objectors withdraw their objection, the objections will carry no further weight with him. The fact that objections have been withdrawn not only means that the objections are not before the inspector and cannot influence the decision but also gives the inspector a comfortable feeling that things are moving towards a consensus.

It is legitimate for an appellant to consider the objections made by individuals and bodies and whether he can satisfy them that their concerns are either unfounded or can be dealt with. If the Ramblers Association are concerned that development may involve the closure of a footpath, the appellant may agree a diversion of that footpath which may be acceptable and permit them to withdraw the objection. Neighbours may be concerned by noise and disturbance. It may be possible to agree with them noise attenuation measures or hours of limitation which will meet their concerns.

Objectors are a loose cannon because the appellant cannot know what they will say. Unless their objections are so utterly unreasonable that he is fairly confident the inspector will pay them no regard, time and energy spent in meeting and dealing with objectors will be time well spent. A person who purports to speak for others, ie that he represents a parish council or residents' association, should have documentary evidence of his authority. If he does not, it may be worth exploring it before he gives evidence. Occasionally representatives act without knowing what the body's views are, and such a witness can be discredited, at least as far as he purports to represent the views of others.

Even if objectors do not withdraw their objections, it will be helpful for the appellant to have gained a complete understanding of their case. He can bring evidence to show that he did meet them and offered reasonable assurances.

9.3.1   Public meetings

A public meeting is sometimes suggested as a way of dealing with third parties. The author strongly recommends that you do not hold a public meeting under

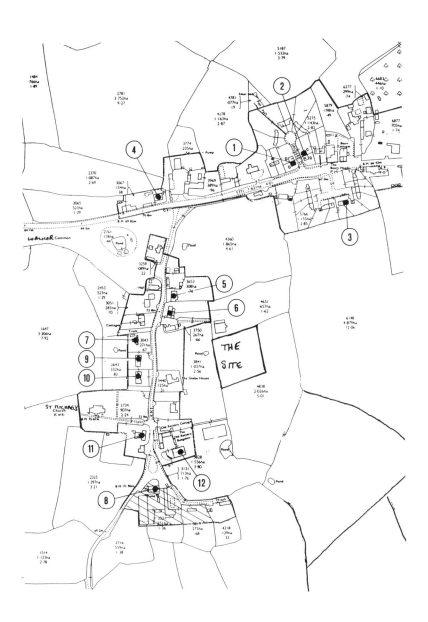

Figure 9.1. Proposed development on a rural site and type of objection.

© Ordnance Survey

SCHEDULE OF REPRESENTATIONS

	Name and address	VA	T	ECA	SOC	OVDL
(1)	J Plumb 1 Orchard Close	x	x		x	
(2)	W Peachy 14 Orchard Close	x	x	x		x
(3)	L Snow S Winters		x	x	x	
(4)	M Hay The Croft			x		x
(5)	J Tor Hill Farm	x	x	x		
(6)	D House Home Farm		x		x	
(7)	F Foot Walks Cottage	x	x			x
(8)	C Black White Farm		x	x	x	x
(9)	L House Home Cottage	x		x		x
(10)	D Jekyll Hyde Cottage	x	x		x	
(11)	E Green Virginia Cottage	x	x			x
(12)	L Parsons The Old Rectory	x		x	x	

Key
VA   Visual amenity
T   Traffic
ECA   Effect on conservation area
SOC   Site is open countryside
OVDL   Outside village development limits

any circumstances. Numbers cannot be controlled, the most vociferous take the stage and nobody listens to anyone else. It is better to arrange to meet small groups of people and quietly discuss their concerns, preferably over a cup of tea. Most people are more reasonable when spoken to individually than at a mass meeting.

9.3.2   Supporters

Those who are likely to support the proposal should not be neglected, whether they have written in or whether it has been ascertained that they are not averse to the proposals. People always object more readily than they support, but the gaps in the ranks of the objectors should be considered. Did the parish council object? If not, is it possible that they will be prepared to come and support the application, if approached sensibly? Immediate neighbours who support the application are worth ten people half a mile away who object but will be unaffected by the development. Appellants too often focus on objectors without giving due consideration to supporters. In reality, it may be easier to gain supporters than to win over objectors.

If the appeal is proceeding by way of informal hearing or by written representation, then it is usually adequate for such a person to write a letter of support. The person can be given the name, address and reference. If there is to be a public inquiry, letters of support are also welcome and will be given due weight by the inspector. It is useful to have one or two supporters appearing in person to provide a counterbalance to objectors.

9.3.3   Petitions

Petitions or identical letters churned out by photocopier or word processor and signed by different people should be avoided by objectors. When all these are collected, it becomes apparent that the weight attached to each individual document or signature must be very little. Moreover, it gives an air of collusion. Petitions received against the proposals should be scrutinised. The terms are often inadequate or misleading. Those signing them are often not in a position to express a view on the information given in the petition itself. Analysis of names and addresses is useful. If skulduggery is suspected someone will have to go through the electoral register and check who is registered as resident at that address. One of the signatories often appears in person. This may be one of the few occasions to cross-examine a third party, particularly if he shows no real understanding of the petition.

9.4   Interference with third parties

It is always wrong to attempt to prevent a third party from expressing his opinion. It is for the inspector under the rules to decide whom he will hear and how long he will give them. It is suggested that those who wish to make representations, either in support or against, should do so individually in their own words. This carries much more authority, even though the handwriting is bad or the spelling leaves something to be desired.

Third parties, whether or not legally represented, must be treated with courtesy and consideration. Neighbours may feel that development prejudices their peace and quiet or the value of their properties. These are important considerations for them. Professional advisers are duty bound to deal politely and quietly with such parties, however emotional they are. It is right to do so; parties should also bear in mind that failure to do so will reflect adversely on their case. If the client or his non-professional representatives cannot be trusted to maintain a professional, courteous approach, they should certainly be dissuaded from taking any part in this aspect of the appeal.

If existing advisers or the client have been very much involved with objectors at the application stage, there may be benefit now in bringing in a new team to deal with the objectors, enabling a fresh start to be made. This may be beneficial not only in dealing with the objectors but also in seeing new ways of tackling problems. Moreover, in planning appeals, the professional practitioner may bring valuable negotiating skills to the team. If there is a substantial body of objection, however, an appellant should consider engaging a specialist consultancy firm to handle this side of the appeal in conjunction with the professional advisers.

9.5 At the hearing

At the opening of the inquiry, the inspector will ask who wishes to be heard and take their names. He will indicate when he intends to make space for them. This is often after the appellant and the local authority have presented their cases, but before the closing speeches. However, members of the public who wish to speak on the same day, because they have taken time off work or have other responsibilities, should be given every opportunity to do so. But if objectors are free to do so, they would be well advised to spend the time listening to the appeal as it is presented and to take advantage of the usual slot at the end. They will have heard all the arguments and be in a position to tailor their representation to deal particularly with points that have not been adequately answered in the course of the hearing.

Objectors often like to make their points and disappear and there may be considerable advantage in arranging for an evening session on the first or the second day of the inquiry. Members of the public can attend, and objections can be heard in a single session. Normally such objectors do not reappear thereafter and no question of intervening later in the process arises. There is a further advantage in hearing objectors at an early stage, as any points raised can be dealt with before the close of the appellant's case.

9.6 Asking questions

Objectors, particularly if they have handed in a written proof of evidence, are sometimes invited by the inspector to ask questions of the various witnesses.

There can be no objection to such a procedure. Inspectors have been known to ask objectors to let them know the questions they wish to put. The inspector will then put these questions to the witness as part of his own questioning. If there are a large number of objectors, this course of action has much to recommend it. It controls the repetitious questions that waste time and the inevitable difficulty that people have in distinguishing between statements and questions. This is entirely a matter for the inspector, although if it is likely to be a problem, there is no reason why the advocate should not raise the question with the inspector at the outset.

Where there are a number of objectors, inspectors often invite them to select a spokesperson to avoid a succession of repetitive evidence. A well-prepared appellant will know how such objectors can be marshalled into interest groupings, and if he has prepared the ground with objectors beforehand, he will be aware of the nature of such groupings. It may indeed be helpful for an appellant to prepare the ground in his preliminary discussions with objectors by setting up a formal dialogue with their representative body to enable objectors to feel comfortable in coming under the umbrella of a representative body.

9.7   Cross-examination of third party witnesses

The cross-examination of third party witnesses must be a decision for the advocate. If the ground has been properly prepared and representations have been dealt with specifically in the proofs of evidence, no cross-examination will be necessary.

The general rule that an advocate should not ask a question unless he knows the answer is a golden rule here. With third parties in inquiries, one does not know the answer and should avoid asking the question. There are, however, limited points where a witness can elucidate questions of fact or where, if he was a signatory to a petition where the objection has been proved by the evidence to be wholly unfounded, the unfounded objection can be highlighted. Even with third party witnesses called by the appellant, taking them beyond their proofs is fraught with danger. This does not arise with professional witnesses who understand the rules and the case they are presenting.

Chapter 10

Secretary of State Decisions

10.1 Introduction

Over 98 per cent of appeals are dealt with by inspectors who are able to make the decision themselves under the Town and Country Planning (Determination of Appeals by Appointed Persons) (Prescribed Classes) Regulations 1981. There are, however, a number of circumstances where cases will not be decided by an inspector but by the Secretary of State himself after receipt of a report from the inspector advising him of the circumstances and usually including a recommendation. This chapter deals with cases the Secretary of State will decide and the relevant procedure.

The first category of cases are appeals against refusal or non-determination of planning applications by a local authority under s 78 of the Town and Country Planning Act 1990 which the Secretary of State recovers for his own decision. These are cases which would otherwise be dealt with by inspectors. The second category is not appeals but applications for planning permission which are called in by the Secretary of State for decision by himself under s 77 of the Act. Since they follow the same procedure, they are mentioned here. Thirdly, listed building consent and conservation area consent appeals cannot in some circumstances be dealt with by inspectors. Fourthly, called-in listed building consent and conservation area consent applications. These are decided on a different basis from the one applying to planning permission and these differences are dealt with in Chapter 13. When decided by the Secretary of State, they will, however, follow the procedure set out in this chapter.

Figure 10.1 shows the rules and regulations relating to appeals determined by inspectors or the Secretary of State.

10.2 General points

Very few cases are decided by the Secretary of State. Such cases are either important or controversial in themselves or linked to another application which is to be dealt with by the Secretary of State. A number of applications are occasionally brought forward to the Secretary of State so that they can be dealt with together. The Inspectorate's report for the year ended 31 March 1994 indicates that only 245 planning appeals were decided by the Secretary of State and 99 applications were called in.

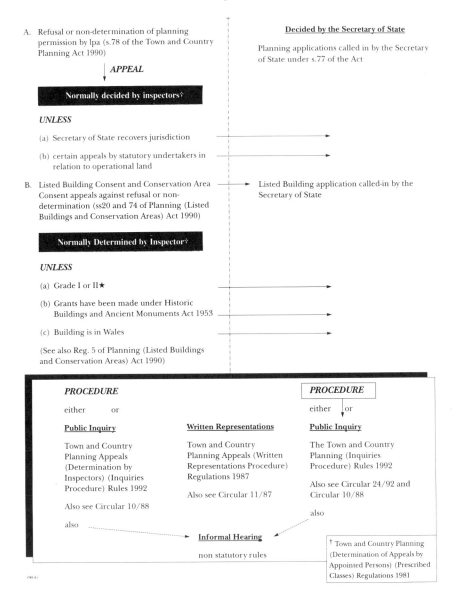

Figure 10.1. Planning appeals and call-in.

In many cases, the developer will know that the appeal will fall to be determined by the Secretary of State because it comes into one of the categories laid down. In other cases he will have a shrewd suspicion that the local authority or objectors will ask for the Secretary of State to take over the procedure. If it is inevitable or probable that this will be a Secretary of State decision, this will have been taken into account at the initial strategy stage. The applicant or appellant, as the case may be, will be prepared for the expense and delay which may result. However, an unexpected letter from the Secretary of State either directing the local authority not to grant planning permission for, say, 21 days (which is the normal prelude to a call in), or indicating that he has recovered jurisdiction is usually a bad sign for the developer. Until the Secretary of State exercises the power, it is always open to a party to write explaining the reasons why this should not be dealt with by the Secretary of State.

There are circumstances where an appellant or an applicant may actively welcome intervention by the Secretary of State. For instance, it may be apparent that it will be difficult to persuade an inspector to be politically adventurous in respect of say development in the national interest. The Secretary of State may take a more robust view. That was the case recently with a green belt development for Boss Trucks where the Secretary of State called in an application and granted planning permission for industrial development in the green belt, giving the very special circumstances relating to national factors as one of his reasons.

Once the Secretary of State has formally indicated that he will be dealing with the matter himself, the developer must either withdraw the application or appeal or carry on. In the majority of cases, a public inquiry will be needed for sufficient information to be available for a proper decision to be made by the Secretary of State. The inquiry will follow much the same course as when an inspector is taking the decision. However, after the inquiry a significant delay will follow while the inspector prepares his report and recommendations, submits them to the Secretary of State and the Secretary of State considers whether to accept the report and issues his decision. The Secretary of State's decision will be final, subject to an application to the High Court on a point of law.

10.3   Appeals recovered by the Secretary of State from the jurisdiction of inspectors

The criteria for recovery of jurisdiction were published in 'Planning: Appeals, Call in and Major Public Inquiries' (Cm 43, 1986). The following are the most important cases where the Secretary of State may recover jurisdiction:

(1) residential development of 150 or more houses;
(2) proposals for development of major importance having more than local significance;
(3) proposals giving rise to significant public controversy;
(4) proposals which raise important or novel issues of development control;
(5) retail development over 100,000 sq ft;

(6) proposals for significant development in the green belt;
(7) major proposals involving the winning and working of minerals;
(8) proposals which raise significant legal difficulties;
(9) proposals against which another government department has raised major objections; and
(10) cases which can be judged only in connection with a case over which inspectors have no jurisdiction.

The criteria only indicate appeals which may be recovered by the Secretary of State. A number of cases which might meet any particular criteria are not in fact recovered. Expressions such as 'giving rise to significant public controversy' must be seen in the national not the local context.

10.4   Called-in applications

In most cases applications made to the local authority will be determined by them. The Secretary of State, however, has an overall supervisory capacity and reserve powers to take the decision out of the local authority's hands The Secretary of State has indicated that he will intervene only when there are compelling reasons why the local authority ought not to make the decision. The basic principle of policy adopted by him is that there must be planning issues of more than local importance involved. The main categories of applications which can be called in are applications for planning permission, for approval required under a development order, applications for listed building consent and conservation area consent and certain applications concerning local authority's own development.

The Secretary of State has a wide discretion. His exercise of the power to call in (or more likely his failure to exercise the power) is difficult to challenge (*R v Secretary of State for the Environment ex p Newprop* [1983] JPL 386). Any challenge will have to be by judicial review on ordinary principles (see Chapter 14). The power is seldom needed if the local authority wishes to refuse the application. If an application is refused, the disappointed applicant can exercise his right to appeal and the Secretary of State can decide at that stage whether he wishes to deal with the appeal himself. As there is no third party right of appeal against the grant of planning permission, if the local authority wishes to grant an application, the only way that the matter can be brought before the Secretary of State is by a call-in at that stage. In order to prevent the local authority from granting a planning permission, it is usual in these cases for the Secretary of State to issue a holding direction under art 14 of the GDO directing the local authority not to decide the application within a certain number of days, giving him time to decide whether to issue the call-in direction.

Before the Secretary of State can consider whether to call in an application, it needs to be brought to the attention of the Department. This can happen in a number of ways. Development not in accordance with the development plan which the local authority do not propose to refuse must in the following circumstances be referred to the Department, allowing 21 days for a decision. A decision on call-in may be taken if the proposals include a development of more than 150 houses or flats or more than 10,000 sq metres of retail floorspace. Certain developments by a local authority may be called in and, most importantly, 'any other development which, by reason of its scale or nature or the location of the land, would significantly prejudice the implementation of the Development Plan's policies and proposals' (Town and Country Planning (Development Plans and Consultation) Direction 1992 (DoE Circular 19/92, Annex 3)).

The local authority is also required to notify the Secretary of State in respect of certain retail floorspace under the Town and Country (Shopping Development) (England and Wales No 2) Direction 1993. The calculation is complex but broadly speaking involves proposals for gross shopping floorspace of not less than 20,000 sq metres, or proposals for between 2,500 sq metres and 20,000 sq metres which when aggregated with other 'relevant shopping floorspace' as defined in the direction will bring the total relevant shopping floorspace for the area to over 20,000 sq m.

Finally, any interested party may write to the Department requesting the Secretary of State to call in an application. This could be the applicant himself, the local authority or third party objectors.

10.5 Listed building and conservation area consent

Similar provisions enable the Secretary of State both to call in such cases for his own decision or to recover jurisdiction on appeal from the inspector. What is at issue here is the importance of the building: appeals in respect of applications for Grade I and Grade II* buildings are automatically dealt with by the Secretary of State himself (Town and Country Planning (Determination of Appeals by Appointed Persons) (Prescribed Classes) Regulations 1981).

There is no formal requirement to submit applications for listed building consent and conservation area consent to the Secretary of State except in cases where the local authority are seeking consent. In most cases the Secretary of State will not take decisions out of the hands of the local authority even in the case of a Grade I building. A very contentious application, say for the demolition or partial demolition of a Grade I or Grade II* building, would undoubtedly be subject to opposition, particularly by English Heritage who would request it to be called in, a request likely to be granted.

10.6 Position of local authority and applicant after call-in

In a called-in application, the local authority are not defending their handling of the application. As they have not had a chance to refuse it, there are no reasons for refusal. The position of both parties is that they are assisting the Secretary of State in gathering sufficient information to reach a decision. This is quite different from an appeal, and the Secretary of State will give both his reasons for the call-in and a statement of issues at the beginning of the procedure. Both of the principal parties are therefore assisted in the preparation of the evidence, which is not confined to matters raised in the statement of issues.

10.7   Written representation cases

Because of the nature of these cases, the scope for the written representation procedure will be reduced. Often the very factors which required the decision to be taken by the Secretary of State will require a public inquiry to be held. However, the appellant or the local authority may suggest that the case should be dealt with by the written representation procedure, which is exactly as set out in Chapter 4 in relation to inspector determinations. However, the inspector will not make the decision but will report to the Secretary of State. The latter will issue a separate report on his determination and the reasons, indicating whether he accepts or not the inspector's recommendation. From the point of view of the appellant and local authority, there is little difference.

10.8   Public inquiries

The public inquiry will be held under rules different from those relating to public inquiries in cases where the inspector is making the decision. These rules are dealt with below. The general advice on handling inquiries and dealing with witnesses given in Chapter 6 relating to inquiries under an inspector are also relevant to Secretary of State inquiries.

The Secretary of State Rules govern such inquiries and Circular 24/92 gives information on them. The objective and the general thrust are similar to those where an inspector makes the decisions. Only the differences are highlighted in this chapter.

10.9   Additional dimension

It is an important feature of Secretary of State cases, and one largely responsible for the additional delay, that one has not only to convince an inspector of one's case (so that he is able to make a fully reasoned recommendation to the Secretary of State), but also the very knowledgeable civil servants in the Department of the Environment and possibly the minister himself. This can be of practical significance, as is illustrated by a case (unreported) involving a new settlement in Hampshire where the Secretary of State issued a letter indicating that he intended to grant planning permission, subject to clarification of various matters. He gave way to a successor before the responses could be considered. His successor then issued a letter indicating that he was minded to refuse the application and indeed did so.

10.10   The Rules

The Secretary of State Rules are framed to take account of the fact that a decision is made by the Secretary of State rather than the inspector and that an inquiry can come about not only as a result of an appeal but also as a result of a call-in.

10.10.1   Pre-inquiry meeting

The first major change from the Inspector Rules comes in r 5 and indicates the procedure for a pre-inquiry meeting. Because of the nature of Secretary of State appeals, it is likely that pre-inquiry meetings will be needed more often than with inspector appeals. The rules therefore make special provision for the holding of such meetings. In particular, the Secretary of State serves the parties with a notice of his intention to hold a pre-inquiry meeting and a statement of the matters about which he particularly wishes to be informed for the consideration of the called-in application or appeal. The statement of reasons is extremely important to all parties, particularly in a called-in application where there may be little public information as to the issues raised. Even if the application is dealt with by the Secretary of State because it falls into one of the contentious categories outlined earlier, the precise reasons given will enable the local authority and the applicant or appellant (as the case may be) to tailor precisely their statement of case and subsequent work.

Where another minister or government department has expressed a view in writing that the application should not be granted or granted only subject to conditions, the Secretary of State is required to include this in his statement and notify the relevant minister. In this way, if another government department have in effect triggered the matter being dealt with by the Secretary of State, they will know from the outset that they have an important part to play in dealing with the issues at the inquiry.

The local authority must publish in a local paper information on the pre-inquiry meeting and on the Secretary of State's statement. The pre-inquiry meeting, or the first pre-inquiry meeting, must be held not later than 16 weeks after the relevant date (the date of the Secretary of State's notice of intention to cause an inquiry to be held). Where a pre-inquiry meeting is to be held, the Secretary of State must give three weeks' notice of it to the local authority, the applicant/appellant and any other person whose attendance is desirable. To effect this notice the Secretary of State may require the local authority to publish, serve and post such notice of a pre-inquiry meeting.

10.10.2   Procedure at pre-inquiry meeting

The inspector presides at the pre-inquiry meeting, determines the matters to be discussed and the procedures to be followed (r 5(9)). He may require any person present who is behaving in a disruptive manner to leave and return only on such conditions as he specifies. The power is given to the inspector to hold further meetings if he requires.

10.10.3   Statements of case

Rule 6(3) provides the timetable for the serving of the statement of case. Where no pre-inquiry meeting is held and it is a referred application (ie a called-in application not an appeal), the appellant's statement of case is due six weeks after the relevant date, ie at the same time as the local authority. In the case of an appeal where no pre-inquiry meeting is held, the appellant's statements must be served nine weeks after the relevant date, ie three weeks after the local authority's statement of case. This is the same provision as for inspector cases.

A person who has indicated a wish to appear at the inquiry may also be required, within four weeks of being so required, to serve an outline statement on the Secretary of State, the appellant/applicant and the local authority.

Where there is a pre-inquiry meeting, both statements of case are due four weeks after the conclusion of the meeting. Copies of documents referred to may be requested of either side.

After receipt of the statements of case the Secretary of State or inspector may require further information which they will specify and such information shall be furnished to the other persons who have also issued statements of case. The local authority must allow access to these statements of case and documents referred to.

Unless he has already done so, the Secretary of State, in respect of a referred application, shall not later than 12 weeks from the relevant date serve a written statement of the matters he wishes to be informed about. This requirement is discretionary in the case of an appeal.

10.10.4   Calling of pre-inquiry meeting by inspector

Where the Secretary of State does not exercise his power under r 5 to call a pre-inquiry meeting, the inspector appointed to conduct the public inquiry may hold one if he thinks it desirable (r 7). Two weeks' written notice is required and r 5(9) applies, ie the inspector presides at the meeting.

10.10.5   Timetable

Where a pre-inquiry meeting is held, r 8 provides that the inspector may arrange a timetable for the proceedings and vary it from time to time, including fixing a date by which proofs of evidence and summaries shall be sent to him.

10.10.6   Notification of inquiry

The time periods allowed are slightly longer than for inspector cases. Unless such a date is impractical, a public inquiry must be fixed within 22 weeks of the relevant date (20 weeks in the case of inspector decisions) or eight weeks after conclusion of the pre-inquiry meeting, unless this is considered impractical. In practice, in any major inquiry more than eight weeks will be required between the pre-inquiry meeting and the opening of the inquiry, since proofs have to be exchanged three weeks before the opening of the inquiry. Until the Secretary of State's statement is received and discussed at the pre-inquiry meeting, the parties may not be able to finalise the work necessary. Four weeks' notice must be given of the inquiry date and inquiry arrangements unless a lesser period is agreed with the applicant/appellant and local authority. This is in line with the inspector rules.

Procedures regarding proofs of evidence, the inquiry and site inspection are the same as for inspector appeals.

10.10.7 Procedure after inquiry

Procedure after the inquiry is naturally different, since the inspector will not be taking the decision himself. Rule 16 provides for the inspector to make a report in writing to the Secretary of State which is to include his conclusions and his recommendations or reasons for not making a recommendation. If an assessor has taken part in the inquiry he will report to the inspector on the matters on which he was appointed to advise. The inspector is required to append a copy of the assessor's report to his own and state whether he agrees or disagrees, giving his reasons for disagreement.

10.10.8 Where the Secretary of State disagrees with the inspector

Additionally, r 16(4) makes provisions for steps to be taken at this stage if the Secretary of State disagrees with the inspector's conclusions. If after the close of an inquiry the Secretary of State differs from the inspector on a matter of fact which appears to be material to a conclusion reached by the inspector or takes into consideration new evidence or a new matter of fact or policy and for that reason, intends to disagree with the recommendation of the inspector, he is required to notify the persons entitled to appear at the inquiry of the circumstances and give them an opportunity of making written representations within three weeks. If he has taken new matters into consideration, he must ask such parties whether they wish the inquiry to be re-opened.

The parties need to bear in mind that the Secretary of State will not rubber stamp the inspector's conclusions. The decision is his and he can and indeed does on occasion take a radically different view from the inspector's. Although he will have received the inspector's conclusions and recommendations, the purpose of the inquiry held by the inspector was to enable all the evidence to be heard, tested and collated so that it could be presented to the Secretary of State in order for him to make his decision. This is a fertile ground for challenge to the High Court and is dealt with in Chapter 12.

Where the Secretary of State disagrees with the inspector's recommendations or intends to take a different view on questions of fact, he has power to re-open an inquiry. He may well do so if there have been significant changes which need to be examined and tested so that he can receive an additional report containing the results of the inspector's investigation and the views of all the parties. He is required to re-open the inquiry if asked by the developer or the local authority if he has taken into consideration any new evidence or a new matter of fact. The re-opened inquiry does not have to be before the same inspector. In some cases it may be sensible to continue with the same inspector because of his knowledge of the case; in others the Secretary of State may consider that a new inspector may be appropriate.

10.10.9   Decision letter

Rule 17 provides for notification of the decision. The Secretary of State's decision may be accompanied either by the inspector's report as a whole or by a statement of its conclusions and recommendations. The persons entitled to be notified of the decision are entitled to see a copy of that report on written application to the Secretary of State within four weeks of the date of the decision. Such persons may also inspect any other documents within a period of six weeks.

Particular problems may arise because of the delay between the inquiry closing and the Secretary of State issuing his decision. Because the decision must be made on the day in the light of all the circumstances relevant at that time, it is possible that there may have been changes either of policy or relating to underlying facts. The case of *Bolton Metropolitan Borough Council and Others v Secretary of State for the Environment and Others (Court of Appeal)* [1994] EGCS 127 illustrates the difficulties. In 1993 the Secretary of State granted planning permission for a regional shopping centre at Dumplington near Manchester. An inquiry had taken place in 1986 and 1987 in relation to a number of different proposals in the Manchester area. By the time the Secretary of State was making his decision in 1993 there had been substantial changes in respect of retail floor space, in government guidance and in the relevant development plans. The Court of Appeal held that the Secretary of State was required to approach his final decision with an open mind despite having made an earlier decision on a preliminary basis; that where the decision letter is silent on a material consideration and where circumstances 'appear to point overwhelmingly in favour of a different decision', the court may infer that the decision maker has not fully understood the materiality of the matters before him.

10.10.10   If the decision is quashed by the High Court

The procedures for re-opening the inquiry on the quashing of a decision under s 288 of the Act are the same as those for inspector cases.

10.11   Major inquiries

Because of the importance of Secretary of State cases, many more of them are likely to be treated as 'major planning inquiries' than is the case with inspector appeals. Reference should be made to the code of practice for major planning inquiries annexed to Circular 10/88. Although the statutory rules are the same, the code sets out useful information on the steps to be taken to ensure that the inquiry is regulated and kept within manageable limits. It deals with matters such as the registration of parties. For such a major inquiry, the pre-inquiry meeting or meetings will be vitally important in the management of the hearing, from the point of view of both local authority and the applicant/appellant.

Chapter 11

Costs

11.1 Introduction

As government advice makes clear, an award of costs is not intended to influence the outcome of proceedings but to act as a discipline to those involved in handling appeals. Far too much attention is often paid to costs, both by local authorities and by appellants, affecting the thinking and actions of the parties at the wrong time and for the wrong reasons. Local authorities on occasion state that the fact that costs may be awarded affects their ability to refuse applications. Local authorities do not make money out of development (in contrast to developers) and therefore should not be required to pay costs at all or, if they are, should pay a nominal amount rather than the astronomical costs that can be run up by a developer on a major project with a full team. On the other hand, developers can be unrealistic in their expectations of local authorities. A local authority may be deciding a hundred planning applications every three weeks. There is clearly a limit to the time that can be spent over every decision and coming back to the developer on every point. Too often developers are seen by local authorities to be aggressive, threatening a costs application before the ink is dry on the cheque for the application fees.

The attitude of both parties hinders open discussion and careful development of the appeal process. Cases have been lost on both sides because of an undue emphasis on the costs position instead of careful analysis and development of the planning merits. That warning having been given, this chapter deals with costs in planning proceedings; when to apply for them, who can apply for them and the criteria on which they are awarded.

Attention has been drawn to the differences between planning proceedings and ordinary civil litigation. This difference is nowhere more evident than in the awards of costs. In the following discussion, practitioners should bear firmly in mind that each party is normally expected to bear its own costs, that costs are only awarded exceptionally for unreasonable behaviour, and that costs decision is not connected to the success or failure of the party at appeal.

The rule is set out in Circular 8/93:

> (1) In planning and other proceedings to which this guidance applies, the parties normally meet their own expenses. . . . Costs are awarded only when what is termed 'unreasonable' behaviour is held to have occurred . . . The word 'unreasonable' is used in its ordinary meaning. . . .

(2) The principle that the parties normally meet their own expenses means that, in proceedings to which this guidance . . . applies, awards of costs do not necessarily 'follow the "event" ' . . . An appellant is not awarded costs simply because the appeal succeeds. Nor are the Planning Authority awarded their costs simply because the appeal fails. An award against a successful party may very occasionally be justified. . . .

(3) The availability of costs awards, on specific application, is intended to bring a greater sense of discipline to all parties involved in planning proceedings. A decision to award costs against one of the principal parties in appeal is not punitive. The great majority of planning appeals *do not* result in a costs application. Awards of costs are only made in 30% of costs applications, on average.

The practitioner should also bear the pragmatic rule in mind that costs awarded are unlikely to meet actual costs of running the appeal. It is not a good business decision to run an appeal simply for reasons of cost even if one believes that there is a good chance of a costs award being made.

11.2   Power to award costs

Section 250(5) of the Local Government Act 1972 enables a minister causing a public inquiry to be held to make orders as to the costs of the parties at the inquiry and as to the parties by whom such costs are to be paid. This is applied to public inquiries by s 320(2) of the Act. This applies to informal hearings by virtue of para 6(5) of Sched 6 of the Act. Appeals under the Planning (Listed Buildings and Conservation Areas) Act 1990 are also covered.

There is a power to award costs for the written representation procedure by virtue of s 322 in the same way as if a public inquiry has been held. The Secretary of State has indicated that costs will not for the time being be awarded in respect of written representation appeals, except for enforcement appeals where costs have been awarded for some time. At present, therefore, neither the appellant nor the local authority is at risk of costs if the written representation procedure is chosen and it is not an enforcement appeal.

A further power was introduced in 1992, enabling costs to be awarded where arrangements have been made for a local inquiry or informal hearing to take place and such inquiry or hearing is cancelled.

The Secretary of State's power to award costs does not run against the Crown and other government departments. If any question arises as to whether unnecessary costs have been caused by the actions of the Secretary of State or of other government departments, there is no power as such to award costs. However, an application should be made to the Secretary of State for an ex gratia payment outlining the circumstances involved. The Citizen's Charter requires government departments to have formal complaint procedures and identify those who deal with them. This may be the best way of forwarding such claims.

11.3   When to apply for costs

It is a normal pre-condition of an award of costs that an application has been made. The time that such an application should be made is set out in Annex 5 of Circular 8/93. If there is a public inquiry or hearing, the application should be made to the inspector before the close of the proceedings. He or she will normally ask before formally closing whether there are any other applications. That is the signal for the advocate concerned to get to his feet (Circular 8/93, Annex 5, para 1). If an arranged inquiry or hearing is cancelled, application for costs should be made in writing immediately and in any event no later than four weeks after confirmation that the inquiry or hearing has been cancelled (Circular 8/93, Annex 5, para 2). Finally, in written representation enforcement cases applications should be made to the Department in writing before the inspector's site inspection (Circular 8/93, Annex 5, para 3).

These time periods are not limited by statute. There should be very few reasons for not making a costs application at the right time. Paragraph 4 of Annex 5 of Circular 8/93 indicates that the Secretary of State will accept late applications only if the party applying for costs can show good reason. Normally a late application will not be decided by the inspector but by the Secretary of State. The opportunity to ask for costs against another party is not an unexpected feature of any case. Provided the advice given in this chapter is followed it should not be necessary, except in the most extraordinary circumstances, to throw oneself on the mercy of the Secretary of State with a late costs application.

11.4   Who can apply for costs?

Either of the principal parties, ie the appellant or the local authority, can apply for costs, as can any third party. The position of each in the various types of appeal will vary and this is dealt with in detail in the next section on grounds for making a costs application.

In relation to called-in inquiries, para 9 makes clear that the role of the principal parties is to assist the Secretary of State in the process of reaching his decision on planning issues. The applicant had a right to make the application which triggered the call-in and the local authority has taken no action which gave rise to the hearing. The principal parties will not be at risk of an award of costs relating to the substance of the case or action taken prior to the call-in. However, partial award of costs may be awarded for unreasonable behaviour such as failure to comply with the procedure rules.

In respect of third parties, there is a general resistance to awarding costs on the basis that parties have voluntarily chosen to enter the arena. They will not have costs awarded to or against them where unreasonable behaviour by one of the principal parties relates to the substance of the case (Annex 4, para 2). Where unreasonable conduct relates to procedural matters and causes unnecessary expense to third parties, they may be in the same position as principal parties. Again, where an inquiry or hearing is cancelled because of the unreasonable conduct by any principal party, third parties may be awarded costs. However, they will need to demonstrate that they had forewarned the applicant and the local authority of their intention to appear before incurring expenses (Annex 4, para 4). If a hearing has been cancelled because a

satisfactory outcome has been negotiated between the principal parties they are
unlikely to be awarded their costs.

Those representing third parties should be particularly aware of the cost
position. Community groups, parish councils and so on may feel particularly
aggrieved if they have raised substantial sums for legal advice and witnesses
and find they are denied at the last minute of their day in court, and to crown
the injury, suddenly discover that they have also to pay their own abortive costs.

11.5   In what circumstances will an award of costs be made?

Paragraph 6 of Circular 8/93 sets out three conditions which must normally be
fulfilled before an award of costs will be made:

(1) one of the parties has sought an award of costs at an appropriate stage
     of the proceedings; and
(2) the party against whom costs are sought has behaved unreasonably; and
(3) this unreasonable conduct has caused the party seeking costs to incur
     or waste expense unnecessarily, either because it should not have been
     necessary for the matter to be determined by the Secretary of State or
     because of the manner in which another party has behaved in the
     proceedings (for example, because an arranged inquiry or hearing had
     to be cancelled or extended, resulting in waste of preparatory work or
     unnecessary additional expense).

If no application is made, neither the inspector nor the Secretary of State will
consider the question of costs. If for some reason an application for costs is not
made at the right time then an attempt will have to be made to persuade the
Secretary of State to accept a late application for costs.

The third point above flows from the basic principle that an award of costs
is not punitive. If the behaviour, however exasperating it is, does not cause
additional cost then it will not found a cost award.

It is not unknown for parties, particularly if acting in person, to fail to respond
to letters, be late, fail to provide copies and generally create difficulties. Equally,
it is not unknown for local authorities under pressure of resources to fail to deal
fully and expeditiously with an appeal. Such behaviour may be ill advised or
unprofessional but unless it can be established that it has actually caused
additional expense, it is a waste of time trying to make a point by way of a costs
application. If the application for costs neglects to identify the additional work
caused by the unreasonable behaviour, the inspector will certainly pursue the
point.

Finally, the most important criterion, that of unreasonable behaviour.
Circular 8/93 gives details and examples of the circumstances which in the past
have given rise to awards of costs. The leading case on costs is *Council of the
City of Manchester v Secretary of State for the Environment and Mercury
Communications Ltd* [1988] JPL 774.

In that case, which is worth reading in its entirety, the council had tried to
argue that in refusing an application because of fears about the potential

hazards of microwaves, they were entitled not to follow the advice of the Health and Safety Executive that there was no public danger and that costs should only be awarded if the reason for refusal was such which no reasonable planning authority could have given. This argument was rejected. The test, then, is whether the behaviour was unreasonable in the ordinary meaning of the word.

11.6 Practical points

Costs awards are won and lost before the advocate ever rises to his feet to address the inspector or before the letter of application is written to the Department. Unreasonable behaviour should be documented at the time, giving the opposition every chance to remedy the matter. The correspondence should concentrate on the planning issues. The letters will speak plainly for themselves if a costs application is made in the future.

Common events giving grounds for an application are as follows.

11.6.1 Reasons for refusal inadequate

Where reasons for refusal are believed to be unsustainable, the authority should be asked for further information or to withdraw the reasons. Lack of a satisfactory answer paves the way for an application on costs to be dated from the date the appeal was lodged on the basis that it could have been avoided if proper information had been forthcoming.

11.6.2 Statement of case and list of documents inadequate

This may be the right time formally to request the local authority to withdraw a makeweight ground of appeal if it is quite clear from the council's statement of case and the appellant's own work that a particular ground, eg highways or disturbance to amenity, cannot be substantiated. Again the appellant is in a strong position, where either outcome is beneficial. He will either get further information to enable him to prepare his case or he has placed on record the request for information which has not been met. The test is not whether there is substantial evidence before the inspector on a particular ground of refusal but whether there is evidence to substantiate their reasons for refusal in accordance with the Circular (*R v Secretary of State for the Environment ex p North Norfolk District Council* 13 July 1994 unreported).

11.6.3 Discussions on evidence

Once statements of case have been exchanged, there is an opportunity to clarify matters of evidence and detail before proofs are finalised. If the local authority refuse to make a person available to discuss these issues, then a brief note indicating that a meeting has been requested and refused should be placed on the record.

11.6.4   Failure to keep to the rules

The main sanction for failing to keep to the rules lies in award of costs. In appropriate cases it is suggested once again that a letter is placed on file saying that the statement of case (or whatever) is overdue and that this is causing difficulties in the preparation of the case, and asking for it to be served before a specified end date. The letter should indicate that if this is not received by that date then the party will instruct the team to prepare work on a broad basis since the information is not to hand which would enable them to focus their work.

The above events also offer local authorities opportunities which they often fail to exploit to clarify issues. If the other side are out on a limb, the authority should ensure that the branch is well and truly exposed. There is no reason why a local authority on receipt of an appeal should not immediately write to the appellant requesting further details in respect of vague grounds of appeal. If those details are not forthcoming and the local authority have to cover more ground than would have been necessary if they had known the reality of the appellant's case, then a letter on file will have underlined the point.

The hearing itself should produce few surprises; both sides will be aware of the points where the other side have difficulties with the case and will have prepared the ground for a costs application if, in the event, the appeal hearing runs true to form and the unreasonable behaviour is confirmed.

11.7   How to protect one's client against an award of costs

If decisions are taken in good time and with proper consideration of the planning merits, there is little risk of an award of costs. But there is no magic formula. Those who have the greatest difficulty understanding the concept may be behaving in a spirit of one-upmanship. A practitioner acting for the appellant who finds that the appeal grounds are unlikely to be properly substantiated, may wish to advise that there is no point in continuing with the appeal. If his advice is rejected, he should opt for the written representation procedure.

If in doubt, the practitioner might like to ask the other side in good time whether they would be prepared not to ask for costs if a certain course of action is pursued. Common sense often prevails when such an agreement is offered, thus removing any residual uncertainty.

Written representation procedure (enforcement appeals only) and informal inquiries offer a quicker and less formal procedure but the general rules as set out above continue to apply. If more information is needed, it should be requested and confirmed in writing. If the other side has been unco-operative or not complied with the procedure, a polite letter will put this on the record.

11.8   Effect of award of costs on the appeal decision

Paragraph 7 of Annex 1 to Circular 8/93 makes it clear that the appeal decision will not be affected in any way by an application for costs. The application for costs will be made and dealt with separately. The inspector or Secretary of State will issue separate letters dealing with the appeal and the award of costs or deal with the award of costs in a separate section of the decision letter.

Nonetheless, some experienced practitioners feel that an application for costs may have a marginal effect on the inspector. An application for costs which is scarcely warranted may give the impression that it is being made to put pressure on the inspector. Most inspectors have in their time worked at grassroots level and fully understand the difficulties.

The author suggests that an application for award of costs should not be made unless there is at least a *prima facie* case. Clients, naturally enough, wish to recover what they can of their expenses and they may well be influenced by normal civil litigation rules. It is to be hoped that most clients will accept professional advice not to press an unwarranted claim.

11.8.1   Counter-claim for costs

Where the other side make an application for costs, there is an argument in favour of making an application for costs as well. This puts into the practice the maxim that attack is the best form of defence. The inspector may take the view that both parties have been at fault to some extent and this is probably not a clear case for an award of costs. The argument is valid only if there are reasonable grounds for putting forward the application even though the considered judgment on the chances of success may not be high.

The circular advises that cross-applications will each be dealt with on their merits as separate applications. Inspectors are familiar with tactics and delaying the close of the inquiry in this way may not improve the client's position.

11.9   Making the application

A costs application should be made briefly, objectively and without heat. A skeleton argument in writing may be handed to the inspector before the advocate makes the application. If only one costs application is being made it will be made and the other side will then have an opportunity to respond to it. If it is known that both sides are to make application for costs, consideration needs to be given as to whether one's own application should precede or follow the other side's application, or whether the two applications should be telescoped together. If a telescoping method is adopted, one side makes his application and the other side answers it; then the second side makes his own application, leaving the starting party to finish with his response.

It is for the advocate to decide how to deal with it at the time. If the two costs applications arise out of two totally different events, they can easily be separated. Frequently, however, the costs applications arise out of the same events, the point at issue being who was responsible.

The application should state clearly what is applied for. In this way the award will be certain and there will be no room for disagreement as to what particular costs have been awarded. The application will be either for all costs from the preparation of the appeal to the decision or partial costs. Such partial costs should be carefully identified. They may be defined by reference to dates, eg from 1 March to 1 October, or by reference to one or more reasons for refusal or a discrete topic.

If a costs application is to be made, the practitioner should warn the client that costs are awarded only exceptionally and may be awarded for part of the heads of expenditure only rather than the whole. Moreover, even if costs are awarded, the costs recovered will not in most cases cover the actual expenditure the client has laid out.

In due course the decision letter on costs will be received. The inspector or the Secretary of State will not determine the *amount* of costs payable.

11.10   Recovery of costs

Recovery of costs can be a minefield for a professional without a clear idea of the procedures. From the legal practitioner's point of view, this is a complication. Just when the case has been won and the practitioner wants to put the file away, he finds that he must deal with the process of recovering costs.

11.10.1   Practical points

The file must not be put away to be dealt with later. It is essential this is dealt with promptly before papers are scattered, while witnesses and the team are still available and their memory is fresh. It may be sensible to write immediately to the client with the costs award to deflate any undue expectations. The client is unlikely to be repaid for the bills he has laid out, partly because some of the expenditure incurred will be disallowed when the claim comes to be assessed and partly because the rates of reimbursement very often do not cover current commercial rates in their entirety. Additionally, the client should be informed that recovery of the costs will inevitably incur solicitor's costs and out-of-pocket expenditure.

As a matter of professional competence solicitors should keep their files complete with attendance notes of all telephone conversations and meetings and indications of the time spent dealing with the case. If there is any possibility of a costs award, this is a pre-requisite for ensuring that the client is able to recover the maximum amount. If an award of costs is made in due course, those drawing the bills to ascertain precisely what is payable will use the file as their starting point. Any sketchiness or omission will mean that there will be no evidence to pursue that aspect of the claim.

Solicitors are strongly advised not to rely on other members of the team. Solicitors, because of their own time recording and billing requirements, can be expected to keep the best records of what was done and the time it took. As soon as the costs application is apparent, team members may be asked to keep a careful note of the tasks they are asked to carry out and the time it takes. The costs draughtsman will go through the files and prepare the papers either for taxation or for the independent costs draughtsman.

11.11   Negotiations

The first requirement is for the parties to seek to reach an agreement on the sum properly payable. Because of the cost, delay and uncertainty of the court's own taxation procedure, considerable effort should be put into this first attempt to reach agreement. It is sometimes thought that it is enough to write a letter to the other side enclosing the bills of the various consultants, with perhaps a more detailed breakdown. But unless the claim is very small and straightforward, it is not the best approach. The costs draughtsman will have to be approached if agreement is not reached to draw a bill in proper form, and it is better to do it at the beginning. Both the solicitor and his client can therefore discuss the initial amount to be put to the paying party and how much can realistically be received on taxation. This information is essential in order for them to place any offer into its context. To refuse a reasonable offer will simply delay the time when payment is received and incur the risk that less may be finally received at the end of the day.

The solicitor is required to meet the costs of drawing the bill and should not pass the costs to the client. The costs draughtsman acting on behalf of the client will draw the bill to maximise what is recoverable. It is suggested that care should be taken to be reasonable here. If an unreasonable bill is submitted, it may bring discussions to a halt. There is an element of horse trading at this stage.

Once the bill has been received from the draughtsman, discussed between solicitor and client and approved, it should be sent off to the other side with a request for agreement. A time limit is usually given for agreement after which the High Court taxation procedure will be initiated. There may be merit in some cases, however, in avoiding High Court taxation by both parties agreeing to appoint an independent costs draughtsman to review the papers and the draft bill and to decide what is properly payable, acting as an expert. Such a suggestion can be included either with the draft bill or immediately the draft bill has been rejected.

If the draft bill has been carefully drawn, it will probably not be rejected out of hand. The more likely response to a correctly drawn bill will be an offer of payment somewhat lower than that in the draft bill. This offer for payment may be acceptable or it may be possible to suggest an intermediate figure which will be acceptable. Once agreement has been reached in open correspondence, no further formal step needs to be taken, providing that the paying party honour their obligation.

11.12   Calculating sums payable

The basic rule is that one is entitled to all reasonable costs properly and necessarily incurred in connection with the matters covered by costs award.

Consequential loss, eg interest charges, holding expenses, management expenses and possibly any depreciation due to market changes or increases in buildings costs, are not recoverable as part of a costs application.

The reasonableness of any action taken for which reimbursement is sought is that of a sensible practitioner considering what, in the light of his then knowledge, was reasonable in the interests of his client (*Francis v Francis & Dickerson* [1955] 3 All ER 836.

The actual rates chargeable can be contentious, particularly in respect of city rates. This was examined in the recent case of *KPMG Peat Marwick McClintock v The HLT Group Ltd* QBD 14 March 1994. The judge held that city professional rates were appropriate and the fact that the plaintiff could have obtained the same services at a much lower price elsewhere was irrelevant. The survey of solicitors' expense rates published by the London Solicitors Litigation Association is a valuable source of information and is a factor to be taken into account by taxing officers when fixing hourly rates for solicitors on taxation of costs.

In calculating sums payable, two points should be noted. Firstly, the receiving party is being compensated for bills he is required to meet. There is therefore difficulty in recovering for services rendered to the paying party which were never intended to be charged. Thus if a legal adviser is giving his services at a reduced rate or even free, he cannot charge the full amount simply because a third party is now paying. Similarly, many witnesses do not expect to be paid. It will be difficult to pass through daily rates for such witnesses simply because someone else is paying. Secondly, VAT is recoverable only to the extent that the receiving party himself has been unable to recover it. If the receiving party is registered for VAT, he will have recovered the VAT chargeable on bills he has received. If he tries to recover the VAT from the paying party, he will in effect have recovered the VAT twice. The VAT element of bills should therefore be ignored, as far as the draft bill to be paid by the other side is concerned, unless the receiving party is not registered for VAT.

Drawing a bill is a specialised task, requiring a knowledge not only of the form in which the High Court likes such bills but also, specifically, of what elements will and will not be allowed on taxation, together with expertise on the rates currently being allowed. The costs draughtsman will charge for his time, but a good cost draughtsman's fees represent value for money.

11.13   Taxation

If no agreement can be reached in a relatively short order, the costs order should be registered with the High Court. The procedure is governed by RSC Ord 62. Costs include fees, charges, disbursements, expenses and remuneration and costs of proceedings (including the taxation itself) as well as costs arising out of or incidental to those proceedings.

The High Court will issue an order which has the effect of making the amount payable a court judgment enforceable in the normal way and interest on the judgment will start to be payable. It will not be enforceable until the amount payable is quantified by the taxation procedure. Once this has been done the receiving party can consider next steps.

Order 62, r 29 of the RSC specifies that the proceedings for taxation must commence within three months of the date of the order. This is in fact honoured more in the breach than the observance. The taxing officer does have power to deprive the receiving party of his costs or reduce them.

It is vital to avoid protracting these proceedings, as the solicitor will become engulfed in new work and put them to the bottom of the pile, while witnesses and others will lose their memory of what happened and be unable to supplement deficiencies in the file itself.

The procedure of taxation is arcane and convoluted. Fees are payable and there is a system for apportioning the cost of taxation. A taxation hearing may be held if it is necessary to argue through various points. These details are not dealt with here. They are properly the purview of the costs draughtsman who is conversant with the most recent practice.

11.13.1   Costs on matters beyond the immediate appeal

The case of *R v Secretary of State for the Environment ex p Westminster City Council* (1989) BLR 23 considered the extent to which matters beyond the immediate appeal in question and the application which gave rise to it may be material to the costs decision. Amended schemes were submitted to the local authority in the weeks preceding a public inquiry and refused by the chairman's casting vote. However, the committee decided that the application which was the subject of the appeal would not be opposed at the local inquiry and duly took that stance. Costs were awarded against the council because the public inquiry was unnecessary. The council sought judicial review of that costs award on the basis that the matters complained of lay outside the ambit of the appeal proceedings. This was rejected by the High Court.

11.14   Challenging an award of costs

An award of costs (or a decision not to award costs) cannot be challenged under s 288 of the Act. It must be dealt with by an application for judicial review under RSC Ord 53. In *North Kesteven District Council v Secretary of State for the Environment* (1989) JPL 445 the High Court held that a costs application was not a matter strictly concerned with the determination of the substantive issues raised on the appeal. A challenge therefore must be made within ordinary public law principles and subject to an initial application for leave. Such challenges are dealt with in Chapter 14 on judicial review.

Worked Example: Specimen Award

LETTER FROM PLANNING INSPECTORATE

Messrs Smith & Jones
134 Newtown Road
Newtown N43 12RAP

Dear Sirs

TOWN AND COUNTRY PLANNING ACT 1990, SS 78 AND 322 AND
SCHED 6 LOCAL GOVERNMENT ACT 1972
APPLICATION FOR COSTS

1. I refer to the application for award of costs against the Red Forest Borough Council which was made at the inquiry held in March 1994. The inquiry was held in connection with an appeal by Europa Electronics Limited against a refusal of planning permission for an application for demolition of a house, erection of extension to existing factory and use of adjacent land as storage at Strait Lane, Red Forest. A copy of my appeal decision letter has been sent separately.

2. The application for costs falls to be determined in accordance with the advice contained in Circular 8/93 and in all the relevant circumstances of the appeal, irrespective of its outcome. Costs may only be awarded against a party who has behaved unreasonably.

3. In support of this application it was pointed out that the Council had failed to substantiate grounds 4 and 5 of the grounds of appeal. This is contrary to the advice given in paragraph 3 of annex 2 of Circular 8/93. The appellant was therefore put to unnecessary costs in dealing with these grounds of appeal.

4. In response, the Council stated that the grounds of appeal were substantiated in their evidence and that this was not the type of case where separate technical information was required and that it was perfectly proper in this case for the evidence to be given by the planning officer on a common-sense basis.

5. I see nothing necessarily unreasonable in the Council deciding to include, as the 4th and 5th grounds for refusal, objection on highway and amenity grounds but they then had a duty to substantiate these reasons at subsequent appeal proceedings. The Council's witness accepted under cross-examination that there was no real likelihood of intensification of industrial use, additional traffic or adverse effects on neighbours. No one else on the Council's side sought to disagree with him or submit evidence on this point.

6. I do not differ from his judgment on this matter and these concessions left no evidence of substance to support the Council's case in these respects. I conclude therefore that the Council failed in their duty to

substantiate these reasons for refusing the application and I regard their conduct in this regard as having been unreasonable.

7.   Taking into account all of these factors I conclude that the application for an award of costs is justified in part.

FORMAL DECISION

8.   Accordingly in exercise of my powers under Section 250(5) of the Local Government Act 1972 and paragraph 6(4) of Schedule 6 to the Town and Country Planning Act 1990, and all other enabling powers, I HEREBY ORDER THAT Red Forest District Council shall pay to Europa Electronics Limited the costs of the appeal proceedings, limited to those costs incurred in rebutting the reasons for refusal numbers 4 and 5, as specified below, such costs to be taxed in default of agreement as to the amount thereof. The subject of the proceedings was an appeal under Section 78 of the aforementioned Act of 1990 against the refusal of the council to grant planning permission for demolition of a house, erection of extension to existing factory and use of adjacent land as storage at Strait Lane, Red Forest for the following reasons.

1.   The proposed development is contrary to Policy GB1 of the adopted Red Forest UDP and would form an alien intrusion into the metropolitan green belt.

2.   The development would serve to extend the boundary of the present built up area into open land alongside the highway and is likely to make adjacent areas of the green belt less defensible against further encroachment.

3.   The proposals involve the loss of a dwellinghouse contrary to policy H1 of the adopted Red Forest UDP.

4.   The proposals would result in an intensification of industrial use and would cause unacceptable additional traffic on the local road network.

5.   The proposals would adversely affect the residential amenity of existing houses along Strait Lane.

Yours faithfully,

A C Smith DipTP MRTPI
Inspector

Chapter 12

Application to High Court to Quash Decision on Appeal

12.1 Introduction

The decision letter received at the end of the appeal process indicates whether planning permission has been refused or granted subject to conditions. The decision may be unsatisfactory, for the appellant, the prospective developer, the local authority or an affected third party. One further avenue of challenge is available: an application to the High Court under s 288 of the Town and Country Planning Act 1990. This chapter deals with the High Court proceedings. A worked example is included for information. Different considerations apply to enforcement appeals which are dealt with in Chapter 13. If this section does not apply, judicial review might be considered (Chapter 14).

The notice of motion must be issued within six weeks of the date stamped on the decision letter. No application is possible after this period (see para 12.3).

The challenge is on a point of law only: there is no challenge on the merits. If the inspector accepted the other side's evidence and on balance rejected the client's point of view, it is probably unwise to waste money by pursuing this procedure. However, if this route is to be explored, counsel will be needed to advise on the merits and to settle the application and affidavit.

12.2 General points

A challenge under this section is sometimes referred to colloquially as 'an appeal to the High Court' but the term is misleading here. The inspector will have looked at the merits of the case in exactly the same way as the local authority considered them when the original application was submitted. The application to the High Court is of a very different nature. The High Court will not under any circumstances look at the merits of the case: the procedure is available only on narrow grounds.

Preparation for defending a High Court challenge will have been begun long before the notice of motion is received indicating that a challenge has been made. Likewise, a prudent party will have prepared the ground for a challenge. If the appeal has been properly prepared and conducted, any point of difficulty will have been fully canvassed before the inspector. He will be in a position to explain the decision he has taken fully and correctly. The only real uncertainty will arise from aspects of a decision letter which are truly unexpected. For example, the inspector or the Secretary of State may rely on an issue which was not canvassed before him or he may omit to consider a relevant factor. Proper preparation of the appeal papers and proper presentation of the case will have strengthened the decision letter as a whole, thus minimising the chances of a successful challenge.

Whether one is advising a party making a challenge against an inspector's decision or resisting such a challenge, the advice must be the same: prepare the difficult ground and make sure that all parties are aware of those difficulties.

It may be appropriate to indicate during the course of the inquiry that if a certain course of action is taken, a party will be prejudiced, and even indicate that they will challenge the eventual decision. A better course is normally to set out clearly the reasons why objection is taken, giving any necessary references in point. This will form the starting point for the challenge in due course.

12.3   Time limits

There is a statutory period of six weeks in which to issue and serve the notice of motion. The period runs from the date the decision letter is signed and date stamped, not the date of receipt (*Griffiths v Secretary of State for the Environment* [1983] 2 AC 51). In that case a decision letter was date stamped and posted on 8 December but not received until 13 December. Mr Griffiths appeared in person before the House of Lords to argue that no person could be 'a person aggrieved' until he actually received notice of the decision. Not so: his application was struck out.

This is a statutory time limit, beyond which the right to make the application is lost. This time limit must *on no account* be confused with the shorter time limit applying to the equivalent High Court challenge in respect of enforcement notices (see Chapter 13).

The statutory time limit was considered in *Low v Secretary of State for Wales and Glyndwyr District Council The Times*, 18 March, 1993, CA. At first instance an application by Mr Low under s 288 was dismissed on the grounds that it was not made within the six-week period of s 288(3). The decision letter was dated Friday 15 March 1991 and refused planning permission. The six-week period expired on Friday 26 April 1991. On 21 March Mr Low had written to the Welsh Office seeking information about the forms to be used for an application to the High Court and on 17 April an official replied, enclosing copies of the kind of notice of motion which might be appropriate. The envelope containing Mr Low's notice of motion was received at the Central Office of the Queen's Bench Division on 26 April, the last day of the six-week period. It was stamped by the Central Office on that date; then there was another stamp partly obscuring the first reading 'Chancery Division received 29th April'. Finally there was a Crown Office stamp for 1 May, which was five days outside the six-week period. The court accepted that it may have been received by the court generally within the time and owing to administrative muddle did not reach the Crown Office in time.

12.3.1   No allowance for Sundays and holidays

Another case illustrates the operation of the time limit (*Stainer v SOSE and Shepway District Council* QBD Oct 19 1992). The inspector had refused an appeal for planning permission. The Secretary of State applied to strike out the application under s 288 on the grounds that it was out of time. The decision letter was date stamped 29 November 1991. The statutory six weeks expired on 10 January 1992. The House of Lords in the case of *Griffiths*, discussed above, had laid down that the six-week period started from the date of the decision, not the date on which the decision was received and the six weeks was absolute.

The applicant was advised by the Crown Office that days like Christmas Day and bank holidays were not part of the six weeks. If that had been the case the time would have expired on 13 January 1992 which was the date on which the notice of motion was lodged. In fact the six-week statutory time includes days like Christmas Day and bank holidays. There is an exclusion of such days in short limitation periods of seven days (RSC Ord 3, r 2) but that did not apply to a period of six weeks. In any event, it only applied to periods of time fixed by the Rules or by any judgment order or direction. It did not apply to a period fixed by statute. The notice of motion was therefore out of time and the court had no jurisdiction to decide the application.

In a quite exceptional case, *Mendip District Council v Secretary of State for the Environment* 29 November 1992 unreported, the court held that there was a power to extend the time for *service* of a notice of motion which had been issued within the time limit. Legal advisers are strongly advised, however, not to delay in considering an application and to make the application and serve the documents in good time.

If the time limit is already approaching, legal advisers may consider issuing and serving the notice of motion within time with an informal notification to the other parties involved that this is a protective measure. If such an application is withdrawn shortly after service, the costs payable in respect of the other side's costs are unlikely to be significant. The costs penalty may be considered worth incurring if required to preserve an applicant's right to take action.

Once a notice of motion been issued and served, negotiations with the local authority and the Secretary of State's legal advisers may be worth while. Cases sometimes arise where a local authority may agree to grant planning permission for a revised scheme in order to avoid scrutiny of an appeal decision which could reflect adversely on its policies or actions. The Secretary of State, having issued the decision letter, cannot withdraw it, but he may be prepared to offer no defence to the application if his legal advisers inform him that an error has occurred.

12.4   What decisions may be challenged?

Section 288 provides a route of challenge for a number of decisions both of local authorities and the Secretary of State in the planning context. The following decisions are covered by s 288:

(1) Decisions of the Secretary of State relating to appeals under s 78 of the Act and called-in decisions under s 77.

(2) Enforcement appeals in so far as the determination relates to the ground which relates to the granting of planning permission or variation, revocation of conditions.

(3) Decisions of the Secretary of State relating to certificates of lawfulness of proposed use and development and certificates on the lawfulness of existing use and development.

Decisions made by inspectors are deemed to be those of the Secretary of State himself for these purposes. (A number of other types of decision may be challenged under s 288 but do not come within the ambit of this book.)

Most decisions of the *local authority* (including determination of planning applications) are therefore not susceptible to challenge under this provision. They will either have to be challenged under section 78 of the Act, which gives a right of appeal to the Secretary of State, or by judicial review. Other notable exceptions are decisions by the Secretary of State which are not final decisions on the matter, ie interlocutory decisions made by the Secretary of State or an inspector.

12.5   Who can challenge the decision?

Section 288 permits any person aggrieved by the decision to make the application. Earlier cases interpreted this narrowly as applying only to parties whose legal right is being infringed. However, a chain of cases beginning with *Turner v Secretary of State for the Environment* [1973] 28 P&CR 123 has established that a common sense view should be adopted. A person who now owns the relevant land (even though he did not at the time the original application was submitted to the local authority) is a person aggrieved (*Times Investment Limited v Secretary of State for the Environment and London Borough of Tower Hamlets* [1990] 3 PLR 111).

The local authority to whom the original application was submitted is authorised to make an application by virtue of s 288(2). Indeed, in practice, any person who is entitled to appear at an inquiry is likely to come within the scope of the section.

A real point must be at issue. A person who accepts the decision but finds the reasoning unacceptable is not a person aggrieved (*TLC v Secretary of State for the Environment* [1985] JPL 868).

12.6   Outcome of the application

The powers of the High Court under this section are limited by s 288(5).

12.6.1   Interim orders

There is a power to suspend the operation of the order or action, the validity of which is questioned, until the final determination of the proceedings. The applicant will in most cases specifically request this protection. It will prevent the planning permission becoming effective until the final determination.

There will be a few occasions when the local authority or a third party will wish to resist such an order as a matter of principle, although it may be appropriate in some cases to make an application for an undertaking in damages. This may be appropriate if, for instance, a decision granting planning permission is challenged. The developer may legitimately feel that having taken his proposals through the local authority approval system and to appeal to the Secretary of State, he should be recompensed for any further delay due to a third party challenge. This will be a difficult decision for those seeking such an interim order. Parties may be unwilling to take a chance on what may be very substantial damages payable. On the other hand if an interim order is not sought, there may be difficulties in setting aside an implemented planning permission. In most cases developers would be well advised not to implement a development where planning permission is challenged. If they have recklessly ploughed ahead despite warnings they may get little sympathy from the court.

It has been established in relation to applications for injunctions that local authorities are not normally required to give an undertaking in damages (*Kirklees Metropolitan Borough Council v Wickes Building Supplies Ltd* [1992] AC 227). The rationale is that local authorities have a public regulatory duty and have no private interest to be protected. It would be possible to argue that this reasoning should extend to interim applications under this section. As a pragmatic matter, it may be necessary for local authorities or third parties to make an interim application and refuse to give an undertaking in damages, leaving it to the discretion of the court whether in those circumstances an interim order will be made.

12.6.2   Quashing the decision

The court may quash an order or action if satisfied that it is not within the powers of the Act or that the interests of the applicant have been substantially prejudiced by a failure to comply with any of the relevant requirements in relation to it. 'Relevant requirements' is defined in s 288 (9) as 'any requirement of [the] Act or of the Tribunals Inquiries Act 1992 or of any order, regulations or rules made under [the] Act or under that Act which are applicable to that order or action'. The two grounds for quashing an action or order are examined in more detail in para 12.7.

The court has a discretion whether to quash a decision. The general rule is that a decision will be quashed if there is a substantial defect unless it would not have affected the outcome. Even if it does affect the outcome, there is still a discretion not to grant relief. In most cases, however, once the applicant has established a substantial flaw in the decision, either because it was outside the powers of the Act or because procedural rules have not been adhered to and this has affected the outcome, the decision will be quashed and remitted for re-determination.

The court may either quash the decision and remit the decision to be decided anew by the decision-maker or uphold the decision. This contrasts with the much broader jurisdiction available under judicial review for the exercise of the inherent supervisory function of the High Court.

12.7   Grounds of challenge

Section 288(b) sets out two grounds of appeal:
  (1) that the action is not within the powers of the Act; or
  (2) that any of the relevant requirements have not been complied with in relation to that action.
In practice the two grounds are often difficult to disentangle and compartmentalising the perceived defect may not be the most helpful approach.

12.7.1   Status of decision letter

The court will apply a benevolent construction to the decision letter which is to be read as a whole as addressed to an informed audience, *Richmond upon Thames LBC v Secretary of State for the Environment and Another* [1994] EGCS 123.

> It is no part of the court's duty to subject the decision made to the kind of scrutiny appropriate to the determination of the meaning of a contract or a statute. Because the letter is addressed to the parties, they are well aware of the issues involved and of the arguments employed at the inquiry, it is not necessary to rehearse every argument relating to each matter in every paragraph (*City of Westminster v Haymarket Publishing Ltd* 42 P&CR).
>
> The Inspector was not writing an examination paper on current and draft development plans. The letter had to be read in good faith and references to policies had to be taken in the context of the general thrust of the Inspector's reasoning (*David Wilson Homes (Southern) Ltd v South Somerset District Council and Secretary of State for the Environment* CA [1994] JPL 63).

12.7.2   Procedural irregularities

A clear case must be found if the application is to succeed. Many of the general principles of judicial review as set out in Chapter 14 apply to applications under s 288. In relation to the first ground in particular a decision which fails the tests of illegality and *Wednesbury* reasonableness or 'irrationality' under judicial review principles will be quashed. The second ground corresponds to the procedural irregularities limb of judicial review.

Planning appeal procedures for written representation and public inquiry appeals are laid down by statutory instruments. These rules require reasons, which are proper and adequate to be given. While there are no statutory instruments dealing with informal hearings, there can be a ground of challenge if the Code of Guidance is not adhered to.

A further ground may be possible if the decision is one which the Secretary of State has taken himself. Such appeals are dealt with in Chapter 10. The

Secretary of State will have received the report of the inspector who held the public inquiry and will then issue his own decision. If he reaches a different conclusion from the inspector on a finding of fact or takes in new evidence which was not available at the inquiry, he must notify the parties and give them at least an opportunity of making further representation (Secretary of State Rules, r 12). He must in addition have sufficient material to enable him to reach such a position. To do otherwise would infringe the principle of rationality.

12.8   Procedure

The action is commenced by way of an originating motion under RSC Ord 94, r 1 and is served on the other parties, ie the Secretary of State (via the Treasury Solicitor) and the local authority, if appropriate.

Evidence is normally by affidavit only. While the applicant must always serve an affidavit, often the Secretary of State will not need to. The affidavit will exhibit the decision letter and any other relevant documents. It should be made by a person who has first-hand knowledge of the matters concerned. If this is not possible, the affidavit should identify the elements which are hearsay and therefore attested only to the best of the deponent's knowledge and belief.

No new evidence is normally admissible in respect of matters which were canvassed at the appeal stage. The court will not permit this procedure to be used as a back door route to re-open issues. New evidence will only be permitted when it relates directly to the challenge itself, eg where there is dispute of fact.

12.9   Effect of quashing the decision

Where a decision letter is quashed, the decision itself is simply erased from the record and matters stand as they were immediately before the decision letter was issued. The decision-maker will have to consider whether to re-open any inquiry or hearing or ask for further information from the parties. Rule 19 of the Inspector Rules provides that where a decision is quashed and a person entitled to appear at the inquiry did appear, such parties must be invited to make further representations and 21 days allowed for a response. A decision will then be taken whether to re-open the proceedings before issuing a new decision letter.

12.10   Costs

The general rule is that unsuccessful applicants not only pay their own costs but also pay the costs of the other parties. However, where a local authority make the application the usual practice is to award costs not only to the Secretary of State but also to the developer if he is represented.

Costs are always at the discretion of the court. If the developer is the applicant, the court will be reluctant to require him to pay both the Secretary of State and the local authority's costs. For this reason, the local authority may not appear on a developer's application although they are often a party to the action.

12.11   Judicial review

If the decision falls within the ambit of s 288, that section will have to be used. If it does not, then s 288 cannot be used since as a statutory remedy it is limited strictly to the words of the statute. Where an application under s 288 is inappropriate, consideration will have to be given to whether judicial review may be appropriate.

The dangers of using judicial review where an applicant is in a position to use s 288 were recently illustrated in *R v Secretary of State for the Environment ex p George Bradley* QBD 14 Dec 1993. An inspector had rejected an appeal by the applicant but the applicant contended that the inspector failed to suggest conditions which could have overcome objections. The court held the inspector was under no obligation to suggest conditions. Moreover, the application was made by way of an application for judicial review precluded by the Act (because an application under s 288 was an available remedy) and was dismissed as inappropriate on that ground. It is possible, however, that there may be cases where there is no effective remedy either under s 288 or judicial review.

Worked Example

IN THE HIGH COURT OF JUSTICE

QUEEN'S BENCH DIVISION

IN THE MATTER of the Town and Country Planning Act 1990, Section 288, and Order 94 RSC

AND

IN THE MATTER of land at Sty Lane, Happy Valley, Wolverton

AND

IN THE MATTER of a Decision by the Secretary of State for the Environment notified by letter dated 25 September 1994

BETWEEN:

MISS J. PIGGIE   Applicant

and

THE SECRETARY OF STATE
FOR THE ENVIRONMENT   First Respondent

and

WOLVERVALLEY DISTRICT COUNCIL   Second Respondent

NOTICE OF MOTION

TAKE NOTICE that the High Court of Justice, Queen's Bench Division, at the Royal Courts of Justice, Strand, London WC2, will be moved at the expiration of 21 days from the service upon you of this notice or so soon thereafter as Counsel can be heard, by Counsel on behalf of the above named Applicant for an Order:

(1) That the above mentioned decision of the First Respondent and notified by decision letter dated 25 September 1994 whereby the Applicant's appeal against a decision of the Second Respondent dated 5 November 1993 refusing planning permission for the erection of a bungalow was dismissed be quashed;

(2) That the costs of this application may be paid by the First Respondent or that such order as to costs may be made as the Court may think fit.

AND FURTHER TAKE NOTICE that the grounds of this Application are as follows.

GROUNDS

(1) The First Respondent's decision was not within the powers of the Act

(2) That relevant requirements have not been complied with.

PARTICULARS

(1) The inspector in dismissing the appeal failed to have regard to a material consideration, namely the planning obligation submitted by the applicant.

(2) The inspector in the course of the inquiry acted contrary to the rules of natural justice and with bias.

(3) Further, the inspector failed to give adequate reasons for his decision and failed adequately to deal with evidence and submissions of the applicant concerning the issues in the case.

(4) The interest of the applicant has thereby been substantially prejudiced.

DATED 15 October 1994

Bacon, Fitch & Co
Market Square
Wolverton

Solicitors to the Applicants

TO:

The Secretary of State for the Environment
c/o The Treasury Solicitor
Queen Anne's Chambers
28 Broadway
Westminster
LONDON SW1H 9JS

AND TO:

The Chief Executive
Wolvervalley District Council
Planning Department
Town Hall Chambers
Wolverton

MISS J. PIGGIE   Applicant

and

THE SECRETARY OF STATE
FOR THE ENVIRONMENT

First Respondent

and

WOLVERVALLEY DISTRICT COUNCIL

Second Respondent

NOTICE OF MOTION

[   ]

Deponent: J Piggie
Affidavit No: First
Sworn on:
Filed on behalf of the Applicant

IN THE HIGH COURT OF JUSTICE   CO 94/1008

QUEEN'S BENCH DIVISION

IN THE MATTER of the Town and Country Planning Act 1990, Section 288

AND

IN THE MATTER of land at Sty Lane, Happy Valley, Wolverton

AND

IN THE MATTER of a Decision by the Secretary of State for the Environment notified by a letter dated 25th September 1994

BETWEEN

MISS J. PIGGIE   Applicant

and

THE SECRETARY OF STATE
FOR THE ENVIRONMENT   First Respondent

and

WOLVERVALLEY DISTRICT COUNCIL   Second Respondent

AFFIDAVIT IN SUPPORT

I, Jasmin Piggie of The Pond, Trotter Lane, Wolverton MAKE OATH AND SAY as follows:

1. I am the applicant in this matter. I applied to Wolvervalley District Council for planning permission to erect a family house in August 1993. This was refused by the Council and I appealed to the Secretary of State in January 1994 against that refusal. That appeal was heard at a public inquiry between 15th March and 15th June 1994. I was present at the hearing of the appeal and each of the matters deposed below are within my own knowledge, or stated not to be so where relevant.

2. There is now produced and shown to me marked 'JP1' a true copy of the decision letter in this matter dated 25th September 1994.

3. In paragraphs 12–15 of his decision letter the inspector recorded the evidence in respect of previous houses on the site. My sisters, Honeysuckle Piggie and Rose Piggie gave evidence as to what had

happened to the previous houses on the site. To the best of my knowledge and belief these paragraphs record the substance of their evidence. In particular, my sister Honeysuckle had erected a house made of straw which had proved totally unsuitable to local conditions. The council advanced no evidence that straw was a suitable building material and indeed the council's witness, Mr J. Boar, conceded in his evidence that brick was the most suitable material.

4. Before the inquiry began I executed a unilateral planning obligation under section 106 of the Town and Country Planning Act 1990 on the advice of my lawyers. There is now produced to me marked 'JP2' a true copy of this document.

5. There is now produced to me an excerpt from the Local Plan marked document 'JP3'. This Policy requires a Wolverton by-pass to be constructed in the Plan period to avoid congestion in the centre of Wolverton. The supporting text indicates that public funding for this road is unlikely in the Plan period and that the council will seek contributions from developers to fund this road. I therefore undertook to provide 6 million acorns for the provision of this road, conditional upon planning permission being granted.

6. In paragraph 22 of his decision letter the inspector states that the construction of the road is not necessary to enable the development to proceed since the traffic generated by my development proposal will not significantly affect the need for the by-pass, and he has therefore not taken the unilateral obligation into account.

7. On the afternoon of the 4th day of the inquiry I had lunch in the Market Cafe at Wolverton. There I saw Mr. Wolfe, the inspector, having lunch with Mr. G. Sheppard who is the leader of the District Council. They were seated at a table by themselves.

8. My witnesses were intimidated by the hostile attitude shown by the inspector and his constant interruptions.

SWORN BY the said JASMIN PIGGIE

on

Before me,

Solicitor/Commissioner for Oaths

CO/ 1994

<u>IN THE HIGH COURT OF JUSTICE</u>
<u>QUEEN'S BENCH DIVISION</u>
<u>CROWN OFFICE LIST</u>

BETWEEN

MISS J. PIGGIE <u>Applicant</u>

and

THE SECRETARY OF STATE
FOR THE ENVIRONMENT

<u>First Respondent</u>

and

WOLVERVALLEY DISTRICT COUNCIL

<u>Second Respondent</u>

<u>AFFIDAVIT IN SUPPORT</u>

[   ]

Chapter 13

Special Considerations:
Enforcement and Allied Appeals
Listed Building Consent
Conservation Area Consent

13.1 Introduction

The focus of this book is on appeals under s 78 of the Town and Country
Planning Act 1990 in respect of applications made to local authorities for various
types of planning permission. However, there are a number of other applications
under the Act and under associated listed buildings and conservation area
legislation. On some occasions these appeals may be directly related to planning
appeals. On other occasions some of the principles and procedures of planning
appeals may be relevant. This chapter deals with these related appeals:

(1) appeals in respect of planning permission for development already
     carried out (s 73A of the Act);
(2) appeals in respect of certificate of lawfulness of existing use or
     development (s 191 of the Act);
(3) appeals in respect of certificates of lawfulness of proposed use or
     development (s 192 of the Act);
(4) appeals against enforcement notices (s 174 of the Act).

All the above provisions are contained in the Act. The Planning (Listed
Buildings and Conservation Areas) Act 1990 contains appeal procedures which
may be relevant to a planning appeal:

● listed building consent appeals (s 20);
● listed building enforcement notice appeals (s 39);
● conservation area consent appeals (s 74).

The coverage of the issues and procedures is not comprehensive but simply
introduces the nature of the appeals and how they may interact with appeals in
respect of planning applications. Each of these has its own peculiarities and
will need to be considered in individual detail. Since this book deals with
appeals, it follows that the decision has already been taken as to what type of
application to make to the local authority. However, in order to put the appeal
into context, it is necessary to distinguish the different types of application.
What is particularly important is whether they are prospective (as is the case
with most applications dealt with in this book) or take place after the event,
when the development has already been carried out. Development carried out
without planning permission may be subject to enforcement action by the local
authority. Figure 13.1 illustrates this aspect.

227

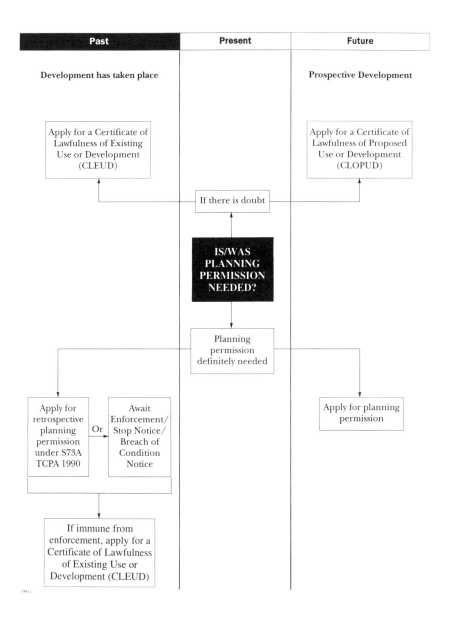

Figure 13.1 Dealing with prospective/retrospective consents.

13.2 Applications for planning permission for development already carried out

Section 73A of the Act permits a retrospective application to be made for planning permission for development which has been carried out before the date of the application. This section can be used when development has been carried out without any planning permission at all or in accordance with a temporary consent or without complying with some condition subject to which planning permission was granted. The section can only be used when the breach has already occurred.

These appeals require special attention. Because a breach of planning control has occurred, the person who has carried out the development and the owners of the land may be faced with the choice of either putting in such an application or dealing with an enforcement notice or breach of condition notice.

13.2.1 Dealing with the breach

There will be an added dimension to the decision to be made on whether to appeal any refusal or failure to determine the application. The application under s 73A of the Act will be dealt with strictly on the planning merits, and the history of how this state of affairs came about and the personal circumstances of the owner are likely to be given little weight.

If no appeal is lodged and the position is not rectified, either by the removal of buildings or the cessation of unauthorised use, the local authority will have to consider further enforcement action. In the case of a breach of condition, the local authority can issue a breach of condition notice and initiate a prosecution. This is something which few landowners would wish to face, and in those circumstances the best advice is either to remedy the breach or make an application under this section. An appeal can then be made against the refusal or non-determination of this application.

If a breach of condition is not in issue, the owner may take a more sanguine view of the situation. Before lodging an appeal, it is suggested that the chances of success should be weighed up. The weight of local policies and local objections should be considered a determining factor. If the application is moving towards refusal, there may be merit in withdrawing the application to avoid a refusal on the planning record. It may then be considered expedient to do nothing and wait and see what the local authority themselves do.

The next step for the local authority is to consider enforcement proceedings and the issue of an enforcement or stop notice. Enforcement notices are dealt with below. Many practitioners believe that inspectors who are faced with buildings which have already been built generally endeavour to make the development acceptable rather than require its removal.

13.2.2 The practical approach

A pragmatic approach is recommended. If what has been done causes clear problems to neighbours or others, the local authority are likely to lose no time in moving to enforcement and if a change of use is involved to issue a stop notice requiring the cessation of the use. To be unco-operative in this situation may simply antagonise further neighbours and the local authority. In an extreme situation, the local authority can seek an injunction without taking any other enforcement action. In these situations the person responsible should either remedy the breach by ceasing the contravention or removing the buildings or make the application for planning permission under this section. If, however, the inspector refuses the application under this section, the issues will have been fully explored and it will be difficult to resist further enforcement action at a later stage.

On the other hand, if what has occurred is relatively low-key, providing that there is no breach of condition and the circumstances do not render an application for an injunction likely to succeed, it may be worth sitting tight and requiring the authority to justify the issue of an enforcement notice. There will be a deemed planning application as part of the enforcement appeal process. The inspector can therefore grant the equivalent of an application under this section as a result of an appeal against an enforcement notice. He will be looking at the wider picture. Arguments other than planning merits can be raised in the course of the appeal.

Appeals under this section are ordinary planning appeals under s 78 of the Act. The advice in previous chapters relating to planning appeal procedure relates to an appeal under this section.

13.3   Certificate of lawfulness of existing use or development

Section 191 of the Act enables any person to ascertain whether any existing use of buildings or other land is lawful, whether any operations which have been carried out are lawful and whether any failure to comply with the conditions or limitation subject to which planning permission has been granted is lawful. This section replaces the previous Certificate of Established Use.

The position is that if development which was unlawful at the time it was carried out is now immune from enforcement, a certificate can be applied for under this section, in effect granting planning permission for the work. Section 73A (discussed in para 13.2) deals with the situation where development has been carried out unlawfully but the local authority's powers to enforce against the contravention still exist. However, where the contravention is immune from enforcement because it has continued over the requisite number of years without enforcement action being taken, the situation can be regularised by means of this section.

13.3.1   Immunity from enforcement

The time limits are complicated but, broadly speaking, are four years beginning with the date of the breach, where the breach is a change of use of any building (or part of a building) to use as a single dwellinghouse; four years if the breach is a carrying out of building, engineering or other operations from the date when the operations were substantially completed; and ten years in the case of any other breach. The single dwellinghouse provision is intended to catch the subdivision of houses into flats or maisonettes.

In an application under this section, what is at issue is a question of fact: were the building operations substantially completed on or before a date which attracts immunity? Did any change of use begin on a date which enables immunity to be gained and has it continued to the present day? These are questions of fact, with no question of planning merits. Any question as to whether the application conforms with the development plan or is seriously detrimental to local amenity is irrelevant. If it can be proved that the development is within the immunity provisions, the certificate will have to be granted, whatever the planning merits.

Advisers should therefore bear in mind that this is not a planning appeal in the ordinary sense. Attention should be focused on what has to be established and the evidence by which it is to be established. The procedure for making the application is prescribed by art 26A of the GDO. Advice is contained in Circular 17/92, Annex 1.

13.3.2   Burden of proof

The circular makes it clear that the onus of proof is firmly with the applicant. This contrasts with the normal planning situation where there is, strictly speaking, no onus of proof. Particular attention should be paid to the provisions of s 193(7). Because of the evidential burden, a local authority may revoke a certificate if information given was false in a material particular or any material information was withheld. Moreover, under s 194 of the Act it is an offence knowingly or recklessly to make a statement which is false or misleading in a material particular or with intent to deceive, or to use any document which is false in a material particular or with intent to deceive to withhold any material information. The evidence tendered at the application stage will be put under close scrutiny, and any doubt as to its validity will no doubt be exposed.

An appeal may be lodged within six months of the date the application is refused or the 'prescribed period' has expired (see Chapter 1). The Secretary of State on appeal is required to grant the certificate if he is satisfied that the authority's refusal (or deemed refusal in non-determination cases) is not well founded. If the Secretary of State is satisfied that the authority's refusal is (or would have been) well founded, he is required to dismiss the application. The Secretary of State does not therefore consider the decision afresh as he does with planning appeals under s 78 of the Act.

Section 196 provides a right on appeal for both the local authority or the appellant to a hearing. At present the decision will be made by the Secretary of State, not an inspector under transferred powers. The usual choice as to written representation, informal hearing and public inquiry applies. The inquiry procedure is governed by the Town and Country Planning (Enforcement) (Inquiries Procedure) Rules 1992. Written representations and informal hearings are dealt with under enforcement notice appeals. Because the evidence will centre on matters of fact, a public inquiry may be needed so that any disputed evidence can be formally presented on oath and subjected to rigorous cross-examination. The normal costs position in respect of unreasonable behaviour applies in relation to such an appeal.

13.3.3 Practical points

Care is needed. While the Secretary of State may not consider the decision of the local authority afresh under this section he is entitled to go a little wider (*Cottrell v Secretary of State for the Environment* [1982] JPL 443).

The evidence needed to make or refute the case should be established. What evidence can be brought to bear on the point? What is the quality of that evidence? How is it to be presented? Evidence over the full ten years is likely to be sketchy or non-existent in certain respects. Appellants should remember that the burden of proof is on them and any gaps in the case will count against them. If the emerging evidence does not support the exact terms of the application which is being made, another application, in terms which are fully supported by the evidence, should be considered.

If development is immune from enforcement this can be immensely valuable since it enables a planning permission to be obtained for development which would on its planning merits almost certainly be refused. The appellant is entitled to take advantage of this section if he is able to do so. If a practitioner is dealing with a non-conforming use which is most unlikely to get planning permission, work on collecting evidence for an appeal against the local authority's refusal of such a certificate may be the best point of attack. In many cases it may be worth employing a professional to track down local people with personal knowledge of the facts who have moved away or previous occupants.

Documentary evidence may be available from a number of sources. There are trade and street directories going back to Victorian times and electoral registers and old rating records, if still available. The local archives may contain relevant material in some cases, in others the local archivist may suggest a local historian, whether professional or amateur, who will know of the existence of relevant material or provide further leads. It is generally possible to obtain ordnance survey maps going back to early Victorian times and to trace through the development of an area. There may also be records within the local authority itself. Building control records often go back a long way and they may even have the original approval drawings for a Victorian house. Similarly, the trading records of a company or individual may give a clear indication of the business which was carried on if this is helpful to the appellant's cause.

13.4 Certificate of lawfulness of proposed use or development

The normal planning appeal situation under s 78 of the Act arises when a person has satisfied himself that planning permission is required for what he intends to do. Section 191 (dealt with in para 13.3) deals with the situation where what has already been done required planning permission but was carried out despite the lack of planning permission. This section looks to the future and enables a person to apply to the local authority for a certificate that what he intends to do does not require planning permission.

The onus of proof is with the applicant. What is in issue is the nature of the proposed use. If the application is refused or if the 'prescribed period' has expired, an appeal may be lodged within six months (see Chapter 1). The Secretary of State will not consider the matter afresh, only whether the refusal or deemed refusal is well founded. If it is, he must refuse the certificate. The inquiry procedure is governed by the Town and Country Planning (Enforcement) (Inquiries Procedure) Rules 1992. Written representation procedure and informal hearings are available. Procedures are dealt with under enforcement notice procedure below.

13.4.1 Question of fact

The principle is that no planning merits are involved in the decision and the section simply offers a procedure for resolving a disagreement between a developer and the local authority as to whether consent is required as a matter of planning law.

Such differences can arise in a number of contexts. Is the proposed development, for example, within permitted development rights in the GDO? Delicate questions sometimes arise as to the exact extent of the original dwellinghouse for the purpose of calculating any extension. Or is what is proposed not development (and therefore does not require planning permission) because both the present use and the proposed use fall within the same use class of the Use Classes Order? Such distinctions often hang on the exact categorisation of the present use and what is proposed and are not always easy to answer.

Is what is proposed ancillary to the principal use of the unit? Questions often arise as to whether a small-scale business carried on from a house is ancillary to the residential use or whether it would constitute a separate use resulting in a mixed development which does require planning permission. Does what is proposed constitute a new planning use of part of the site? This may occur when an ancillary use is intensified, eg a previous servant's flat is used as a separate residential unit.

Other situations where disagreements arise include those where the use itself was not covered by an express permission, ie was in existence in 1947, and doubts exist as to the extent of such lawful use of existing buildings; and where an existing use is covered by a planning permission but this is ambiguous in its terminology, ie 'agricultural haulage yard'.

It may seem a little devious to gain consent for a development which would not be permitted under an ordinary application. However, if there is a possibility that a contentious or non-conforming development can be brought within the terms of such a certificate it will be immensely valuable. An applicant is entitled, after all, to deal with planning law as he finds it. It is important for practitioners to be fully conversant with the rules which may permit a proposed use or development to be established as lawful under this section. The appeal procedure is the same as for certificates of lawfulness of the existing use under s 191.

13.5   Enforcement notice appeals

If the local authority believe that a breach of planning control has occurred, they may issue an enforcement notice requiring steps to be taken to remedy the breach, whether this is a change of use, the erection of a building or structure, or failure to comply with a condition or limitation. There is a right of appeal. Because of the criminal penalties which may result, enforcement appeals may become more legalistic and focused on technicalities than planning appeals under s 78 of the Act. A material error which causes injustice may well invalidate a notice (*Patel v Betts* (1977) 243 EG 1003). This general illegality point should be borne in mind when considering an appeal and if necessary argued as a separate point in addition to the grounds set out below.

13.5.1   Statutory time limit on appeals

The right of appeal (s 174 of the Act) is subject to a statutory time limit. Outside this period the notice becomes effective and the right of appeal is lost. The rules require the notice to be served at least 28 days before it comes into effect. The enforcement notice will indicate the date on which it takes effect. Some of that time may already have expired before the recipient seeks advice. The practitioner should act promptly, as failure to do so may result in a negligence action. The appeal must be *received* by the Inspectorate before the enforcement notice takes effect.

There are two quite separate limbs to an appeal against an enforcement notice.

13.5.2   Grounds of appeal

The grounds are set out in s 174 of the Act. Firstly, there will be a deemed application for planning permission (*Ground A*). The advice given in previous chapters relating to planning appeals is therefore relevant to dealing with the deemed planning application. The normal planning fee will be payable and the Inspectorate will inform the person concerned of the fee required.

The second limb relates to the breach of planning control. *Ground B* covers a situation where the matters complained of have not occurred. This is a pure question of fact (eg the local authority allege that a certain field has been used as a Sunday market on every Sunday since Christmas) and may be challenged as a matter of fact.

Ground C concerns matters which, if they occurred, do not constitute a breach of planning control. The ground here is that what is alleged to have occurred is either not 'development' (perhaps because it is within the Use Classes Order) or is for some other reason permitted development.

Ground D concerns a breach which is immune from enforcement. If the relevant time periods have elapsed (see para 13.3.1), the enforcement action is time barred and the notice will not be upheld. The cut-off date is the date when the notice is issued.

Ground E is that copies of the enforcement notice were not served as required by s 172 of the Act. A person who appeals automatically forfeits this ground. The Secretary of State has power to disregard any failure to serve if the person concerned has not been substantially prejudiced.

Ground F is that the steps required by the notice are excessive. What is required by the enforcement notice to remedy the breach may depend on the exact situation before unauthorised development took place or may be more than required to deal with the breach.

Ground G is that the period for compliance is too short. This is a question of reasonableness in all the circumstances.

The Inspectorate publish a guide to procedure which should be obtained before an appeal is lodged. Copies of the notice and appeal form should have been received with the enforcement notice itself. The address for lodging enforcement notices is the Department of the Environment (PLUP 2), Tollgate House, Houlton Street, Bristol, BS2 9DJ (fax: 0272 878782; from 16 April 1995: 0117 987 8782). In Wales the address is the Secretary of the Welsh Office, Cathays Park, Cardiff CFl 3NQ (fax: 01222 825150).

If the statutory time period is close to expiring, a fax should be sent to the Inspectorate stating that the fax is the formal lodging of an appeal against an enforcement notice, giving the details of the enforcement notice and faxing a copy. The fax should also give the grounds of appeal and state that full details will follow.

13.5.3   Appeal procedure

The appeal procedures are governed by the Town and Country Planning (Enforcement Notice and Appeals) Regulations 1981 and are very similar to the procedures for ordinary planning appeals. Enforcement appeals, unlike those relating to appeals in respect of certificates of lawfulness of existing or proposed use or development, are normally decided by an inspector (not the Secretary of State). The onus of proof in respect of evidential matters in relation to breach of planning control rests with the appellant (*Nelsovil v The Minister of Housing and Local Government* [1962] 1 WLR 404).

13.5.4   Should you appeal?

The decision on whether to appeal should, in the author's view, be taken firstly at a short-term pragmatic level, followed by a more measured look at the situation as a whole. In many enforcement cases the short-term pragmatic course of action will be to appeal immediately. This is because the right of appeal is lost if an appeal is not lodged within the time limit, and because an appeal suspends the operation of the enforcement notice and delays the time when it takes effect and must be complied with. An immediate appeal thus preserves the rights of the party receiving the notice and gives time for any remedial measures to be discussed.

Once the enforcement notice becomes effective and the period for compliance has expired, the danger is that the local authority will be able to enforce compliance, either by prosecution, injunction or carrying out the necessary works themselves to remedy the breach and recharging the costs to the landowner. If the discussions with the local authority are ultimately successful, the local authority can withdraw the enforcement notice. If, on the other hand, after further consideration it is apparent that there is no defence to the enforcement notice and that there is a real risk of costs being awarded if the procedure is not aborted, then the appeal can be withdrawn.

13.5.5   The longer-term view

Because of the repercussions of an enforcement notice, the balance will often tip more quickly in favour of appeal than it will in respect of an ordinary planning matter. If no appeal is lodged the enforcement notice will become effective and the appellant will have to comply with it. He may therefore think that it is worth appealing whatever the strength of his case. The lodging of an appeal will suspend the enforcement notice and thus give him more time to deal with the situation. Since the local authority do not have to be certain that there has been a breach before issuing the enforcement notice (it need only 'appear' to them that a breach of planning control has occurred), the appellant may wish to test the local authority's evidence. When scrutinised formally it may prove weak.

There are a number of dangers for an appellant. Costs can be awarded even on the written representation procedure for an enforcement appeal. If the case is very weak, the appellant may be buying the extra time at considerable cost. Appealing may also exacerbate the situation with the local authority and neighbours and harden attitudes, so that a compromise position may be difficult to negotiate.

If the contravention is a change of use for which the local authority can serve a stop notice, an appeal may not effectively suspend the action of the enforcement notice. In other circumstances, if what is complained of is a breach of condition, the local authority may issue a breach of condition notice. There is no appeal against such a notice and failure to comply will be an offence (s 187A of the Act). The only way of setting aside such a breach of condition notice is by judicial review. Judicial review is dealt with in Chapter 14, where an example of a challenge to a breach of condition notice is given.

If there is no case at all for an appeal the appellant should be advised to comply with planning requirements. It may be unwelcome advice to the appellant that he has a weak case and should move quickly to remedy the situation before further costs are sunk into a hopeless case, but such advice should be given robustly if required.

13.5.6 Other powers

Appellants' advisers should not limit themselves to considering only procedures under the Act. A breach of planning control may involve breaches of other legislation. A local authority has wide powers to deal with noise under the Control of Pollution Act 1974 and the Environmental Protection Act 1990 and to deal with overcrowding and housing conditions under the Housing Act 1985. There are also powers under the Building Act 1984 to deal with unsafe structures or structures dangerous to health.

13.6 Taking stock of the chances of success of an enforcement appeal

By the time an enforcement notice is served, there will normally be a documented history to the matter. The local authority will have carried out investigations and discussions with the alleged contravenor. In some cases they may have issued a planning contravention notice with a request for details of ownership. The practitioner should ensure that he has the whole story from his client, whether his client is the local authority or the contravenor before pulling together the various strands and advising on the merits of an appeal. In most cases advisers will wish to appeal on as many grounds as possible.

Many practitioners feel that where buildings have been erected, an inspector will be reluctant to require their removal if the appellant can advance cogent reasons why planning permission should be granted or can suggest measures or conditions which would remedy the damage caused by the contravention.

Neither an appeal including the ground that planning permission ought to be granted nor a separate planning application retrospectively may protect against the power of the local authority to seek an injunction in an appropriate case to restrain a breach. This was discussed in the case of *Runnymede Borough Council v Harwood (Court of Appeal) The Times*, 22 February 1994.

13.7 Evidence

Whatever appeal route is chosen, gauging the quality of the evidence will be an important part of assessing the merits of an appeal. If the local authority have done their homework properly, they will have collected evidence, from their own officers or from neighbours, on the exact circumstances in which the contravention occurred and they will be able to document it. Bearing in mind that the onus is on the appellant, those advising him will need to assemble what evidence they can in favour of his case. While the evidence of the alleged contravenor himself is admissible, it should be backed up by corroborative evidence, either documentary or from other parties.

Enforcement appeals, unlike ordinary planning appeals, often concentrate on the actual events which have occurred rather than on policies. It is for this reason that evidence is often taken on oath. It will therefore be crucial to ensure that the quality of evidence is the best that can be obtained and that pertinent and credible witnesses are available.

There are no hard and fast rules. The owner of the land and his relatives may be best placed to give evidence as to what has occurred and may be very credible. All too often, however, they are seen as self-serving and do not stand up well against the weight of evidence of neighbours who have kept detailed diaries of what has occurred. Personalities tend to come to the fore and feelings can run high. Objective, independent evidence is rare and valuable. Will the witnesses used 'come up to proof' at the inquiry? Many non-professional witnesses, who may be happy to help in the informal situation of an interview in a solicitor's office or their own home, will be uncomfortable in an inquiry and easily led into giving the answer the questioner wants. Apparently 'helpful' witnesses — ie those with a tendency to talk too much — generally prove to be a handicap.

If an appeal is unlikely to succeed or the evidence is thin, it may be sensible to ask for the written representation procedure where the costs will be less than those involved in an informal hearing or a public inquiry.

13.7.1   Application to regularise the breach

In some circumstances a planning application will have been lodged to regularise the situation before the enforcement notice is issued in an endeavour to persuade the local authority to delay issuing the enforcement notice until the results of that planning application are known. If this has not been successful, an enforcement notice will be issued. Those advising the owner or occupier served with the enforcement notice will have to consider whether to proceed with that application as well as with the enforcement appeal, which of course contains a deemed application for planning permission itself.

The application for planning permission may not cover precisely the same ground as that covered by the enforcement notice. The enforcement notice will have been tightly drawn by the local authority in accordance with their evidence while the planning application may be wider in that it represents what the landowner really would like as opposed to simply reflecting the existing situation. This is particularly so in relation to a change of use which has occurred without planning permission. Indeed, once the terms of the enforcement notice have been considered, it may be right to lodge a separate planning application under s 73A, if the enforcement notice falls short of covering completely the desired use.

It is disappointing to win an enforcement notice appeal only to discover that permission is granted for the use complained of in the enforcement notice and the owner still has a site on which he has planning problems. Commonly, the enforcement notice will specifically allege unauthorised use of a small part of a site, say for storing building materials. Planning permission on appeal would normally only relate to that particular use and will not enable the use to intensify or spread over the whole site. A properly framed planning application, if successful, will rectify the problem. It will normally be unwise to rely on a separate planning application alone and not to appeal the enforcement notice.

13.7.2 Confidentiality

Confidentiality can prove a real problem in enforcement appeals, both for the local authority and the appellant. A great deal of the evidence will be centred on past history. First-hand information will normally be available from present and past neighbours and present and past occupiers of the land. Many of these witnesses will be reluctant to come forward and become involved in a problem which does not directly concern them. This reluctance may be heightened by the fact that evidence will be taken on oath if a public inquiry is held and the knowledge that their identity will be revealed to the other side. After all, neighbours have to continue to live next door to the occupier of the land and they may feel intimidated. The question of confidentiality is dealt with in more detail in para 2.6 in relation to appeals generally, and this holds true of enforcement appeals.

A number of approaches may be used to deal with the problem. If the written representation procedure is used, letters from witnesses are normally acceptable and will be taken at face value. If there is a real conflict of evidence, however, the inspector may feel that he must see the witnesses and a public inquiry or informal hearing will be held. While the names of the witnesses will have to be given, it may be possible in some cases for their addresses to be given c/o of the agent acting for the appellant or c/o of the local authority. However, if the proximity of the witnesses is important to their evidence it will normally be essential to give their address so that the first-hand nature of their evidence can be established. The local authority, however, may be in a position to rely principally on the enforcement officer or some similar person.

The appellant's advisers should carefully review the evidence and who will give it as part of the consideration of the appeal process. The occupier himself will normally be willing to give evidence, but his evidence may not extend over the time or over all the matters on which evidence is required to be given. Both his evidence and that of people closely connected with him, whether they are members of his family or employees, may lack the independence which will weigh heavily with inspectors when considering conflicting evidence. If the appellant has already engaged a planning professional before the enforcement notice is issued, such a person may have first-hand evidence and may be in a position to deal with a number of questions of fact. Where possible, documentary evidence should be collected. It is difficult to refute and does not involve personal conflict between individuals.

13.8 Challenge in the High Court

Section 289 of the Act provides a challenge to the High Court in respect of enforcement appeal decisions in a similar way to challenges under s 288 of the Act in relation to decisions on planning appeals. There are, however, important differences. One is the statutory time limit: the application for leave must be made within 28 days of the receipt of the decision letter. Although the court has power to extend this time limit, they will do so only in exceptional cases.

The right course must be to act promptly. It is essential to remember this time limit is *shorter* than the six weeks applying to a challenge on a planning appeal under s 288.

The right of appeal is limited in these challenges to the appellant, the local authority or any other person having an interest in the land to which the notice relates. There is no right of appeal for an 'aggrieved person' as under s 288 nor a right of appeal for parties other than the appellant, even though they may have been served with the notice.

The challenge is limited to a point of law and the grounds are broadly the same as under s 288, ie the court will not look into the merits. The deemed planning application which forms part of the enforcement appeal must be challenged under this section not under s 288. The court's power is limited to remitting the matter to the Secretary of State for re-determination. There is also a requirement for leave to be obtained. No criteria are laid down for the granting of leave but its purpose is to filter out totally unmeritorious cases.

In general, an enforcement notice will not become effective while the challenge is pending. However, this challenge should not be used by an appellant simply to put off the day when he has to comply with the notice. He may either not get leave or the local authority may obtain an interim order under s 289(4A) of the Act that the notice or part of the notice shall have immediate effect.

When in doubt appeal. But the practitioner should take stock of the situation before doing so. It may be necessary to encourage the client to comply with the law.

13.9   Listed buildings

13.9.1   Introduction

This section deals with appeals against the refusal or deemed refusal of an application for listed building consent and appeals against listed building enforcement notices. The Town and Country Planning (Listed Buildings and Conservation Areas Act 1990 (the Listed Buildings Act) provides control over work carried out to listed buildings. This control is entirely separate from the controls over development under the Town and Country Planning Act 1990. Whenever development is proposed to a listed building, professional advisers therefore need to consider whether an application for listed building consent is also required.

13.10   Planning appeals involving listed buildings

In certain circumstances, an application for planning permission may have implications for listed buildings. This occurs when a planning application affects a listed building or its setting. Section 66 of the Listed Buildings Act requires the local authority to have special regard to the desirability of preserving the building or its setting or any features of special architectural or historic interest which it possesses.

This will arise in two situations: where the work proposed affects both a listed building and its setting and requires listed building consent. In this case, there will be two applications under the separate jurisdictions, but they will usually be dealt with together. It also arises where no application for listed building consent is required but a planning application affects a listed building or its setting. A change of use, for example, will not need listed building consent but will need planning permission.

The importance of the setting of a listed building varies and each case will have to be looked at on its own merits. The test is broadly visual and if the proposed works cannot be seen together with the listed building, it is difficult to see how it can affect its setting.

13.11   What work requires listed building consent?

The requirement to apply for listed building consent is based on criteria completely different from the requirement to apply for planning permission. It is a common misconception that only exterior changes are subject to listed building control, and the correct test is set out in s 7 of the Listed Buildings Act:

> . . . no person shall execute or cause to be executed any works for the demolition of a listed building or for its alteration or extension in any manner which would affect its character as a building of special architectural or historic interest, unless the works are authorised.

The test, therefore, is whether the works would affect its character, not whether they can be seen from the outside.

It is dangerous to assume that works will not affect the character because the owner or the architect considers that the affected parts of the building are, viewed subjectively, of little merit or originality. There is an increasing emphasis on the integrity of buildings and, unless what is proposed is like-for-like repair, it is suggested that discussions should take place with the local authority. In most cases, they will require an application so that the precise extent of the work can be identified and be subject to control.

It is an offence to carry out work which requires listed building consent without that consent. Contravention arising from a casual approach may involve considerable expenditure in putting matters right. A salutary example is *R v Leominster DC ex parte Antique Country Buildings Ltd* [1988] 56 P&CR 240 where a timber-framed building was dismantled, packed in cases and sold to America by the landowner for a sum in the region of £3,000. The local authority issued a listed building enforcement notice and were able to prevent the shipping of the timber-frame abroad and require those concerned to re-erect the building in its original location.

13.11.1   Criteria for consent

The criteria for consent will also be applied on an appeal against a refusal or deemed refusal of listed building consent. The overriding consideration will be the preservation of the building or its setting or any features of special architectural or historic interest (s 56). General advice is given in PPG l5 which should be scrutinised closely if such an appeal is contemplated.

13.11.2   Appeals

The general appeals procedure is similar to that on planning applications. Additionally it may be argued on appeal that the building is not of special architectural or historic interest and should be removed from the list. In some circumstances, compensation may be payable if listed building consent is refused on appeal.

13.11.3   The listing

It is not difficult to discover whether a building is listed. A local authority search will reveal a listing and the local authority will normally provide a copy of the certificate of listing. The certificate will give a brief description of the building, the class of listing and any particular features. Care should be taken in interpreting the listing. Listings are not always right and the applicant's own listed building adviser will normally be able to add further information. It should be remembered that even if a feature is not mentioned, it may be important.

13.11.4   Work which always requires listed building consent

Certain classes of work always require consent. They are demolition of a listed building and works which affect the exterior. Replacement windows frequently give rise to problems and double glazing contractors are not always forthcoming with the information that they cannot be installed without listed building consent. The exterior repainting of a listed building may require listed building consent unless it is identical to the existing surface. Consent is also required for works which substantially interfere with interior features such as staircases, fireplaces, doors and panelling.

13.11.5   Grade of listing

Buildings are listed into three grades. *Grade I* covers buildings of exceptional interest. Only about 2 per cent of listed buildings are in this grade. Any works whatsoever to such buildings should be the subject of consultation with the local authority and English Heritage. *Grade II** covers particularly important buildings. Only some 4 per cent of listed buildings fall into this category. These are very often starred because of their interior features. *Grade II* comprises buildings of special interest which every effort should be made to preserve. The vast majority of buildings fall into this category.

13.12   Presumption in favour of preservation

For planning permission the general presumption is that permission should be granted unless the development would harm an interest of acknowledged importance (PPG 1). Listed buildings, however, are part of our heritage which should be preserved for future generations. There is therefore a strong presumption that such buildings and their features should be preserved.

Any appeal ought to be progressed with the assistance of a specialist on listed buildings. There are many chartered town planners and surveyors with expertise in listed buildings, and in a case of importance, a suitably qualified architect will be of great help in designing the changes sympathetically and justifying the changes.

A number of the considerations which apply to planning appeals also apply to listed buildings appeals but against the background of a presumption in favour of preservation. An application to demolish a listed building will have to be underpinned not only with an exceptional replacement but also with well-documented reasons as to why the present state of affairs cannot continue, either because of the cost of repairs or because the building no longer has any use which will permit its continued economic existence. Particular care also needs to be given to the curtilage of a listed building when considering works within the grounds of a listed building.

The ground of appeal that the building should not have been listed should not be neglected. Some buildings are listed in a hurry when development proposals are submitted and such spot listing may not survive a closer scrutiny. There is a view that listing has been a little indiscriminate, particularly in respect of Victorian buildings, and that there are now too many buildings listed which are not exceptional. Any such argument will have to be supported by specialist advice.

English Heritage (in England) and the Royal Commission on Ancient and Historic Monuments (in Wales) will be consulted by the local authority when an application for listed building consent is received. At the moment, English Heritage have the power of direct refusal of a listed buildings application in London. Outside London, their recommendation to the local authority will weigh heavily in the balance. If a local authority are minded to grant planning permission against the advice of English Heritage, English Heritage may request the Secretary of State to call in the application. The Secretary of State's criteria for dealing with listed building consent himself rather than leaving it to an inspector are set out in Figure 13.2.

13.13   Appeals

An appeal is lodged against the decision of the local authority in respect of listed building consent application in much the same way as against a planning application. A separate appeal form will have to be lodged even though the linked application for planning permission may also be appealed at the same time. The appellant should indicate on the form that there is a linked planning

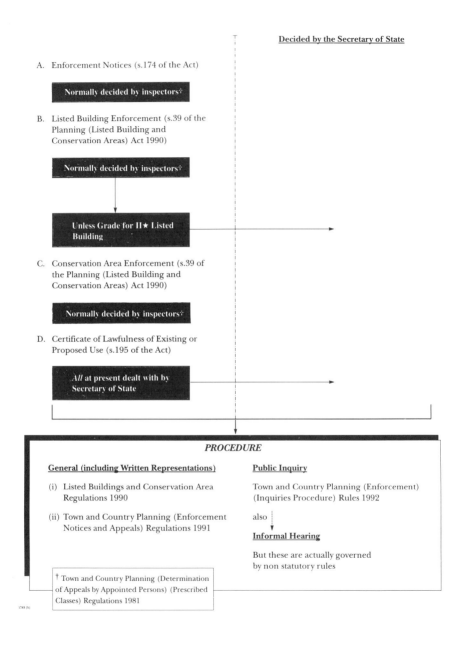

Figure 13.2. Enforcement and Allied Appeals: Inspector and Secretary of State cases; relevant rules and regulations.

application. In practice the two appeals will be dealt with together. It follows that if a listed building consent application or appeal is to be determined by the Secretary of State, then a similar direction will be made in respect of the linked planning appeal or application. Likewise, if a planning application is called-in or dealt with by the Secretary of State himself, the listed building consent application or appeal is likely to be dealt with in a similar way.

13.13.1   Separate planning and listed building appeals

There is no formal requirement for an applicant to proceed simultaneously with the planning procedures and the listed building procedures. However, in most cases it will be expedient to do so. The planning application will be dealt with in any event with special regard to the listed building. It will be difficult in many cases to progress a listed building application where a planning consent is also required without submitting at the same time full details of the planning permission which is being sought. Frequently, demolition will not be permitted until the new building has been approved and contracts let for the redevelopment. The better view is normally to regard both planning application and listed building application as intricately linked and mutually supportive.

On some occasions, other action is appropriate. For example, an owner may take the view that the building should not have been listed, particularly if it has been listed recently. He may request the Secretary of State to reconsider the listing, and if this is successful the building will be delisted. The planning application can continue without listed building complications. The danger is that if this fails and the listing is confirmed, it will be more difficult to attack the listing on appeal.

A building is sometimes listed after planning permission for building work has been obtained. Because of the separate nature of the jurisdictions the listing will not invalidate the planning permission. But since listed building consent must be obtained before the work is carried out, it will in effect make the planning permission incapable of implementation without listed building consent. Advisers will have to consider whether the existing planning permission is still acceptable in the context of the new listed building. If so, listed building consent alone need be applied for. In many cases, it will be as well to reconsider the whole issue in the light of the listing and to submit a new planning application specifically tailored to the new status of the building and continue with both planning application and listed building application in tandem.

A change of use will not require listed building consent but may require consideration of listed building matters (see para 13.11).

13.14   Listed building enforcement notice

Where work which required listed building consent has been carried out without such consent, the local authority may, as well as prosecuting those responsible, issue a listed building enforcement notice requiring restoration to take place.

There is no time limit for issuing such notices. This contrasts with the ordinary planning immunity periods for breaches of planning control. Works which require both planning permission and listed building consent may be immune from enforcement as regards the planning element but subject to enforcement under the listed building regime. An owner may therefore be liable for breaches of the listed building regime which were carried out by his predecessors.

13.15   Listed building enforcement appeals

Appeals against listed building enforcement notices are governed by s 39 of the Listed Buildings Act. In particular it should be noted that Ground of Appeal A allows, *inter alia*, an appeal on the basis that the building is not of special architectural historical interest; Ground B that the matters alleged do not constitute a contravention, ie that listed building consent was not required; and Ground C that the works were urgently necessary in the interests of safety or health and that listed building consent ought to be granted.

The appeal must be made before the date specified in the notice as the date which it is to take effect on by sending the notice properly addressed and pre-paid so that in the ordinary course of post it would be delivered before that date (s 39(2)). The listed building enforcement notice is suspended pending the determination of the appeal. The appeal is governed by the Town and Country Planning (Enforcement Notices and Appeals) Regulations 1981. Inquiry procedure is governed by the Town and Country Planning (Enforcement Inquiry Procedure) Rules 1981.

13.15.1   Other remedies of local authorities

The local authority have the same remedies for failure to comply with an effective listed building enforcement notice as they have in respect of planning contraventions, ie the ability to carry out the works themselves and to recharge the costs, injunction and prosecution.

13.16   High Court challenge

Section 65 provides for an appeal to the High Court against the decision of the Secretary of State on a listed building enforcement notice appeal. The provision is similar to that relating to enforcement notice appeals under s 289 of the Town and Country Planning Act 1990. Application for leave must be made within 28 days.

13.17   Conservation area consent

Conservation areas are designated by the local authority. A local search or search of the planning register will reveal whether a particular building is within a conservation area. There are two principal consequences of a building being sited in a conservation area. First, special attention is paid to the preservation and enhancement of the conservation area, and secondly, conservation area consent is required for demolition.

Section 72 of the Listed Buildings Act requires any application under the Town and Country Planning Act 1990 or under the Listed Buildings Act to pay special attention to the desirability of preserving or enhancing the character or appearance of that area. Planning applications for works within conservation areas will be subject to this additional criterion. In *South Lakeland District Council v Secretary of State for the Environment* [1992] 1 All ER 573 the House of Lords accepted that the character and appearance of a conservation area could be preserved not only by proposals which improved the appearance but also by development which did not harm the area.

Demolition in a conservation area requires conservation area consent. While demolition generally has been brought within a planning control (but subject to complicated permitted development rights and exceptions), demolition of individual listed buildings and buildings in conservation areas requires individual consent. (Demolition includes partial demolition or removal of part.) The purpose of this is firstly to protect buildings which, although not listable in their own right, nonetheless add a group value to the conservation area; and secondly to ensure that the conservation area is not affected by unsightly gaps where demolition has taken place but development is not immediate. It will normally be a requirement of conservation area consent that a building shall not be demolished until the authority are satisfied that a suitable new building will be erected immediately.

Applications for conservation area consent and conservation area consent appeals will be dealt with broadly speaking as listed building consent applications and appeals. The code in respect of conservation area requirements is extremely complex.

13.17.1 Listed buildings in conservation areas

If a building is both listed and in a conservation area, it is exempt from conservation area consent and will simply be dealt with under the listed building provisions. Certain small buildings and other structures are exempt. These will have to be looked at in detail. PPG 15 deals with these precise requirements.

Chapter 14

Judicial Review
and Other Avenues

14.1   General principle

Judicial review is inappropriate where statute provides a method of review, whether by way of appeal or otherwise. Many planning decisions are subject to such appeal and are backed up by preclusive clauses, which means that the decisions are final and subject to only limited challenge by way of judicial review (*R v Secretary of State for the Environment ex p Ostler* [1977] QB 122). There is therefore less recourse in the planning arena to the supervisory jurisdiction of the court under RSC Ord 53 than there may be in other areas of the law. It follows that if the decision being questioned is the grant or refusal of planning permission by the local authority and the person concerned is able to appeal to the Secretary of State under s 78 of the Town and Country Planning Act 1990, this will preclude an application for judicial review.

If the decision complained of is the grant or refusal of planning permission by the Secretary of State or his inspector on appeal and the grounds of challenge fall fairly within the statutory challenge provision of s 288, then again judicial review is not advisable. Similarly, if the decision is that of the Secretary of State on a called-in application under s 77 of the Act and the challenge falls within the provisions of s 288, s 288 should be used. The situation is not, however, absolutely clear cut and is discussed in detail below.

Categories of decisions for which no statutory challenge procedure exists are therefore suitable for judicial review. These cover a challenge to an award of costs or the failure to award costs (*North Kesteven District Council v Secretary of State for the Environment* [1989] JPL 445. Judicial review should also be used where the decision complained of is not a final decision and it is necessary to challenge it immediately. This will normally relate to procedural matters, ie refusal to receive evidence, to adjourn hearing or to decline to register the application. Finally, judicial review is appropriate for final decisions where the challenge lies clearly outside the scope of the statutory challenge provisions, eg fraud. The grounds of challenge under s 288 of the Act in relation to planning decisions and under s 289 (relating to enforcement decisions) have been dealt with in earlier chapters.

An illustration of judicial review in the planning field is the case of *R v London Borough of Ealing ex p Zanuddin The Independent,* September 5 1994.

The council had issued a breach of condition notice. There is no statutory appeal provided in the Act and the notice was therefore challenged by judicial review. Planning permission had been granted for a mosque, together with associated facilities and 22 houses, subject to a number of conditions, one of which stipulated that no part of the development was to be occupied until both the community building and the residential units had been satisfactorily completed. The council, believing that a breach had occurred by the holding of an act of worship before the mosque was completed, issued the breach of condition notice requiring such activity to cease until the building was completed. The court looked in detail at the conditions and the events which the council alleged amounted to a breach. In the event the court held that there was no breach and rejected the council's interpretation of what had occurred as a matter of planning law. The application was therefore granted and the breach of condition notice quashed.

14.1.1   Preclusive provisions

Section 284 contains preclusive provisions. The determination of planning applications by local authorities is outside the scope of this section. A decision on an adjournment does not fall within these provisions (*Co-Operative Retail Services Ltd v Secretary of State for the Environment and City of Wakefield Metropolitan District Council and William Morrison Supermarkets* [1980] 1 WLR 271). There is doubt as to whether refusal to entertain an appeal at all is within the preclusive provisions. The view was expressed in *Child Grey v Secretary of State for the Environment* [1977] 33 P&CR 10 that it would be but this was doubted in the *Co-Operative Retail Services* case mentioned above. The better view is that judicial review is likely to be available. Such judicial review should not affect the appellant's position. The right course will be to lodge the appeal and if the Secretary of State refuses to accept the appeal, to apply for judicial review. If this is successful, the Secretary of State's decision will be quashed and the appeal will become live again.

14.1.2   Failure to exercise statutory challenge

Various preclusive provisions apply in relation to listed building decisions and enforcement notices. The position of principle is that if the party represented by the practitioner has a right of challenge, and this is not exercised within the time limits laid down, then the right of challenge will be lost and an application for judicial review will not be acceptable as a substitute.

14.1.3   Cases where judicial review may be available despite existence of appeal procedure

If there is a right to challenge a decision but the person concerned is not one of those who may take advantage of the appeal procedure or the grounds of challenge fall outside the statutory appeal procedure, judicial review may be available. Judicial review was therefore appropriate to review the legality of a condition attached by a local authority to the grant of planning permission in (*R v London Borough of Hillingdon ex p Royco Homes Ltd* [1974] QB 720. It was also appropriate in *Davy v Spelthorne Borough Council* (1983) 81 LGR 580 to review the loss of statutory right of appeal owing to advice tendered by the local authority where fraud was alleged.

Judicial review was used to review the grant of a certificate of lawfulness of existing use in a case which concerned the established use certificate procedure (*R v Sheffield City Council ex p Power and Others*). Three applicants were all residents in the parish where owners of land had made an application for an established use certificate in respect of clay pigeon shooting. The three neighbours did have a sufficient interest to bring the proceedings, but they were not within the appeal provisions and were therefore able to review the decision of the council, arguing that the certificate should not have been issued on the basis that there had been insufficient evidence before the council to justify its issue. The council had failed to circulate notice within the area concerned and had they made proper inquiries the certificate would not have been issued. The council also resisted the application on the basis of delay but in the circumstances this was held not to be the fault of the applicants. The application was granted and the certificate of established use quashed. Similar reasoning would, it would seem, apply to the new certificate procedure.

14.2   Interim applications: should one let the procedure run its course?

It may occasionally be better to let a procedure run its course and take the point at the next stage. For instance any question as to the legality of a local authority's handling of a planning application or the legitimacy of the reasons for refusal may be cured by an appeal to the Secretary of State by the applicant because the inspector will decide the question anew. Exception was taken to the way in which a planning application was handled in the case of *R v Swansea City Council ex p Elitestone Limited* [1992] JPL 1143. This concerned an application for judicial review by the owner of land who wished to demolish the chalet-type wooden structures on the land and replace them with conventional housing. The local authority declared the area a conservation area at a meeting of two members where the requisite three clear days' notice of the meeting had not been given as required by the Access to Information Provisions of the Local Government Act 1972. In that case, the application for judicial review became academic when the council subsequently declared the conservation area at a meeting which did conform with the rules. Since there is no appeal as such against the designation of a conservation area, judicial review was the only course available to challenge that designation.

Similarly, where it is believed that members wrongly disregarded professional advice tendered to them in refusing an application, an appeal is usually a better remedy since the inspector will look at the whole decision again. The normal result of judicial review is simply to remit the case back to the local authority. Judicial review will therefore not normally achieve the consent that an applicant for planning permission is seeking.

Likewise in the course of an appeal hearing in many cases it will be more sensible to await the final decision letter and challenge that for procedural impropriety under the statutory challenge provisions of the Act rather than take immediate action under judicial review. There are, however, exceptions. For instance, if the question arises as to whether evidence should be received, it may be expedient that the matter should be dealt with before the inquiry proceeds. If it is left until the determination is made and the decision is quashed, it will then be necessary to re-open the inquiry and start again. In such circumstances an application for judicial review may be entertained and indeed it would be wise to ask the inspector to adjourn the inquiry pending the outcome. If he refuses, the High Court may be asked to order an adjournment of the inquiry pending the outcome (*R v Secretary of State for the Environment ex p Royal Borough of Kensington and Chelsea* [1987] JPL 567).

14.3   Who can apply for judicial review?

An applicant must have sufficient interest to allow him to institute a claim. An individual who is personally affected clearly has a sufficient interest. Difficulties may arise, however, in respect of representative bodies. Normally a representative body whose individual members are financially affected will also be able to issue proceedings (*Covent Garden Community Association v Greater London Council* [1981] JPL 183). A neighbour may apply for review of a decision which affects him or her and to which objection has been made (*R v North Hertfordshire District Council ex p Sullivan* [1981] JPL 752).

A greater problem arises in relation to interest groups which have no financial interest or whose members have no personal involvement in the outcome. In the notorious case of *R v Secretary of State for the Environment ex p Rose Theatre Trust Company* [1990] 1 PR 39, the Rose Theatre Trust was held not to have standing to bring judicial review despite the fact that the trust was formed specifically to preserve the Rose Theatre.

This decision has been subject to significant criticism and in recent cases a more liberal approach has been taken. A useful discussion is contained in the case of *R v Canterbury City Council ex p Springimage Ltd* [1993]. There a distinction was made between the generality of the public on the one hand and a person who has a particular interest in the matter above the generality. In that case a person who had acquired land for development and believed that his prospects of obtaining planning permission were adversely affected by a decision to grant planning permission for a similar development on another site was held to be a person who was particularly affected and had standing.

In the case of *R v Poole District Council ex p BeeBee* [1991] 2 PLR 27 a very fine line was drawn over the right to argue the fate of the sand lizards at Canford Heath. The British Herpetological Society were held to have sufficient interest to seek judicial review of a planning decision because the Society had been associated with the site for 20 years and had made financial contributions to it. However, the judge indicated that the World Wildlife Fund would not have been able to bring such proceedings.

Interestingly enough, Greenpeace had standing to challenge British Nuclear Fuels in respect of the new THORP plant at Sellafield (*R v HM Inspectorate of Pollution and Ministry of Agriculture, Fisheries and Food ex p Greenpeace Ltd*). The court emphasised the fact that Greenpeace were not 'meddlesome busybodies' but a respectable and responsible organisation. It is difficult to reconcile this with the *Rose Theatre* case (which the court declined to follow) and the remark, admittedly *obiter*, in the Canford Heath case that the World Wildlife Fund would not qualify.

While the courts are retreating from setting an artificial barrier at the outset by interpreting narrowly the requirements of standing, if there is any doubt as to the acceptability of a representative body, it may be better to put forward an individual as a nominal applicant or preferably a nationally recognised body of whose standing there is no doubt. Such bodies do have a stature and ability to speak from wide experience which is valuable in many such cases.

The grant of planning permission without receiving representation from a body who had been told that their representations would be considered was reviewable (*R v Swale District Council ex p Royal Society for the Protection of Birds* [1991] 1 PLR 6).

14.4   Time limit

Order 53 of the RSC requires an application for judicial review to be made 'promptly, at any rate within three months' of the relevant decision. The temptation to think that three months is the time limit should be resisted. The courts have consistently held that 'promptly' is the right test and is quite separate from the three month cut-off. A salutary case in point is that of *R v Swale Borough Council ex p Royal Society for the Protection of Birds* [1991] 1 PLR 6. An application for judicial review was made within the three-month period, albeit towards the end of it. The court dismissed the application on the basis of undue delay: the planning permission the subject of the challenge had been issued and a third party was entitled to rely on it. Very substantial loss would have resulted if the planning permission was quashed and there was a very real public interest issue in ensuring that if such decisions were to be challenged they should be challenged at the earliest reasonable moment. Furthermore, the local authority had not been warned of the challenge. The result was that although the court indicated that the Royal Society for the Protection of Birds had a good case for the quashing of the decision, it did not fall to be decided because of the delay.

In the case of *Greenwich Council and Cedar Transport* which involved a challenge to the setting of the council rate, the High Court indicated that even a delay of a few days could be serious where a decision affected a large number of people.

The three months is not, however, a statutory bar. In an appropriate case the courts will entertain an application even after three months as the case of *R v Stratford upon Avon District Council ex p Jackson* (1985) 51 P&CR illustrates. Eight months had elapsed between the decision complained of and the seeking of judicial review. The court accepted that there was good reason for the delay because time had been spent trying to persuade the Secretary of State to call in the application and there had been delay in granting legal aid. However, the court emphasised that if substantial hardship or prejudice to the rights of third parties had been involved, relief would have been refused.

Although the question of delay is argued at the leave stage and leave may be granted, the issue may be raised again and the application still dismissed for undue delay at the substantive hearing (*R v Swale District Council ex p Royal Society for the Protection of Birds* [1991] 1 PLR 6. The time limit runs from the date of the decision to the application for leave (*R v Stratford upon Avon District Council ex p Jackson* (1985) 51 P&CR).

For the sake of completeness it should be borne in mind that in certain circumstances the validity of a decision may be raised as a defence against a matter arising out of the decision (see *Wandsworth LBC v Winder* [1985]). Such a defence will by-pass the normal time limits.

It is of limited validity in the planning field where most decisions will either be subject to preclusive clauses preventing them being raised in subsequent proceedings or there will be no private rights infringed which would permit the defence to be raised.

14.5   Orders available under judicial review

Judicial review is wider in its scope than the challenges under ss 288 and 289 of the Act where the court may only quash the decision and remit it back to the decision-maker to make the decision again, remedying the defect identified by the High Court.

14.5.1   What can be covered in an application for judicial review

Judicial review is now free from the earlier narrow rules. The *quid pro quo* is that Ord 53 must be used if what is at issue is review of an administrative decision. It is not possible to use the ordinary writ procedure, for instance, for breach of statutory duty (*O'Reilly v Mackman* 1982 3 WLR).

Application for judicial review may include an application for orders of *mandamus,* prohibition and *certiorari.* It may also include an application for a direction or an injunction if it is just and convenient for these matters to be dealt with in this way and a claim for damages if it arises from a matter raised in the application.

14.5.2   Court's discretion

It should be borne in mind that the court is exercising the inherent supervisory jurisdiction. The exercise of such powers is always within the discretion of the court. If judicial review is contemplated, it will be important to ensure that the decision-maker is made aware of the views of the objecting party, if possible before the decision is taken. A full letter should be written setting out the facts, the matters complained of and the action required, stating that an application will be made for judicial review if the decision-maker persists.

This will have two beneficial effects: it will ensure, firstly, that the decision-maker and any third parties affected are fully aware of the decision and not taken by surprise. This will protect the position of the applicant in any future judicial review proceedings. Secondly, it will give the decision-maker an opportunity to respond and, unless the decision-maker is *functus officio*, to reconsider the decision. This has the virtue of enabling a prospective applicant to consider the decision-maker's position before embarking upon judicial review. The decision-maker may have a legitimate position which was not apparent on the initial information. Should judicial review proceedings become necessary it may serve to restrict to a certain extent the prejudice suffered by an affected third party. If he took action which a prudent person would have avoided in the circumstances, the High Court is unlikely to afford him sympathy. This might be the case, for instance, if a planning permission is implemented despite early notification that it was subject to challenge. The judge in the *Swale* case particularly criticised the applicant for failure to give timely warning of the likelihood of challenge.

While the court's general discretion is very wide, the applicant can probably hope for no more than to have the decision quashed and remitted to the decision-maker for a correctly made decision. The High Court will not place itself in the position of the decision-maker:

> It is important to remember in every case that the purpose is to ensure that the individual is given fair treatment by the authority to which he has been subjected and that it is no part of that purpose to substitute the opinion of the judiciary for that of the authority constituted by law to decide the matters in question (*Chief Constable of N. Wales Police v Evans* (1982) 1 WLR 1155).

It is often possible, however, to read between the lines of the High Court judgment, and it will be difficult for the decision-maker, who will also read the judgment with great care, to reach the same decision again. The court may, for instance, indicate that had a certain factor been taken into account it is most unlikely the decision could have been the same. But in many cases judges are anxious not to influence the decision-maker. Most judgments will therefore simply indicate what is wrong with the decision complained of and leave the field open for the decision-maker to retake the decision. Inherent in this procedure is the possibility for a decision being remitted for redetermination, redetermined, challenged again for another reason, and remitted again. Theoretically, there is no limit to such challenges although in practice they are most unusual.

14.6   No review of merits

The commonest reason for a party seeking legal advice as to whether a decision can be challenged is because the decision is adverse to his interests and he thinks it is wrong. He is questioning the merits of the decision. The courts, however, in their supervisory capacity, will not review the merits.

A decision may be considered 'wrong' if a flaw in the decision-making process has led to an incorrect decision. It is the teasing out of the flaw in the procedure from a common sense view of 'wrongness' that is the purpose of the analysis which follows. However wrong the decision may appear in a common sense evaluation, if it cannot be faulted procedurally, then an application for judicial review is unlikely to be successful.

14.6.1   Grounds for judicial review

Although the grounds for judicial review can be considered under separate headings, such an analysis can be misleading, and it is safer to work first of all from first principles than to find a pigeonhole into which the case can be put. The spectrum analogy, indeed, may be more helpful, as it was set out by Lord Hailsham in *Aberdeen District Council v London & Clydesdale Estates* [1980] 1 WLR 182:

> When Parliament lays down a statutory requirement for the exercise of legal authority it expects its authority to be obeyed down to the minutest detail. But what the Courts have to decide in a particular case is the legal consequence of non-compliance on the rights of the subject viewed in the light of a concrete state of facts and a continuing chain of events. It may be that what the Courts are faced with is not so much a stark choice of alternatives but a spectrum of possibilities in which one compartment or description fades gradually into another. At one end of this spectrum there may be cases in which a fundamental obligation may have been so outrageously and flagrantly ignored or defied that the subject may safely ignore what has been done and treat it as having no legal consequences upon himself. In such a case if the defaulting authority seeks to rely on its action it may be that the subject is entitled to use the defect in procedure simply as a shield or defence without having taken any positive action of his own. At the other end of the spectrum the defect in procedure may be so nugatory or trivial that the authority can safely proceed without remedial action, confident that, if the subject is so misguided as to rely on the fault, the Courts will decline to listen to his complaint. But in a very great number of cases, it may be in a majority of them, it may be necessary for a subject, in order to safeguard himself, to go to the Court for declaration of his rights, the grant of which may well be discretionary, and by the like token it may be wise for an authority (as it certainly would have been here) to do everything in its power to remedy the fault in its procedure so as not to deprive the subject of his due or themselves of their power to act.

The spectrum thus covers at one extreme a decision which is so fundamentally flawed that it is not worth the paper it is written on, and at the other extreme a decision which is subject to a minor error of little consequence. Into the former category would come the issuing of an enforcement notice without informing the recipient of the right of appeal. In the latter would be some trivial mis-spelling of a name or address where there is no doubt as to who the recipient was and as to whether he had received the document.

Once a flaw is apparent, the decision-maker would be wise (as Lord Hailsham indicated) to go back and correct the defect if he can, so that the decision is beyond doubt. In some cases, once the decision is taken or the document issued, it may not be possible to reconsider it. Once a planning permission has been issued a local authority can take no further steps in respect of it. However, in many cases it is possible to deal with the situation; for example an enforcement notice can be withdrawn and reissued in proper form. In many cases it may be possible to indicate that the difficulty can be circumvented, for instance a new application can be requested which will permit a new decision to be taken.

The recipient is in a difficult position if the decision is not one that the local authority can reconsider in some way or if he cannot persuade them to reconsider the position (if they are able to do so). In most cases, as Lord Hailsham indicated, it would be unwise simply to treat the decision as a nullity. There may be occasions when this is the correct course but such a decision must be taken on legal advice so that the chance to challenge is not lost.

The grounds of appeal for judicial review can be dealt with under three headings:

(1) illegality;
(2) *Wednesbury* unreasonableness or irrationality;
(3) procedural impropriety.

14.7   Grounds of appeal

14.7.1   Illegality

A public body must act within its powers and use them for the purpose for which Parliament has given them, without dishonest or ulterior motive, (*DON v SOSE* QBD 8.2.94). If there are relevant policy guidelines, it must follow them but it must not blindly follow a policy without taking into account all relevant considerations. The decision-maker may not fetter its discretion. It must decide each case on its merits, taking into account relevant considerations and ignoring irrelevant ones.

14.7.2   *Wednesbury* unreasonableness or 'irrationality'

The second category of failure to meet the strict standards applicable to public bodies must be seen in the context of such bodies being required to act within the ambit of their powers, exercising them reasonably at all times. Actions which might be quite unimpeachable for private individuals must be carried out in accordance with public law principles by public bodies. Examples include ethical bans (*R v Somerset County Council ex p Fewings and Others The Times*, 10 February 1994).

'Unreasonable' means 'such that no authority properly directing itself on the relevant law and acting reasonably' could have reached that decision (*Associated Provincial Picture Houses Ltd v Wednesbury Corporation* [1948] 1 KB 223).

When exercising a discretion it is clear that taking irrelevant considerations into account or improper motives will also cause a decision to be set aside on the basis of irrationality.

14.7.3   Procedural impropriety

The third useful point of approach is procedural impropriety. A decision can be challenged on the basis that the decision-making process was flawed. The final outcome is irrelevant.

Public bodies are under a duty to act impartially and fairly. It is not enough that there is no bias, there should be no appearance of bias. The scope of the duty will vary according to the particular decision involved. The principle that no man should be judge in his own cause probably applies to every administrative act but the opportunity for an oral hearing may not exist. There is always a right for an affected party to make his views known to the authority but often the responsibility is only to receive a letter. The courts have expanded the ambit of the duty to act fairly to include the concept of legitimate expectation that certain things will happen.

There is no common law rule that decision-makers must provide reasons although in some cases there is a statutory obligation to do so. However, if inadequate reasons are given, the authority risks the court on judicial review imputing arbitrary and unreasonable reasons.

14.8   Procedural matters

Procedural matters are straightforward. They are governed by RSC Ord 53.

14.8.1   Application for leave

An application for leave is required and is made *ex parte* to a judge by filing in the Crown Office a notice in form 86A and an affidavit verifying the facts relied on. Copies of the forms and notes for guidance of individuals are obtainable from the Crown Office. It is not necessary at this stage to notify the other party, but if the advice in this chapter has been followed the other party will be aware of the proposed application and may even ask for copies of the papers at this point.

It is possible that the respondent (the local authority or the Secretary of State), may choose to intervene at the application for leave stage, requiring an *inter partes* hearing. Many experienced practitioners feel that if there are good grounds for challenging the application at the threshold, either on the basis of locus of the applicant or of undue delay, it is as well to deal with it at this stage. This is a two-edged weapon and often frowned on. Counsel's advice should certainly be sought before such a procedure is considered. The disadvantage is that such arguments can be advanced with full force only once. If they have failed at the preliminary stage, they will lose force if advanced later when more information may be available.

The applicant may request an oral hearing to avoid the judge dealing with it without a hearing. This may be expedient if the case is felt to be marginal and matters need to be explained orally to the judge. The judge may himself order a hearing. If the application for leave is refused without a hearing, the applicant may renew his application for leave within ten days of service of the notice of the judge's refusal. Leave can be granted subject to terms in respect of costs and security for costs.

It is strongly suggested that counsel's advice is sought by the applicant before the application for leave is made so that both the application itself, the grounds and the supporting affidavit can be settled.

14.8.2   Supporting evidence

The supporting affidavit is a crucial document and should be settled by legal advisers after full consideration of the matters to be established, ensuring that all relevant information is before the court. The affidavit must make a full disclosure of the case, warts and all, and skill is needed to ensure that it is as short and pertinent as possible and yet contains all the relevant information. Since the procedure will advance by way of affidavit evidence, with additional affidavits discouraged, the first affidavit is clearly extremely important. Oral evidence is almost never required or permitted.

Careful consideration should be given as to the best person to swear the affidavit and whether there should be more than one affidavit. The High Court operates under strict rules of evidence and first-hand evidence is superior to a reliance on statements given 'to the best of one's knowledge and belief'. In some cases the proper deponent may be the official person responsible, perhaps the chief planning officer who has all the information available rather than an officer serving under him.

14.8.3   Interim relief

Where leave is granted, the court may stay the proceedings to which the application relates if the application includes application for an order of prohibition or *certiorari*. In any other case, the court can grant the same interim relief as could be granted in action begun by writ.

14.8.4   Notice of motion

The application for leave must be accompanied by the notice of motion. Once leave is received, the originating motion will be served and must be entered for hearing within 14 days after the grant of leave. At least ten days must elapse between the service of the notice of motion and the hearing.

14.8.5 Expedition

Attention should also be given at the beginning as to whether an application for expedition ought to be made. Delay on hearing for a non-urgent case of judicial review can be 12 months.

14.8.6 Affidavit in reply

Upon receipt of the papers the respondent has an opportunity to file an affidavit in reply. Rule 53(6) requires this to be made as soon as practical and in any event within 56 days after documents have been served on him.

14.8.7 Other procedures

There is provision for discovery, cross-examination, etc, but they are very much the exception and almost never necessary for a planning appeal. Rule 53(9)(ii) requires an applicant who wishes to have a decision quashed to lodge a copy of the decision verified by affidavit. This will normally be in the basic affidavit.

14.8.8 Costs

Costs for judicial review follow the High Court practice, ie they normally follow the event. An unsuccessful applicant will therefore have to pay not only his own costs but the costs of the public authority whose decision he has challenged.

14.9 Conclusion

While there is little overlap as regards jurisdiction between statutory rights of challenge granted by the Act and judicial review, there is considerable overlap between the grounds of challenge under the statutory challenge procedures and judicial review. Those involved in High Court challenges may therefore find it appropriate to consider the general advice on grounds given in this chapter. Some cases decided following the exercise of statutory rights of challenge may likewise be illuminating in the context of judicial review.

14.10 Other avenues

If none of the obvious alternatives will meet the case, then there are one or two more obscure avenues which may offer some assistance, although they are in the nature of a last resort or 'desperate measures'.

14.10.1 The local government ombudsman

If the complaint concerns a decision by a local authority, recourse can be taken to the local government commissioner appointed under the Local Government Act 1974. The ombudsman will investigate any administrative act or default which took place (normally within 12 months of the complaint) but not:

(1) if there is already a right of appeal or remedy of law unless the ombudsman believes it would not be reasonable for the person concerned to resort to that remedy;
(2) if the matter affects all or most of the inhabitants of the authority;
(3) if it is the question of the merits of a decision taken without maladministration in the exercise of a discretion.

This last restriction is extremely important. The ombudsman will not be concerned with the merits of the case, only with whether the person has been subject to maladministration. This was succinctly stated by Lord Donaldson MR in *R v Local Government Commissioner ex p Eastleigh Borough Council* (1988) QBD 855: 'Administration and maladministration have nothing to do with the nature, quality or reasonableness of the decision itself'.

The ombudsman has wide powers to investigate and issue a report. However, he has no power to overturn a decision. His power is limited to publishing a report, naming the persons concerned if he considers it appropriate and recommending that a financial payment should be made to reimburse the person concerned. This is not therefore a very satisfactory remedy in the planning arena where interested parties will wish to ensure either that something happens or that it does not happen. Financial recompense will be a poor substitute for achieving that objective.

14.10.2   The district auditor

The Local Government Finance Act 1982 established a revised system of appointment and powers of auditors. They have wide powers to take action if a local authority has already or is about to take action which would involve unnecessary or unlawful expenditure by the authority. The auditor himself has powers to initiate judicial review of a decision for failure to act which would have an effect on the accounts of the body (the Local Government and Finance Act 1982, s 25D). In an extreme case the auditor has power to recover sums where loss or deficiency has been caused by the wilful misconduct of any person. This would apply to both elected members and officers of a council. Such surcharging can lead to disqualification of the members involved.

This is clearly inappropriate in most circumstances in the planning field. There may be exceptional circumstances where questions could arise in this context. One might be where an appeal has been refused by an inspector who clearly indicated in his decision letter that the application was only unacceptable because of certain specific matters. If a revised application is submitted to the local authority incorporating the changes required and the local authority persist in refusing the revised application, there may be a case for clearly warning the local authority that they will be liable for costs on appeal and that in view of the decision already made the expenditure is unnecessary and due to the wilful misconduct of the members if they refuse the planning decision on the second occasion. Such a step should not be undertaken lightly but it is an option that may be considered in an extreme case.

14.10.3   Local authority officers

As a final resort, there are people employed by the local authority who have responsibilities as to the conduct of its affairs. The chief finance officer and the monitoring officer have obligations to ensure that the council is conducting its affairs properly and within the law. Either of these (or the chief executive, if there is one) may be worth consulting. However, in the planning field the position is unlikely to be sufficiently clear cut to enable an effective recourse to be had to either the chief finance officer or the monitoring officer.

14.10.4   Parliamentary ombudsman

The parliamentary commissioner for administration will deal with complaints in respect of maladministration on the part of an inspector or the Inspectorate. However, reference can be made only by an MP (who does not have to be the complaining party's local MP). The parliamentary ombudsman has no power to question the merits of the decision reached.

Index